# COUNTRY MUSICIANS

# COUNTRY MUSICIANS

From the editors of *Guitar Player, Keyboard,* and *Frets* magazines.

**Edited by Judie Eremo**

**Foreword by Roy Clark**

A GPI Book
Cupertino, California

Grove Press
New York

Published by Grove Press, Inc.
920 Broadway
New York, N.Y. 10010

Special thanks to Country Music Magazine for their cooperation.
Published originally in *Guitar Player, Frets,* and *Keyboard* magazines.

Library of Congress Cataloging-in-Publication Data

Country musicians.

    Includes index.
    1. Country musicians—United States. 2. Country music—United States
—History and criticism. I. Guitar player. II. Keyboard (Cupertino, Calif.)
III. Frets. IV. Eremo, Judie.
ML385.C65 1987      784.5′2′00922      87-11875
ISBN 0-802-13003-8

Designer: Paul Haggard

Manufactured in the United States of America

First Edition 1987

10 9 8 7 6 5 4 3 2 1

## PHOTO CREDITS
### Cover Photo: Scott Newton

Page v: Carl Fleischauer; viii, 4: Les Leverett; 3, 28: Courtesy of the Jim Halsey Company; 7: Jim McGuire; 9: Jim Atkins; 10: John Knowles; 13, Paul Natkin; 15, 50, 53, 79, 85, 87, 104, 107, 132, 139: Jon Sievert; 17, 19: Courtesy James Burton; 23 (left): Cynthia Green; 23, right, 89, 91, 95, 108, 121, 122 (bottom), 141, Courtesy Of The Country Music Foundation Library And Media Center; 24, 217: Kathy Gangwisch; 33: Courtesy of Epic Records; 35, 36: Jim Hatlo; 39: John Lee; 41: Al Hagensen; 43, 46: Edward Silverman; 45: Charles E. Richardson; 49: Brant Gamma; 57: William Purcell; 59, 62: Steve Caroway; 65: Billy Easley; 67: Woody Woodward; 71, 72, 124, 127, 128: Bob Krueger; 80: David C. Blood; 83: Courtesy of Capitol Records; 97, 98, 122 (top): Doug B. Green; 100: Jim Marshall; 115: Joan Balzarini; 116: Courtesy of Shure Brothers, Inc.; 119: Courtesy of RCA Records; 131: Bill Honker; 134: Fred Styles; 137: Courtesy of Kathy Gangwisch & Assoc.; 145, 148: Melody Gimple; 147: Bill Irby.

Back cover: (clockwise from center) Les Leverett, Courtesy of Kathy Gangwisch & Assoc., Billy Easley, Courtesy of Roy Clark, Courtesy of Merle Travis, Courtesy of Joe Maphis, Jon Sievert, Courtesy of Larry Dickson/Epic Records, Walden S. Fabry.

# CONTENTS

# INTRODUCTION

Country music is now recognized and appreciated as one of the most authentic, important, and popular musical legacies of our American culture. Culled from a unique combination of English, Irish, European, and African traditions, the music has evolved into a sophisticated commercial vehicle respected throughout the world. What started out as spontaneous music jamborees on the back porches of Southern and mountain communities has become an established art form, and is supremely successful in the world of big business. Its unequivocal appeal stems from our own grass roots.

*Country Musicians* is a collection of articles from *Guitar Player*, *Keyboard*, and *Frets* magazines. It reflects their own unique interest—the music. What are artists' techniques, what equipment do they use, and who are their influences?

*Country Musicians* is not meant to be a definitive encyclopedia of country music. Rather, it features a valuable sampling of musicians who represent a broad range of styles in the country music medium, with interviews and profiles of top personalities dating from 1976 through the present.

A warm thanks to the many writers and photographers whose work appears in this book: The editors and columnists of *Guitar Player*, *Frets*, and *Keyboard* magazines from whose work this book was derived; Jon Sievert for his special help and expertise, and particular thanks to Roy Clark who wrote the Foreword to this book, which clearly comes—as does the work of all these country musicians—from the heart.

Judie Eremo

1

# FOREWORD

The first sounds I ever heard were country music. My dad Hester, and his brothers Paul and Dudley played house dances, and our house was one of them. I thought for the first five years of my life that they were the only ones that played music. When I was about five years old, we got our first radio—and I was tuned into a world of country music. Even the static seemed to have rhythm.

Born and raised in the southwestern part of Virginia, I was about ten years old when we moved to Washington, D.C. Country music was a little harder to find at first; but like everything else in life, if you look for it you'll find it.

Washington, in those days (the late '40s and '50s), had many fine country musicians (as it does today). What an environment to grow up in! There was local radio, television shows, night clubs, and square dances—all great places to pick and get experience.

As I got out in the world I met some great musicians; local at first, then in some of the touring bands that came through the area. One thing about country pickers is their willingness to share their knowledge. This sharing is where I got my schooling.

Young musicians today have an even wider source, with television, records, and great magazines like *Guitar Player* and *Frets*. Who knows, if I would have had that kind of help, I might have become something (yuk, yuk)! I think there's a difference between guitarists and pickers. Pickers are like blondes: they have more fun. I'm a picker.

There are so many fine pickers around today, and so many who have left their mark. Surely the world is a much richer place because of COUNTRY MUSICIANS.

*Roy Clark*

# THE MUSICIANS

# CHET ATKINS

By Don Menn

CHET ATKINS HAS DONE MORE FOR THE GUITAR THAN anyone can say. An entire picking approach bears his name. "Atkins-style" is his two-, three-, and four-finger development, inspired by the thumb and one-finger style that his idol, Merle Travis, poured into an ear plastered to a radio speaker back in 1939. On "Chinatown, My Chinatown," cut around 1956, Chet pioneered the use of artificial harmonics, a little steeler's gimmick now used by guitarists of all styles. Though Les Paul set much of the recording world rolling with his technological acrobatics, Chet Atkins also made important breakthroughs for recorded electric guitar. He bent ears with seminal examples of tone modifications now considered commonplace: With engineers Bob Ferris and Ray Butts, he came up with a reverb in 1955 on "Blue Ocean Echo" [*The Best Of Chet Atkins*], a tremolo in 1956 on "Slinkey" [*Mr. Guitar*], and a wah-wah in 1959 on "Boo Boo Stick Beat" [*Teensville*]. He even concocted a nifty, in-sync boom-boom-boom with a bass octave doubler (the "invisible bass man" he called it) around this time, not to mention a fuzztone before anyone else (though he never could figure out where to use *that*).

"Mr. Guitar" is only part of Chet's name. "Nashville Sound" belongs on his I.D., too. He, more than any other single being, created it. In 1957, RCA vice-president Steve Sholes, who had signed Chet as an artist to the RCA Victor label in 1947, made Chet his administrative successor. Atkins became manager of RCA's Nashville office (his real impact went back even further, since he'd been working with Sholes on a free-lance basis since 1951). In 1968, Chet became vice-president in charge of country music (and any and everything). Over the last three decades he has discovered, produced, and counseled four dozen of the biggest country, rock, and pop artists. Some were cautious at first working with a guitarist-turned-producer, but Chet eventually won the confidence and helped the careers of artists such as Don Gibson, Perry Como, Charley Pride, Waylon Jennings, Eddy Arnold, Jerry Reed, Lenny Breau, Bobby Bare, Skeeter Davis, Jim Ed Brown, Rosemary Clooney, Jessi Colter, Dottie West, Jimmy Dean, Jimmie Driftwood, Al Hirt, Homer and Jethro, Sonny James, Willie Nelson, Boots Randolph, Charlie Rich, Hank Snow, Porter Wagoner, and on and on. And Chet was the person who brought pianist Floyd Cramer to Nashville and suggested he learn to play with that "bent-note" piano tweak that became his and Nashville's favorite keyboard embellishment.

His force crossed over: In 1954, Chet, along with others, encouraged Sholes to sign the biggest star of rock and roll, Elvis Presley, and it was Chet who led the sessions on such hits as "Heartbreak Hotel" and "I Want You, I Need You, I Love You," hired the sidemen Elvis kept throughout his career, and even played some rhythm guitar on those and other Presley staples. Throughout the late '50s Atkins played *lead* guitar on Everly Brothers hits such as "Bird Dog" and "Dream" (later Hank Garland worked with Chet, Phil, and Don on other sessions). He signed jazz vibist Gary Burton. He even got Paul McCartney to record "Walkin' In The Park," a song written by the ex-Beatle's father.

In an interview with John Wilson in *The New York Times,* April 7, 1974, Chet denied his importance in all this: "'The Nashville sound' is just a sales tag," he said. "I don't think there is such a thing. The studios in Nashville are like the studios anywhere else. If there is a Nashville sound, it's the musicians." Still, he was the one who hired those musicians, signed many of the pop stars that came to matter commercially, listened to what they played, and told them what worked and didn't work about their playing. In order to broaden country music's appeal, and to just plain surprise the public, he even began adding horns and violins to country music—took it "uptown," something for which he has subsequently apologized because he believes the resulting crossover sound came close to crossing out a unique musical identity. Even so, it is always a pat on the back and not a gauntlet at the feet when people around Nashville say, "If Chet likes it, it'll sell."

He is one whose wisdom has kept ahead of his success. He knows where he—as well as all this potential mammon—came from. Johnny Cash once rhapsodized about Chet: "The down-trodden flock to him because he remembers what it was like to be in a cornfield on a side of a hill in Luttrell, Tennessee."

Outside that town, June 20, 1924, on a 50-acre farm, Chester Burton Atkins began his life as a malnourished, Appalachian waif. His name itself seemed like a stray: "There used to be

some trucks that ran around," he explains, "the C.B. Atkins Moving Company, and my dad [James Arley Atkins] used to see those signs on them. I guess he liked the 'C.B. Atkins' part, so he just made up 'Chester Burton.' There was a senator from Nebraska by the name of Burton, and I think that's where he got that part of the name. I don't know where he got the Chester. I kind of always wished he would have forgotten that. But that's it; that's my name."

He grew up in a family rife with luthiers, musicians, and divorce ( his mother remarried three times and his father five). Inspired by relatives, especially his brothers Lowell and Jim, Chet was playing ukulele when he was four or five. He picked his way through various pieces he'd heard on the family's windup gramophone and through a radio he and neighbors built when Chet was 11. Inspired by George Barnes, Les Paul, Charlie Christian, Carl Farr, and the few other guitarists on record and radio of the day, Chet, nonetheless, intentionally avoided imitating them. It cut him then and still cuts him deep to hear himself compared to anyone.

The day he cites as one of the most important of his whole life was one in his early years when he vowed to become a guitarist after seeing a blind street musician. He became single-minded in the pursuit of his goal. In 1929, his brother Jim left home, teaming up later with Les Paul in 1938 and keeping Chet informed about the world of music outside of the east Tennessee hills. In 1935, Chet moved to Columbus, Georgia, to live with his father. By then, he spent most of his time with a guitar in hand, sometimes even practicing in the bathrooms at school to luxuriate in the natural echo of the stall. In 1942, Chet got his first real job as a professional musician. He was hired as a fiddler with Bill Carlisle and Archie Campbell on WNOX, Knoxville. In the same year, he made the important switch to full-time guitar playing. He held the position of staff guitarist at WNOX for four years, before skipping out and over the waves of some rough radio jobs elsewhere from which he was usually fired for being "too modern" or "not commercial enough."

Chet the guitarist had a brief fling at being Chet the vocalist in 1946-47. His first significant instrumental recording was "The

Galloping Guitar" produced in Atlanta's Fox Theatre in 1949. That cut, in and of itself, reversed the vocal trend that had been developing at the *Grand Ole Opry.* That, anyway, is what some people would say. Chet shrugs off the claim in the previously cited interview with John Wilson: "You can only eat so much caviar, then you want something else. I filled a void as an instrumentalist. There were no others around."

His first LP, *Chet Atkins Plays Guitar,* came out in 1951. Since then he has recorded in the neighborhood of six dozen others on both electric and nylon-string guitars (he switched away from steel-string acoustics in the '50s when he discovered classic guitar strings did not tear up his nails). He records in enough styles to prove that no one need be entrapped by his or her background: Classical, jazz, country, pop, and theatrical standards are all part of his repertoire.

\* \* \* \*

*W*HEN YOU FIRST BECAME INTERESTED IN THE *guitar, and heard George Barnes, Les Paul, and others on the radio, was your goal to become an electric guitarist?*

Not really. I continued to play acoustic guitar. For quite a few years after I had an electric I played a steel-string acoustic a lot, simply because back in those days amplification was so crude. I used a DeArmond pickup, and the strings were not properly balanced. That pickup was the adjustable kind that you attach to the tailpiece, so it was kind of hard to balance each string so that they were all at the same volume. It was difficult to play finger-style on an electric guitar then because of the imbalance. Those pickups tended to work with the bass strings and the first string pretty well, but the wound third didn't pick up at all. I think a lot of this was due to the curvature of the bridge.

*Do you think that the initial reason for your use of the electric was simply to make yourself better heard?*

Yes, but I didn't use it much to play solos when I was doing radio work. I mainly used an acoustic guitar for that, although with an orchestra I played an electric. With them I would play single-string lines and rhythm, so it worked out well that way. Also, when I worked a lot with small combos in clubs on Friday and Saturday nights I would use an electric to play single-line melodies and then turn it down to play rhythm. But I never played an electric on records til about '48 or '49.

*At that point were you differentiating between your electric and acoustic styles?*

Right, if I was working with a combo or a country group. But I played most of my solos on the acoustic. I had an electric pickup in 1947, but if you listen to my first records from back then you can hear that I was playing an acoustic guitar; it was a Gibson L-10.

*What advantages do you think the electric guitar offers you today?*

You have the volume when you're in an auditorium, or when you're playing with a group of musicians. Another advantage is the amount of sustain you're able to get with an electric. The electric also has an entirely different tone quality that one doesn't get with a nylon-string guitar. A major disadvantage with the electric—at least for me—is the lack of control when I'm playing solo, because sometimes, if I don't set the amp exactly right it will be too loud and I will have difficulty playing. I play with both hands, naturally, so I can't usually stop in the middle of a tune to readjust the volume if it's too high. That's the big disadvantage; another is the wear and tear on my nails. I don't play more electric onstage because the steel strings chew up my nails. I play a lot of my solos on acoustic.

*What percentage of a Chet Atkins show is acoustic?*

It's half acoustic and half electric. For the first half of the show I go out and do two or three acoustic tunes by myself, and then Paul Yandell comes out and accompanies me on his acoustic. And we do the rest of the first half by ourselves. Then we have an intermission. For the next set the whole band comes out, and then Paul and I come out and do the rest of the show on electric.

*Do you feel more comfortable on an electric or an acoustic guitar?*

It's weird—I feel comfortable with *both,* because I have played them for so many years. It takes me just a few seconds onstage to get acclimated to the difference in neck width.

*What do you feel are the major advantages and disadvantages of an acoustic instrument?*

The lack of sustain is a definite disadvantage. You know, if you're trying to duplicate the sound of an electric—particularly on the treble strings—a nylon-string guitar doesn't sustain enough. Also, the nature of the instrument makes it difficult to amplify properly. When you get into an auditorium, a lot of the soundmen think that you've got to knock the people over with volume. They can turn it up too loud, and you then get feedback. I would rather have people strain a little to hear me than have a booming, loud sound that resonates and can feed back.

*Would you say that country music is more electric than acoustic now?*

Yes.

*How do the bluegrass fanatics relate to this change?*

I don't know. I'm not in touch with the bluegrass musicians that much. Bluegrass people are a cult. Years ago I remember they didn't even talk to us; they had their own thing going and we had our thing going. But it's changed now, although I'm still not in touch with bluegrass people very much.

*Do you classify yourself as a country artist?*

Yeah, I guess so. And I don't like to play for country audiences. I don't like to work the *Grand Ole Opry.* I never did, though I worked it for years, because all the time you're playing there are kids running up and down the aisles, and they're hawking song books and popcorn out in the aisles, and everybody's standing behind you talking about going fishing next week. It's a very difficult show to work. And all the time I'm on, everybody else in the audience is looking up at the ceiling wondering when Roy Acuff is coming on. But the country fans are more devoted, and they stick with you. You can have one hit and play for the rest of your life. So it comes down to survival, and you survive more with those country folks.

*It used to be that even pop singers at least had guitars around their necks and were thumping away on them; but now, more and more of them just hold the microphone and sing. Is the guitar going out of country music?*

I think some people look pretty amateurish when they just stand out there and pick and sing—it's like radio in the '30s or '40s. Now, if they do it right like Roy Clark and make faces and

**Chet Atkins with one of the many Gretsch electrics that he co-designed.**

the past 20 years country music has been moving more and more uptown, and for that there are a lot of reasons—the war, country people have moved to town, they have become acquainted with pop music, and so on. Because of this, their tastes have changed.

*So you feel that it's a natural change, and not necessarily a commercial one?*

I think it's natural, and it's determined by the disc jockeys, the record-buying public, and the musicians. Musicians have very little to do with it, though, because we put on records what we think will sell. If something does sell, then we make more of it. That's the reason country music moved uptown. also, there are social reasons. Back when I first got into the business, there was a lot of bigotry and prejudice towards country music: Middle-class people were afraid to say they liked it because people would look down on them. They thought they were supposed to like folk music and jazz; they wouldn't admit they liked country. But country music in the past few years has become respected. Its songs have become more palatable to city audiences, and some of the musicians are now big stars on television, like Glen Campbell, Johnny Cash, and people like that. So it's socially accepted now to like country music. Rhythm and blues once had the same problem.

*Does the electric guitar sound pretty to you?*

Yes. I love the sound of it, although I don't like a lot of highs. Most of the time, I tend to use the two pickups combined together. Sometimes, on a very raucous tune I use the pickup close to the bridge. I will also use it when I play a real foot-stomper. But most of the time I use the two pickups combined; very seldom do I use the pickup closest to the fingerboard by itself, because it's too bassy. I don't like it too trebly, either; I like a mixture and a pretty sound.

*How do you approach a solo?*

First I learn the melody, and then I learn the chords from sheet music or from a record. Then I try to use substitution chords here and there that will make the tune a little more interesting. For instance, in place of an *Fm* I would use an *Ab6/9,* or in place of a *C7* I sometimes use a *Gdim* going to *F.*

*Were there any specific books that you learned from?*

The first of the classic guitar books that I ever had were by Pascual Roch. He had a book out in three volumes called *Modern Method For Guitar* [1924, G. Schirmer]. He was one of Francisco Tarrega's students. Ezra Carter, the Carter Sisters' father, gave me those three volumes around 1949 or 1950. I don't think they're still in print. The George M. Smith book *Modern Guitar Method* [Guitarists Publications] was a good one, and still is. I had that book early. I think I had the old Manoloff books, but they didn't have much in them that I didn't already know.

*And how did Ezra happen to have those Roch books?*

That old cock was into everything. He would have spells: If he wanted to repair radios, he'd take a course and learn how to repair a radio. He once decided he wanted to build roads for the people up in Poor Valley and East Tennessee or up in Virginia where he lived, so he bought a bulldozer and built roads. He was into all kinds of things. I don't know how he became interested in classical guitar; I never asked him. But he had those books, and he gave them to me. He didn't play, so maybe he thought his daughters would pick up the stuff. He was a wild

entertain, it's great. And Glen Campbell does it—Glen plays the hell out of a guitar, you know; he can play with anybody. So it depends on who it is.

*Many country singers are just holding microphones now.*

I think they think it looks more professional to hold the mike, you know. You can gesture more and everything if you're not holding the guitar. That's probably what it is, just showmanship. All country acts want a pop hit—they want a crossover hit. And they'll do anything to get it. I mean they'll make a slightly pop record and try to keep their country audience. We've all done that, because you triple your sales if you get a crossover hit. Country music is in a pretty bad state right now because of that. But fortunately there are some records coming along which are pure country that are selling. I hate to see country music die, where you turn on the radio and you can't tell if it's a pop record or a country record and it's that way now. It's gotten so it depends on geography—where you're from—as to whether you're country or not.

*Do you think that when country music first started to become more popular that you played a part in changing the guitar from acoustic to electric?*

I was accused of, and I've apologized for, moving country music too far uptown. But I did very little, compared to what has been done since I almost quit producing. When you're making records, you are trying to keep your job; you're trying to make money for the company you work for. You're compelled to try new things because you're trying to sell a record. The public wants to be surprised. You give them new effects or they won't buy. So you get into a slot where you move in a certain direction, and if they tend to buy that then you give them more of it. Because of this, the music moves in certain directions. So, for

**World-famous as an electric guitar stylist, Chet Atkins also excells on classical guitar.**

old guy—a great person. I had an awful lot of respect for him and Maybelle, and for the girls.

*Was music always an important part of your life?*

Yes, from the very beginning. My brother Jim, when he was at home, played guitar; and then my dad did a little, too. And so I started. I was playing ukulele when I was four or five, and then I tried guitar—but first I was dragging it through the yard, tying a string to it and filling it up with dirt. After my mother was divorced from my dad, she married a guitarist by the name of Willie Strevel. She stayed at the old home place, and my dad moved to Georgia. I stayed with my mother till I was 11. My stepfather played guitar with a thumbpick and his fingers—he'd go out and cut a toothbrush handle off and make a thumbpick from it. We played a lot with a "case" knife, too. That's what we called a kitchen knife. Slide guitar is what that was, you know, but I gave that up when I was about eight years old.

*Did people in your area get together often to make music?*

Yes, we would. Out in the country people will come and stay a while. You don't invite them, they just come. We used to have one boy that we called "Knucks," because he carried a pair of brass knuckles. He was one of those guys that was tone deaf but could play three chords, and he'd sing some mountain song in one key and play guitar in another, and we would brag on him and tell him how great he was. He never suspected we were putting him on.

*What jobs did you have before playing music professionally?*

I worked on a farm a lot, but I never got paid anything for it and I didn't take to that too well. You know, we had a lot of farm work—tobacco, peanuts—I never raised any cotton like Johnny Cash, but could have if my dad had known how to raise it. My dad was a fellow who loved to farm, but he didn't like to do it himself. He'd love to hire people or get his kids to do the work. He was really just a music teacher.

*Did he have an instrument that he concentrated on?*

He played piano, mostly, and fiddle. And he sang—he gave concerts singing classics like "Ave Maria." He was into that stuff where they roll the r's when they sing. My first memory of him was doing his vocal exercises. He hated hillbillies. He hated the simple folk music stuff; he thought it was ignorant and dumb. Of course, I rebelled. I liked it. He didn't like guitar, either.

*How many hours a day were you working chores as opposed to practicing?*

I'd get up very early, feed the stock, get my breakfast, and go to school. A lot of times I'd keep a guitar over at school, or take it with me. I'd always practice at recess and lunch. I'd go to the men's room and practice because there was an echo. Nobody used echo, but to me it sounded beautiful. The boys that had money would be shooting dice, and I'd practice guitar. I would walk to school in the morning because the bus would come by my house and then go 25 miles further and pick up other kids, so it was about an hour or so ride. So I'd walk about four miles to school. In the afternoon he would go right by my house, so I would ride home. And I might practice a little, or work—whatever I had to do. And chop wood, if it was in the winter, for two fireplaces—my dad and his wife's room, and my room. Then I'd stay up to 12:00 and practice at night, and listen to the radio and get four or five hours' sleep. One morning I was setting the milk down. We had a cream separator; I had to do all that job. Well, I set the milk down and woke up on the floor. I'd learned all about masturbation about that time, and I was running off a batch every few hours, and I fainted, and the milk turned over all over me, and I fell. I turned over the kerosene can, and the milk and kerosene were all over. So after that, my dad said, "You've got to start getting some sleep, kid; you can't stay up and pick that damn guitar till 12:00. So he started making me go to bed at night. But I was run down. I had asthma, too. I was a pretty sickly kid.

*Were you missing school because of the asthma?*

Sometimes I would, but most of the time I went. I'd huff and puff and go on.

*Did your dad teach you music?*

Well, sometimes I would go with him and listen to him teach piano—if there was a pretty girl, I'd go in. Other times I'd sit out in his A model, and I could still hear them playing tunes that he had written, and piano selections, simple things. Then he'd tune pianos a lot, too, and I'd go watch him do that, and he tried to teach me how to do that, but I could never hear the beats like he could.

*Do you have a good ear?*

Not really. It's fairly good. I've got a low note I can hit, and so I can tune up pretty close to standard pitch with my voice. I can hit a low *E*—I know just about where *E* is. And I can sit and think, hear a chord or a tone and then visualize the guitar and figure out pretty close where it is. But no, I don't have perfect pitch.

*What instrument were you first interested in?*

I always wanted a fiddle. We always had a guitar around, and my dad would come in and bring us instruments after he left home. He'd say, "Yeah, kid, I'll bring you a fiddle some day," and I guess he thought I was too young. He'd bring mandolins and guitars. Finally our uncle Joe came in from Nebraska, and he heard I wanted a fiddle. So he brought me a fiddle on his next trip. It had been struck by lightening. It was lying by the side of the house or something over in a corner, and the lightning struck the side. The top was busted in 22 different pieces, and somebody had done a great job of putting it back together. he had a bow with it, but the bow didn't have any hair in it. So we went out, me and my brother Lowell, to old Bob, our old white horse. Lowell said, "Fatty"—I was fat then—"you hold his tail." I held it, and Lowell cut off a strand of hair and we glued it in that bow. Then we went up to a fiddle player and got some rosin from him. So two weeks later I worked a job. We played over at the school for a sick person, and I knew two tunes. I think they were "Redwing" and "Sally Ann" or something like that. I was so little—I was only eight or nine years old—that the fiddle wouldn't fit under my chin. My sister and a cousin were operating the curtain at the show, so they thought, "He's going to drop it!" And so they closed the curtain right in the middle of my tune.

*Was that the end of the performance?*

No. Also during that show we did a comedy routine. We did blackface comedy and stuff, but a guy was arresting another guy, and he pulls out a pistol and shoots. He didn't have any blanks—he had a real pistol. And he turned it and shot into the wall. It was about a .45, and it put out every light in that building. They were kerosene lights. Did you know a gun will do that? The concussion will. It put out every damn light in that building.

*Was that your first fiddling job?*

Yeah, I didn't get any money for it, but somebody did—some sick person we were playing for. Somebody was dying with TB. They had a lot of TB out there in east Tennessee, and

my sister died with it when she was 26. Back then they didn't have any drugs for it. I remember when I was a kid, when somebody would get sick, why we would get together and put on a show and turn the money over to the person who was sick. My first job was when they opened up a grocery store. Me and my brother played, and we got $3.00 and some watermelon. I was in that store the other day—they've added on to it. It's a supermarket now.

*When did you first get an electric guitar and amp?*

When I was 15, Eleanor Roosevelt started a thing called the NYA, the National Youth Administration, to keep kids busy in the summertime. It was kind of like the WPA, only for kids. I was part of it, and we built a gymnasium at Mountain Hill School near where I lived, in Hamilton, Georgia. I saved enough money to buy an amp, but we didn't have electricity. You see, we lived out in the sticks. Well, I ordered an Amperite pickup for my guitar from Allied anyway. It was basically just a coil of wire and a magnet that you clamped to the back of the bridge. Then I got a PA system: ordered the amp from one place, a case from another, and tubes from still another—just to save a dollar or so. I put it all together and was ready to go. There was electricity over at the Mountain Hill School, but it was direct current, DC. My amp was made for AC, so I couldn't use it; it would have blown my amp up.

*How did you power it then?*

My dad used to go to town on Saturday and teach, so I would go with him. I also took my guitar and amp down to the church there, 25 miles away in Columbus, where my dad was the choir director. I would plug in and play and afterwards take it all back home again and wish for electricity.

*Did you ever get into any trouble with the pastor?*

No, he loved it. Parson Jack Johnson, the Baptist preacher, was the person who first wanted to put me on radio. He had his own show—30 minutes on WRBL on Saturday morning at ten o'clock. He heard me play when he came out to the farm. He said, "You sing alright. I'm going to have you on my radio program." So I'd sing hymns, play guitar, and he'd preach for 30 minutes. That was around '38 or '39. I got my first fan letter there. Somebody wrote in. I think the first song I ever sang was "Where Is My Wandering Boy Tonight?" That's an oldie but goodie. I was about 14, I guess.

*When did you begin to do studio work?*

When I went to Nashville I started recording right off with Hank Williams and all the big names. I worked the studios till about 1957. I was on every record that Hank made until he died—from 1950 on. The last record I made with him was "I'll Never Get Out Of This World Alive." And he died a few days later. He'd make a cut and then fall over in his chair, and one fellow would say, "He's so skinny his ass rattles like a sack of carpenter's tools when he walks." He was into morphine and stuff. He got a shot in Knoxville, and he had already taken some and didn't tell the doctor, and it put him to sleep.

*Were you ever restricted by record producers or television producers?*

I've had them try to get me to change tunes, and all that. That happens like when you work the talk shows. I remember a director once said, "Would you mind playing it faster?" I said, "I can't play it any faster, I'm sorry. If I play it faster, I might mess up and embarrass myself." You always have that, because those guys don't know anything about guitar playing. They just want something flashy and a lot of jumping around. As far as TV goes, what I prefer to work, really, is PBS [Public Broadcasting System], because you can do an hour or 30 minutes and do your own thing, and come across a lot better—I can. It's difficult when you're just a guest on some show and play one tune.

*Why did you leave studio work?*

After I started A&R [artist and repertoire] work and producing other artists, I just couldn't keep doing session work. You know, I'd try to play, and then you go in and listen to the cut, and it's not what you thought—it's not the balance you thought you had at all, so I'd hire Grady Martin or someone. I played on other people's records—I played on all the Everly Brothers' hits. I didn't realize they had so damn many hits. I heard a medley on TV the other night—"Dream," "Bird Dog," "Bye Bye Love," When I first got the job as A&R man, the first hit I had was recording "Oh Lonesome Me" by Don Gibson. He wrote "I Can't Stop Loving You" and "Oh Lonesome Me" in one day.

*Did you play on Don Gibson's "Sea Of Heartbreak"?*

Yeah, me and Hank [Garland]. We got so Hank and I would play duets. But we don't deserve a lot of credit for those. They're great solos, but Don was the one who would come up with them. I'd say, "What do you want us to play?" Well, he'd hum some wild damn thing that we'd learn, and it'd be different than anything we would think of. If we played a chorus, we'd play some jazzy something, and Don, he'd hum something and say, "Play this." And we'd get something similar to it, and it would turn out to be great.

*And that's how that style of solo originated?*

Well, it wasn't my idea. See, all these things are accidents. Like the style I play is an accident, because I was so far out in the damn sticks I didn't know any better.

*Did you ever appear on any of Elvis Presley's records?*

Yes. I played on "Heartbreak Hotel" and "I Want You, I Need You, I Love You"—things like that. I played rhythm and Scotty Moore played lead. Elvis came in and did some more sessions after those first ones, but I don't remember any of the tunes. I never played electric on those records. With Elvis I hired the band, and he wound up using those guys for years. I hired Floyd Cramer; he'd just moved to town. And I tried to hire the Speer Family as singers, and I couldn't get them, so I got the Jordanaires. They wound up working with Elvis for 10 or 15 years. You never realize when you do a little something what effect it'll have on people's lives. It just turned out he liked the guys, you know, and he used them when he would come back.

*Do you ever sit and play just to relax?*

Oh, that's all I do.

*If you go on vacation, do you take your guitar?*

Always. I always do. Sometimes I don't play, but I want it with me for some reason or other—it's a security thing. I guess. And if I'm bored I just pick up the guitar and improvise, and half a day will go by real quick, just because I enjoy it so much.

*Is it true that you sometimes fall asleep with the guitar on your lap when you have bouts with insomnia?*

I still do that, yeah.

*Do you still suffer from insomnia?*

I don't have any trouble going to sleep; I wake up too quick. That's always been my problem. I go to sleep in five minutes, any time after I've been up a few hours. But I wake up after about six hours. And I don't feel like playing then. Actually, I think I'm much more creative in the morning—I think I can get up, I can write better and everything, because my mind's clear and all my inhibitions have surfaced.

---

## A SELECTED CHET ATKINS DISCOGRAPHY

**Solo albums** (on RCA/Victor): *A Session With Chet Atkins*, LPM-1090RE; *Chet Atkins In 3 Dimensions*, LPM-1197; *Stringin' Along With Chet Atkins*, LPM-1236; *Finger-Style Guitar*, LPM, 1383; *Chet Atkins At Home*, LPM-1544; *Hi-Fi In Focus*, LPM-1577; *Chet Atkins In Hollywood*, LPM-1993; *Hum And Strum Along With Chet Atkins*, LPM-2025; *Mister Guitar*, LPM-2013; *Teensville*, LPM-2161; *The Other Chet Atkins*, LSP-2175; *Chet Atkins' Workshop*, LSP-2232; *The Most Popular Guitar*, LSP-2346; *Down Home*, LPM-2450; *Caribbean Guitar*, LPM-2549; *Our Man In Nashville*, LSP-2616; *Travelin'*, LPM-2678; *Guitar Country*, LSP-2783; *Progressive Pickin'*, LSP-2908; *From Nashville With Love*, LSP-3647; *It's A Guitar World*, LSP-3728; *Class Guitar*, LSP-3885; *Solo Flights*, LSP-3922; *My Favorite Guitars*, LSP-3316; *Christmas With Chet Atkins*, ANLI-1935; *The Best Of Chet Atkins*, AHLI-3095; *Picks On The Beatles*, ANLI-2002; *The Best Of Chet Atkins, Vol. 2*, AHLI-3558; *Chet Atkins Picks The Best*, ANLI-0981; *More Of That Guitar Country*, LPM-3429; *Hometown Guitar*, LSP-4017; *Lover's Guitar*, LSP-4135; *Solid Gold '69*, LSP-4244; *Yestergroovin'*, LSP-4331; *For The Good Times*, AHLI-4464; *Pickin' My Way*, LSP-4585; *Picks On The Hits*, AHLI-4754; *Chet Atkins Discovers Japan*, LSP-5047; *Alone*, APLI-0159; *Chet Atkins Goes To The Movies*, AHLI-0845; *Award Winners*, AHLI-2262; *Best Of A Great Year: Vol. 2*, CLP2-0449; *Good Old Country Gospel*, AHLI-4778; *Greatest Hits Of The '50s*, ARLI-0044; *Greatest Hits Of The '60s*, ARLI-0045; *In Concert*, CLP2-1014; *Now And Then*, VPSX-6079; *This Is Chet Atkins*, VPS-6030; *The Night Atlanta Burned*, APLI-1233; *American Salute*, AGLI-3965. (On Columbia): *Stay Tuned*, FC 39591; *Street Dreams*, FC 40256. **With Lenny Breau:** *Lenny Breau Trio*, Adelphi, ADP 5018l. **With others:** (on RCA/Victor): *Chet Atkins And Hank Snow: Reminiscing*, LSP-2952; *Chet Picks On The Pops: Arthur Fiedler*, LSC-3104; *C.B. Atkins and C.E. Snow—By Special Request*, LSP-4254; *Me And Jerry*, AHLI-4396; *Me And Chet*, ANLI-2167; *Superpickers*, APDI-0329; *The Atkins-Travis Traveling Show*, AHLI-0479; *Picks On Jerry Reed*, APLI-0545; *Great Moments At The Grand Ole Opry*, CPL2-1904; *Chester And Lester*, AHLI-1167; *The Best Of Chet Atkins And Friends*, APLI-1985; *Guitar Monsters*, AHLI-2786; *The First Nashville Guitar Quartet*, AHLI-3302; *Nashville's Greatest Instrumentalists*, ANLI-2181. **With The Nashville String Band** (on RCA/Victor): *The Nashville String Band*, LSP-4274; *Down Home*, LSP-4363; *Identified*, LSP-4472; *Strung Up*, LSP-4552; *The Bandit*, LSP-4659; *The World's Greatest Melodies*, LSP-4771.

# JETHRO BURNS

**By David Grisman**

KENNETH "JETHRO" BURNS HAS HAD A MANDOLIN IN his hands for most of his life. He is certainly one of America's living musical legends. For more than 30 years, he and his guitar-playing partner, Henry Haynes, wreaked havoc with our national funnybone as "Homer and Jethro" on radio, records, TV, and in personal appearances. Little did we realize that beneath the facade of corny jokes and zany antics were some truly serious jazz musicians.

In 1963, with the release of their first instrumental album, *Playing It Straight,* Jethro made a landmark contribution to mandolin playing in the idiom of mainstream jazz, a style which he pioneered. More recently, and particularly since the death of

Homer in 1971, Jethro has focused more and more of his time and energy toward mandolin playing, composing, and teaching. He has made numerous recordings and often appeared with his good friend, [guitarist] Steve Goodman, [*Ed Note: Steve Goodman died of leukemia in 1984*] in addition to cutting a solo album, *Jethro Burns*. He has also been part of notable musical collaborations with Vassar Clements and Sam Bush, Joe Venuti and Eldon Shamblin, Chet Atkins, and the Nashville String Band. There are more than 30 "Homer And Jethro" albums, and Jethro's most recent release is *Back To Back,* a classic jazz mandolin encounter with veteran electric mandolinist, Tiny Moore. His book, *Jethro Burns, Mandolin Player* (Mel Bay Publications) is the first ever devoted to this new style, and has firmly established itself as an essential reference work for a whole new crop of mandolin pickers.

I first made Jethro's acquaintance in 1973, when I stopped off in Evanston, Illinois, where he lives, to take a mandolin lesson. Since that time, Jethro has become both a friend and a musical influence. He shares such relationships with many of us mandolin players. When you hang out with Jethro for any length of time, two things become readily apparent: This man has got to be one of the funniest guys on the face of the earth, and he can play the hell out of a mandolin.

\* \* \* \*

*AT WHAT AGE DID YOU FIRST BECOME INTERESTED IN playing the mandolin?*

At age six. I got my first mandolin from my oldest brother, Aytchie. He brought an old 'tater bug' [roundback] style mandolin home and gave me strict orders not to touch it. So as soon as he went to work in the saw mill, I got it out and started pickin' around on it. I got a couple of things to sound right, and he said it was OK. The first tune I learned to play was "Little Brown Jug." Then a guy named John Henry Gibson, who played a little mandolin and a lot of fiddle, taught me how to pick out melodies on the mandolin.

*What attracted you to the mandolin?*

I liked the sound of it, and when I got to be about ten years old, my father went out and bought me a real fine Gibson mandolin. He paid a whole lot for it. It was an "A" model with a round soundhole. I played that for many years, but all of a sudden I got involved in playing with other musicians, and it wasn't loud enough. We played fiddle tunes and hoedowns. I complained about it not being loud enough, so my father went out and bought me a Gibson banjo-mandolin, and those things were *loud!* I didn't really like the sound of it, it was just loud.

*When did you start professionally?*

I started playing professionally with Homer [Henry Haynes] at the age of 12 at WNOX in Knoxville, Tennessee. We both showed up to audition for a talent contest. I was with my brother, and Homer came in with two other guys. They had a fiddle, guitar, and bass. We played "Nola" and "Sweet Georgia Brown." When the auditions were over, the station manager, Lowell Blanchard, pointed to me and my brother, and to Homer and this other rhythm guitar player, and said, "I want you guys to sit down and just jam!" So we sat there and played "Sweet Georgia Brown" and "Lady Be Good." He said, "All right, you guys won't even be in the contest, *but* we're gonna hire you as staff musicians! You'll go to work on Monday morning." The

program that we worked on was from 12 noon till 1:30, so they made arrangements for us to get out of school. We'd go to school up until it was time to leave, then do the program, then go back. The group was called the String Dusters. After a few years, my brother and the other guitarist each got married, and they didn't want to travel. In the meantime, me and Homer had been working up these comedy routines just for fun, so when the group split, we said, "We'll just do this!" We had been given the names "Homer" and "Jethro" by this same guy, Lowell Blanchard. He got "Jethro" out of the Bible, and "Homer"— well, down South, all the village idiots are called "Homer!" This guy taught us so much about show business. I hung around him and picked his brain, because I knew that he knew all the stuff that I wanted to know. Really, I give him credit for everything I've ever done, because without him, I wouldn't have done anything. He couldn't teach me how to play; but he taught me how to talk, sing, and all the other stuff I had to know.

*When did you and Homer start on your own?*

In 1937. We just played locally. In 1939, we went to Renfro Valley, Kentucky, and became part of the *Renfro Valley Barn Dance.* At that time we had something going that was really great, in that we fed both NBC and CBS. Both networks! We had a program on CBS, called *Monday Night In Renfro Valley,* coast-to-coast. And on Saturday we did the *Barn Dance,* also coast-to-coast. In those days there was no TV, so network radio was good as you could get.

*Who were your musical influences at that time?*

We were listening to [guitarist] Django [Reinhardt] and [violinist] Stephane Grappelli, and I got to copying these guys. Then I got to listening to the big bands, like those of Benny Goodman and Tommy Dorsey. The thing that always impressed me about Django was the fact that he'd play one of these runs that'd be like three city blocks long, and that thing just sang!

*Do you remember the first time you heard Django?*

Yes, I sure do. He was playing a tune called "Clouds." This was in Chattanooga, about 1936 or 1937. It came over the radio station where I was working, WDOD. When I heard that, I said, "My God, I never heard such a sound in my life!" We'd hear the Quintet [Le Quintet du Hot Club du France] do "Clouds," "Sweet Georgia Brown," and "Swing Guitars." When you heard it, you felt so helpless because here was a bunch of guys in France who were playing our music so much better than we were.

*What about [guitarist] Eddie Lang and [violinist] Joe Venuti?*

Oh sure. I always thought that Eddie Lang was the greatest guitar player I ever heard, because he was the *first* guitar player I ever heard. He played some great solos like "Pickin' My Way," "Feelin' My Way," and even Rachmaninoff's prelude in C♯ minor. Then I got to hear the things he did with Venuti. I've still got those records at home. But to me, Eddie Lang influenced me as much as Django or anybody else. Venuti, now there's another one there! I used to see him when he had a group playing in Las Vegas at the Golden Nugget. The first time I met the guy was quite an experience. That was a couple of years ago, when I recorded with him.

*How did that come about?*

He was playing at a jazz club in Chicago called Rick's, so Flying Fish Records lined up this album with Venuti, [pedal steel guitarist] Curley Chalker, and [guitarist] Eldon Shamblin.

**Well-known for his early comedy duet with Homer Haynes, Jethro Burns is a virtuosic bluegrass mandolinist.**

When I first met Venuti, he wasn't impressed at all, and he kept saying, "Jethro, can you play . . . ?" After a while, I got tired of this and said, "Joe, don't ask me 'Can you play?' I can play any damn thing you can! Why don't you say, 'Play "Lady Be Good" or "'S Wonderful!'" or whatever?" I thought he was questioning my ability to play. We became buddy-buddy. Anytime I'd play any kind of a nice lick, why, he'd give me that big smile, and then he'd kick the tempo up! I did another album with him just a month before he died. He asked me to come in and do some cuts with him. He was very sick with cancer. One time we played, and all of a sudden he just got up and said, "I don't feel like playing anymore." He put his violin in the case, and walked out of the studio. That was the last we saw of him. The next thing we heard was that he had gone to Seattle and died. It was so heavy. I loved the guy, because, man, he was so crotchety. I'm the same way, but I don't have the prestige to get away with it like he did!

*How come all the other country musicians you worked with ended up sticking with fiddle tunes, while you got into Django and jazz?*

I liked the fiddle tunes, but there was no challenge there. It was no fun to play 'em, you learned 'em one way. Now, the Django stuff—that was fun. I mean, you could play it a thousand times and play it different every time. That was more of a challenge.

*Were there other mandolin players who inspired you?*

There was a guy named Paul Buskirk. I heard Paul many, many years ago in Memphis, when he was in Eddie Hill's band with the Louvin brothers. He was just incredibly fast. There was another guy, Doug Dalton. When I knew him, he was playing with Clayton McMichen and the Georgia Wildcats, out of

Louisville, Kentucky. Then he came to Knoxville, and boy, he was just hot! He was the first guy I ever heard that played octave strings on the mandolin. He'd put an octave on his *D* string and on his *G* string. It sounded great. He played real nice chord solos. He was out of a group called the Whippoorwills. They had the exact same instrumentation as we did with our String Dusters; in fact, that's where they got the idea; mandolin, two guitars, and bass. They did a lot of our arrangements, tunes like "Don't Be That Way" [Benny Goodman's theme]. They asked if it was okay with us, because our group had dissolved. We said, "Sure, we don't care!" We all heard Bill Monroe, but never got excited about it. Then of course there was Dave Apollon.

*When did you first see him?*

He came to Cincinnati with a vaudeville review in about 1947. I saw him in Dallas later. In a way, the reason I admired Apollon so much was that not only was he playing this great mandolin, but he was one of the funniest guys that I'd ever seen; I mean this guy was just hilarious! Years later, I met Dave in Music City in Hollywood. I played him a few cuts from the *Playin' It Straight* album. He said, "You are influenced by Django!" We didn't play together, but I heard him many times at the Desert Inn in Las Vegas. He inspired me. I didn't try to copy him.

*Did you aspire to become a jazz mandolinist?*

No. Homer and I really wanted to be a comedy team. We were both drafted in '41. It was like being part of a John Wayne movie. After the war, we went back to WLW in Cincinnati where we were featured on several shows. One was *Doodle Sockers,* a completely insane comedy program with a band and everything, like *Laugh In,* except on radio. It was during this time that I met my wife. My wife and Chet Atkins' wife were a twin-sister singing team at the station—the Johnson Twins. When we first moved to Cincinnati, we couldn't find a place to stay. Chet Atkins had a room at the YMCA, and he had an extra bed, so he invited me to move in with him. I lived there for three months and all we did from early morning till late at night was play.

*How did the idea of "fracturing" popular tunes come about?*

We began recording for King Records, doing just straight lyrics, except we hoked up the music a little. This was about 1946. We made a whole bunch of records for King. Then, in 1949, we got a chance to go to RCA Victor, which was number one. They wanted a different format. They said, "How would it be if you did parodies on songs, like do some funny lyrics?" So we said, "Fine." The first tune they laid on us was "Baby, It's Cold Outside," which was written by Frank Loesser. So I sat down and wrote a parody on the thing. Now, once I'd gotten it written, they had to get Frank Loesser's approval. He had to hear it and decide whether we could do it or not. So I read the lyric over the phone to him, and he said, "Okay, that's very funny. However, when you do it, I want 'with apologies to Frank Loesser' on the label!" That's the way we did it, and it was a hit.

*How were you recording when you reached your high level of popularity in the '50s?*

At the point that we're talking about, we had all signed contracts with RCA—Chet, and Homer and Jethro. Every time one of us cut a record, why the other guys were sidemen on it. Homer and Jethro would have a background of Chet Atkins on guitar, Jerry Byrd on steel, Charlie Grillion on bass, and on a lot of things, George Barnes on guitar. George was the ultimate perfectionist. He was the kind of guy that would walk in and say, "Well, if you don't make any mistakes, there ain't gonna be any!" He was that good.

*Were three guitar players too many?*

No, because Homer played rhythm, and Barnes and Chet just traded off leads. They stayed out of each other's way pretty well. I always liked to work with Barnes because he came up with all these real exciting runs. You were never sure where they were going to end, except they always ended right.

*What about the instrumental Homer and Jethro albums; what prompted them?*

We used to do instrumentals in our act, and we finally decided that we were going to do an instrumental album whether the record company liked it or not. We just demanded it. Luckily, at the time we were in a position where we could lean on them. Now they have released those things in Japan. We also cut lots of instrumentals with Chet Atkins, like "Main Street Breakdown," "Barbershop Rag," and "Galloping Guitar."

*When did you start writing tunes?*

Probably eight or ten years ago, after my partner died. I had a lot of time on my hands. I started to put some things together, then put 'em on tape. Now I've got a long list. Some of the original things I've done, I'm so proud of. Maybe nothing will ever come of them, but by God, they were *mine*. Writing is such a kick, man. My main thought is just to get the thing down on tape, that melody line. I wish I had some kind of formula where you could just sit down and put the good stuff down. I can't do it. I get one good line, and ten bad ones. Once in a while, I'll luck out, where I get one to go all the way through.

*When did you begin using electric mandolins?*

When I was on WLS, on the *National Barn Dance*, we had many outdoor dates, like fairs and festivals; and the music from the midway completely destroyed you. Then I started to amplify my mandolin, and Homer started to amplify his guitar. The first one I had was an A model with a pickup. Then later on I got an F-5 with a pickup on it. That was really the only way you could be heard over this noise. I used a Fender 4-string for a while. At the time, it was fun, but I didn't really like it because you couldn't use tremolo. I wanted to get back to those good old double strings. I can't really say that I like the pure electric tone. To me, the utlimate mandolin sound comes from the F-5 and the A-5, acoustically. I still would rather play acoustic.

*When you listen to music for your own enjoyment, what do you listen to? Count Basie?*

Yeah, I still listen to the old stuff. I like the new stuff, but as far as playing goes, I just like to stick to the old standard things. It's gotten to where there's almost as much prestige in knowing all those things as there is in playing say, disco or whatever's happening—which you can play with your three fingers taped behind your back! Myself, I like the Basie-Ellington type things,

and they are really a challenge because they are tough to play. I still fall back on a lot of Django things. You can listen to Django forever and ever, and think you've heard everything he ever played, and all of a sudden you put on an album and hear something completely new. Like "Tears"—my God, what great stuff on the mandolin!

*Do you read music, and have you ever studied other instruments?*

I have learned how to read music a dozen times in my life, and I always forget it. When I was about 17 years old I learned to read from a guy named Henry Farrel, who taught guitar in Knoxville. My brother took guitar lessons from him and Chet Atkins took a few. I took about six lessons on guitar. I did this primarily to help my mandolin playing, because the mandolin didn't have the chords that I wanted. In other words, I could play a melody on the mandolin, but I wouldn't know the chord changes and everything. I figured that the guitar would give me the advantage of knowing what the changes would be, and then I could translate them on mandolin. I never considered myself a guitar player.

*How do you feel about your recording with Tiny Moore [Back To Back]?*

I think it's going to be the greatest thing that ever happened to me. I've told people about it, and they flip. It was a big thrill to get to pick with Tiny, not to mention [bassist] Ray Brown, [drummer] Shelly Manne, and Eldon!

*Are there any other projects you'd like to do?*

The one that really interests me now is a *solo* mandolin album, which you suggested to me. Some of these good old standards that haven't been played to death.

*What kind of instrument are you playing these days?*

Right now I'm playing a brand new Washburn mandolin. A lot of people turn their noses up at them because they're not old and they're not Gibson, but I pick a mandolin that plays for *me*.

*What makes a good mandolin player? What was the hardest thing for you to learn?*

I think the big thing is fingering, because I think a lot of guys could play a hell of a lot better if they would play the fingerings the way they were meant to be played. Now, they lock themselves into the bluegrass chords, which ties up all four fingers on all four strings. There's no reason to do that. A lot of guys do not use the little finger for some reason or other. I went for a lot of years where I didn't use my little finger.

*What do you think about the state of the mandolin right now? Has it changed at all since you started?*

One thing I think is that it's gotten to be a respectable instrument; whereas before, everybody *doubled* on mandolin. I was always put off by guys who said, "Well, I play mandolin as a sideline." Well I play mandolin full-time, and to me that is where it's at right now.

---

**A SELECTED JETHRO BURNS DISCOGRAPHY**

**Solo albums** (on Flying Fish): *Jethro Burns*, FF 042; *Jethro Live*, FF 072; *'S Wonderful! Four Giants Of Swing*, FF 035. *Tea For One*, Kaleidoscope (dist. by Flying Fish), KLD 14. **With Homer (Henry D. Haynes):** *It Ain't Necessarily Square*, RCA, LSP 3701; *Playin' It Straight*, RCA, LSP 2459. **With Wade Ray:** *Down Yonder*, RCA Camden, CAS 2145. **With Tiny Moore:** *Back To Back*, Kaleidoscope, F-9. **With Larry NcNeely:** *Rhapsody For Banjo*, Flying Fish, FF 025. **With Norman Blake:** *Norman Blake*, Flying Fish, FF 701.

# JAMES BURTON

**By Steve Fishell**

**J**AMES BURTON IS THE CONSUMMATE SIDEMAN OF HIS generation. As a lead specialist, he virtually set the standard for country rock a decade before the genre even existed. A master of understatement, he elevated the lead guitar fill to art form status. And Burton is one of the few guitarists (if not the only one) to forge a lucrative session career *after* tasting fame as a teen guitar star. Unlike the Larry Carltons, Steve Lukathers, and

Lee Ritenours, who catapulted from distinguished studio careers to pop and rock stardom, Burton shifted gears into reverse, from high visibility as Ricky Nelson's right-hand man onstage, in the studio, and on television, to the less glamorous confines of the recording studio—playing on TV and film scores, radio jingles, and record dates.

His first recording session was Dale Hawkins' 1957 hit

"Suzy-Q," featuring James' hypnotic signature riff and searing, string-pushing solos. Since then, Burton has played on one ground-breaking session after another in a career that spans almost 30 years—an imposing length of time to remain successful in *any* business, let alone the rarified, high-pressure atmosphere of the studio.

In the '50s, he was the smiling Telecaster-slinger at Ricky Nelson's side every week on *The Adventures Of Ozzie And Harriet*, one of the first television series to regularly feature rock and roll. With country singers Merle Haggard and Buck Owens, he helped define the now-famous "Bakersfield sound" in the early and mid-'60s. Then it was back to the TV screen, as a member of *Shindig*'s house band, the Shindogs. A few years later, visionary singer/songwriter Gram Parsons hired Burton's services for what was to become one of the seminal country rock albums. Shortly thereafter, he helped Emmylou Harris' Hot Band live up to its name. In 1969 when Elvis Presley decided to go back on the road for his first live appearances in years, James Burton was the logical choice to lead the band.

These days—juggling the touring schedules of John Denver and one of Elvis' contemporaries, Jerry Lee Lewis—he continues to inspire the guitar community at large.

From the King and the Killer to the Chairman Of The Board, Burton's studio and road credentials are a veritable who's who of the pop, country, and rock and roll genres. Although he is best known as a country and rock specialist, his studio chops have fueled a wide range of projects by artists as diverse as Nat King Cole, Johnny Cash, the Byrds, Tom Jones, Waylon Jennings, Henry Mancini, Judy Collins, the Supremes, Johnny Mathis, Buffalo Springfield, Ray Charles, the Commodores, the Monkees, Kenny Rogers, Dean Martin, and Frank Sinatra. "I play many different styles of music," he explains, "and I think that's the secret of being a studio musician—making a smooth transition from one style to another. Being a rock and roller doesn't mean specifically that you're only into rock and roll."

Being a "versatile specialist" may seem like a contradiction in terms, but over the years Burton has laid down one example after another of an immediately identifiable stylist fitting into a variety of settings. Who can forget the sputtering, syncopated solos of Merle Haggard's "The Lonesome Fugitive" or "Working Man's Blues," the subtle fills on Emmylou Harris' "Too Far Gone," or the trademark chicken pickin', spitting style on Elvis' live comeback version of "Mystery Train"? Burton has refined his country and rock and roll chops with equal mastery: He is equally poised curling a tasty signature flourish around a ballad's chorus line or plunging pell-mell into a double-time country cooker.

Burton's technique is as singular as his musical prowess. Armed with a Fender medium flatpick between his thumb and index finger *and* a National fingerpick on his middle finger, his self-taught style befuddles onlookers. "It's just the way I started doing it," he shrugs. "I didn't notice anything peculiar until I went into a music store one day and some guy said, 'Man, you're doing it all wrong.'"

The northern Louisiana town of Shreveport, near the east Texas border, is about as far removed from the recording studios of Burbank and Hollywood as one could imagine. James Burton was born there on August 21, 1939, and because of his early interest in the local radio station, his parents bought him a Silvertone acoustic guitar "to beat on" at the age of 13. "I

listened to KWKH in Shreveport," he recounts. "Clarence Gatemouth Brown had a night show there that was all blues and rock." Through KWKH, Burton was exposed to blues greats such as Lightnin' Hopkins, Muddy Waters, and Howlin' Wolf, as well as country music heroes, including Hank Williams, Lefty Frizzell, and Chet Atkins. Learning quickly, he acquired his first electric, a Rex copy of a Gretsch cutaway electric, and studied furiously. "I'd listen to records, and I could hear all of these ideas," he states. "I'd hear a lick and learn to play it, but I'd do it my own way. Also, I really admired the way people like Hank Williams and Lefty Frizzell sang, and I got into their style of singing and overall feeling. I thought that this was how a lead instrument should treat a line—like a lyric—and that was always my approach to playing a solo."

The Rex only lasted three months. James wandered into J & S Music in Shreveport and experienced love at first sight: "When I saw my first Fender Telecaster, I said, 'That's it; I gotta have one of these.' It just felt so right to me." The brand-new blonde '53 maple-neck proved James' instincts to be right. It wound up on innumerable hits by Dale Hawkins, Ricky Nelson, Bob Luman, and others. It is now safely ensconced in the James Burton collection for life.

"I went professional when I was 14, just working private parties and club gigs, and actually getting money for it," Burton remembers. "Money was something that you didn't think about—it was always just for the thrill of playing. I'd skip school to be able to play guitar." His parents remained musically supportive, but, in his words, "I'm not sure that they were real happy about my working clubs at that age. To play in those clubs, you had to go to the police station and get a permit if you were underage. You'd go in, play the gig, and leave."

He became familiar with other musicians around town, including some members of the staff band for the popular regional radio program, the *Louisiana Hayride*. Similar in format to the *Grand Ole Opry*, the *Hayride* was a live concert broadcast to several surrounding states from Shreveport Municipal Auditorium over KWKH on Saturday evenings. "Horace Logan was the producer and co-emcee of the *Hayride*," James reminisces, "and he asked if I would do some shows and join the staff band. I was 14 at the time. We played behind guys like George Jones, Jim And Johnny, Billy Walker, and Johnny Horton. The musicians had to be up on the records—we stayed on top of that. There were very few rehearsals. I ended up playing for almost a year with the staff band."

Young James became fascinated with the bending, vocal qualities of the steel guitar: "I got into playing steel about a year after I started on the electric; I got into playing single-note steel—'Steel Guitar Rag,' and that type of thing." Soon he was injecting that sliding, sustaining tone into his guitar playing: "I worked the *Hayride* with a fantastic steel player named Sonny Trammell. He had a touch on the steel that could make it sound like a guitar. We started switching licks—I would play steel licks, and he would play guitar licks."

James' interest in steel later led him to pursue the slide dobro, an instrument he commands with skillful precision. The dobro became his ace-in-the-hole for studio calls in the '60s, and producers would come to demand the Burton dobro sound as much as his other guitar playing.

Through his work on the *Hayride*, Burton met and worked with a flurry of great early rock and country artists. He recorded

James Burton (right) onstage with Elvis in 1969. James did all of Elvis' studio work, movies, and concerts from that year until the King's death in 1977.

"Suzy-Q" with Dale Hawkins in 1955, at age 15. "We actually recorded that in the radio station at KWKH," James details. "It was very basic. We had three microphones for the drums, bass, guitar, and vocals—not unlike a bunch of guys just sitting around your living room." James originally wrote the song as an instrumental before Hawkins put words to it. Burton's now-famous guitar lick is one of the most instantly recognizable lines in rock music. "That's the basic style that I enjoy playing," he offers. "It's like the Chet Atkins style, but he does more of a country-pop type of picking with the bass, rhythm, and the lead at the same time. I took the same idea, but did it my way, in more of a blues bag. It's just a style I created for myself."

Hawkins and his band played clubs and roadhouses with names like the It'll Do Club in Louisiana, but James soon grew tired of that and joined Bob Luman's band before Hawkins hit the road in 1956. Things started happening faster and faster. He played guitar on Luman's hit singles "My Gal Is Red Hot" and "Red Cadillac And A Black Moustache" (both covered by neo-rockabilly singer Robert Gordon) and worked the *Hayride* steadily with him. Horace Logan, Luman's manager, arranged for the band to travel to Hollywood in 1956 to play in a movie called *Carnival Rock*. While in California, Ricky Nelson met James. Ricky recalled the moment, "The first time I heard him was in the office at Imperial Records. He came from the *Louisiana Hayride*, and I was looking for a band at that time. I was 16, and so was James. I heard this guitar playing at the end of the hall and thought, 'Wow!,' I loved the way he played."

The *Ozzie And Harriet* show was a national pastime in 1957, watched weekly by millions of viewers. Ricky began appearing on the show in 1952, portraying himself on the family series. Starting in 1957, he often closed the segments with a two-minute "live" vocal performance. Ozzie Nelson invited James to join the on-camera backup band for these segments, and this eventually led to James' full participation in Ricky's recording career.

Before James' timely trip to California, renowned country guitarist Joe Maphis had played on all but one of Ricky's earliest 1957 hit recordings for Verve and Imperial, including "Be Bop Baby," "Have I Told You Lately That I Love You," and "I'm Confessin'." (Barney Kessel was lead guitarist on Nelson's first hit, "I'm Walkin'.") Upon James' arrival, several tunes were recorded with both guitarists onboard: "Joe Maphis played on the very first sessions that I recorded with Ricky, which were

'Waitin' In School' and 'Stood Up.' He played the solos, and I only played the rhythm chinks." Eventually, the Nelson road schedule became too hectic for Maphis, and he was replaced permanently by Burton.

The period that followed remains one of the most innovative stages in the development of rockabilly guitar. Although at times Ricky was clearly emulating the classic Sun recordings by Elvis and Carl Perkins, whom he greatly admired, tracks such as "Believe What You Say," "It's Late," "Shirley Lee," "Milkcow Blues," and "Hello Mary Lou" are clearly milestones due to their self-assured precision and tonal development. Burton's round, full bass notes and crystaline, hard-driving highs wrote the book for state-of-the-art Fender tone. "I had a Fender Deluxe and a Twin at that time," James specifies, "but I was using a Fender Vibrasonic with a 15″ Lansing speaker quite a bit on the early sessions with Ricky. I've still got that amp. I also used a Fender Concert a lot. I liked a lot of presence and clear notes: I didn't really like that fuzzy or thin sound. Those early records required a bright sound, not the Buck Owens sound. But when you played chords, you had to have a lot of highs to get the fullness."

"Believe What You Say," with its raunchy string-bending and commanding tone, was the first song to feature Burton on lead. As Ricky told *Guitar Player*, "I think he was probably the first to come up with anything like slinky strings. When we recorded 'Believe What You Say,' I remember him coming into the studio and going, 'Hey, listen to this! He'd put banjo strings on his guitar so that he could bend them way up."

James recalls that the discovery was made in an effort to facilitate smoother string-bending for his bluesy style: "It was the perfect balance all the way across the fretboard. I could use the four light banjo strings, and then just regular D and A strings for the fifth and sixth strings. It was so easy to go from one string to another. I said, 'This is for me,' and I had them gauged and started using them all the time."

Jimmy Haskell, Imperial Records' A&R man, was responsible for capturing on tape what the band played. James Kirkland, who left Bob Luman's band with Burton, played bass, and Earl Palmer was on drums on the early sessions. Later Joe Osborne became the regular bassist. "I had a lot of freedom," says Burton, "but everything was very precise. The main thing that we were concerned about was, 'Is the tone right?' I'm a tone freak. You've got to have the right tone to make it work. I think if you do a ballad, you should have a nice mellow tone. With a good tone and good playing, you're way ahead in the ballgame."

Along with the recordings came those wonderful television appearances—with Ricky and band burning through "Believe What You Say," "It's Late," and other current hits each week. And always there as Ricky's guitar-slinging right-hand man was James Burton, with his penchant for inching two steps forward and grinning directly into the camera while soloing. "You know, Rick used to like to close his eyes a lot when he was singing and getting into the feel of the song," James recalls. "I guess that was one of his trademarks. And I'd be over there and get to cuttin' up, and Ozzie would say, 'Hey, you're going to have to cool it.' [*Laughs.*] He wanted us to have a good time but not to overdo it." On some segments, Burton sported a new Gretsch Chet Atkins model or a Rickenbacker: "I switched off a lot with the Gretsch and other guitars, but that was just for fun and looks. My main guitar was always the '53 Tele, and I used it on all the records."

The hits just kept on coming into the '60s. James enjoyed the security of his lead guitar niche with Ricky, but his exclusive contract prohibited any outside work and he began to feel stifled: "It got to the point where Ricky stopped traveling altogether. We'd only work one month out of the year during the summer, so it got to be very boring for me. When the phone would ring, I'd have to say, 'Well, no, I can't do this or that.'"

The situation reached a head in early 1965 when the increasingly in-demand guitarist was called by Johnny Cash to play dobro on a TV pilot for a new musical show called *Shindig*. "I called Rick to ask him if he would mind if I did the show," the guitarist recounts. "The producers said they wouldn't even put me on camera, just put me off to the side. Rick seemed to be unhappy about this and said, 'I wish you wouldn't do this, because your sound is my sound.'" Eventually, though, Nelson's manager called Burton back with the go-ahead, and James began doing session work.

The *Shindig* pilot was an instant success and the show was picked up by ABC in April 1965. Burton became the show's permanent lead guitarist as a member of the Shindogs, along with Delaney Bramlett on bass, Glen D Hardin playing piano and arranging, Joey Cooper on rhythm guitar, and Chuck Blackwell on drums. "We would go in three days a week and do the tracks in the studio," Burton details. "Some of the stuff would be done live during the taping, but we prerecorded almost 90 percent of the tracks for lip-synching." The show presented a broad cross-section of music, with artists such as Muddy Waters, Ray Charles, Howlin' Wolf, and Chuck Berry, along with the cream of the British invasion bands—the Rolling Stones, the Dave Clark Five, and the Beatles.

The high visibility of television served as a catalyst for James' rising session demand in the later '60s. Calls came in from all sectors of the pop music field. "I was doing like four to six dates a day and sometimes up to 25 sessions a week," Burton declares. "It was day and night." These were the halcyon days of the record date "specialist"; players with a unique identity and style were called in to sweeten and embellish specific tracks on an artist's project. Burton participated on countless such record dates, but several stand out as musts in any essential James Burton discography. His twisting, hound-dog style slide dobro meshed perfectly with Buffalo Springfield's seminal country-rock vision on "A Child's Claim To Fame" [*Buffalo Springfield Again*], recorded in 1967. The song perfectly blends James' fretted dobro work with his seemingly endless vocabulary of rising and falling slide dobro slurs for a timeless double-tracked dobro duet. The record introduced a generation of rock listeners to the dobro sound outside of its traditional bluegrass mold.

Judy Collins' 1968 hit "Someday Soon" [*Who Knows Where The Time Goes*], is a marvelous example of country ensemble teamwork, perfectly meshing Burton's graceful, economical Telecaster fills with steel sage Buddy Emmons' impeccable accompaniment. "That was a great album," James says. "Buddy and I had a feel together that was real nice. That's how you make hit records—teamwork. No one guy in the group is making it happen; it's team playing." James is specific about his lead and fill requirements. "You have to let your playing breathe; I think you have to treat it like a lyric. It's not how much you play, it's what you play and where you play it. It's usually what you *don't* play that makes it."

Burton also made some classic contributions to deep country at that time. Capitol Records producer Ken Nelson called him to add some snappy Tele bite to several Merle Haggard and Buck Owens projects in Bakersfield, California. These early sessions teamed James with the influential pedal steel stylist, Ralph Mooney. Their early collaborations on songs such as Haggard's "The Bottle Let Me Down" led to their own duet instrumental album for Capitol in 1966 called *Corn Pickin' And Slick Sliding*. The LP showcases both players' bright, crisp, decidedly Fender guitar tones, with James also joining in on dobro for a colorful blend of styles.

The Haggard sessions produced other milestone tracks, including "The Lonesome Fugitive" and "Workin' Man Blues." "I guess I cut several albums with Merle," says Burton. "The first thing I did was real country, with me and Ralph doing 'The Bottle Let Me Down.' There was a song that I played on with Ricky called 'I Just Can't Quit'; it had a horn sound on it like twin horns, and Merle wanted to know if I could play some of that style on his record." The cut "Workin' Man Blues"—whose solo closely resembles Burton's earlier effort on Nelson's version of "Milkcow Blues"—features another style James had perfected during his days with Nelson—the muted, staccato, "chicken pickin'" string attack. He explains: "It's that spitting on the strings. It's sort of like being a drummer, playing the notes and the drums at the same time. You can hear it on a song of Ricky's called 'Sneakin' Around.'"

Burton also graced hit singles by Buck Owens, including "Open Up Your Heart And Let The Sun Shine In." The guitarist remembers one incident during those sessions: "We cut one song with a 6-string bass, and were getting ready to do a second tune when Don Rich, Buck's lead guitarist, suggested to Buck that I should do a lead on it. So I took out my Tele, and we started running it down. I played an intro and we got into a solo, a turnaround, and Buck got to listening to my solo and forgot to come back in singing. There was a big pause there, and Buck just started laughing—he blew the take. It was that chicken pickin' sound that captured Buck on 'Open Up Your Heart.'"

A busy and highly lucrative studio career would seem to be very difficult to forsake, and in 1969 the decision was a tough one for James when he got *the call*. Joe Esposito, aide-de-camp to Elvis Presley, phoned to say that Elvis would like to speak with James; moments later the King was on the line. They chatted for two hours like lifelong friends as Elvis explained his wish for James to help him assemble a road band for his forthcoming tour. Burton agreed. "It was a tough decision," he admits, "but I thought it was a good one at the time. Actually, the concert schedule with Elvis still gave me time for session work. We'd go

James played with Elvis at the Las Vegas International Hotel comeback in August '69 and continued with the King until his death in 1977. "I did all of his studio work, movies, everything. It was great," he enthuses. "In the studio, he preferred singing live when cutting the tracks, to capture the live feel. He never did like to overdub, unless it was very necessary. Rather than overdub, he would just go in and do another session. He wouldn't spend a lot of time on one song either—maybe three or four takes. If it didn't happen for him, he would move on to something else. We did several albums at his house at Graceland in Memphis. Mobile units from New York came in. They parked the trucks out back, and we all set up in the den. Just a little family deal."

In spite of a hectic touring and recording schedule, James

managed to record a solo album for A&M Records in 1971. *James Burton* was cut in Nashville with the help of Elvis' longtime producer, Felton Jarvis, and a host of session regulars, including Jerry Carrigan, David Briggs, Norbert Putnam, Charlie McCoy, and Chip Young. Burton served up a tasty version of Presley's "Mystery Train," along with a wall-of-sound rendition of Leon Russell's "Delta Lady," and a snaky cover of "High Heeled Sneakers" on dobro.

In 1972 yet another connection was made that would result in far-reaching musical consequences. Gram Parsons, the visionary of country rock, contacted Burton regarding an upcoming album project. "Well, Gram said, 'I think I've got a deal to do an album, and I really want you on it,' " Burton recounts. "Merle Haggard was originally going to produce, but that fell through." Parsons' manager, Ed Tickner, put together a deal with Warner Bros. that provided for Gram to hire the studio band to go on the road, beginning with the second release. The band Parsons put together for the first album, *GP*, included three members of the Presley backup band (Burton, Glenn D Hardin on piano, and Ron Tutt on drums). Emory Gordy, Jr., Elvis' bassist, joined them on the second album, *Grievous Angel*. The records are modern country treasures, and their futuristic impact contines to this day.

A *Grievous Angel* tour never took place, due to Parsons' untimely death in late 1973, but the groundwork was laid for a hot touring band led by the album's harmony vocalist, Emmylou Harris. "Emmylou was singing on the album," recalls James, "and when Gram passed away, Tickner started managing Emmy; he had made the same plans for her that he had made for Gram."

The following year, Emmylou and producer Brian Ahern began work on *Pieces Of The Sky*, using the same core of musicians from the Parsons sessions. The resulting album features some of Burton's most profoundly lyrical playing on songs such as "Boulder To Birmingham" and "Too Far Gone." The touring band assembled in support of the album was dubbed the Hot Band, and the subsequent live dates, driven by James' hot-rod Tele, were nothing short of blazing.

Burton recorded a second LP with Harris and the Hot Band before departing in 1976, due to conflicts with Elvis' tour schedule. *Elite Hotel* captured the full spirit of the band, mixing live cuts with studio tracks. Burton's melodicism is captured throughout. The album highlights compositions by Rodney

Crowell, Buck Owens, Hank Williams, and Gram Parsons' "Las Vegas" with its exploding guitar support. Regarding the song's rapid-fire, staccato intro, Burton laughs, "I always wanted to play banjo. I just love doing stuff like that. I feel good when I play something that I'm excited about. I used the same thing on Gram's version of the tune, and I thought, 'Well, there's nothing I could do that would feel any better.' "

The crack Hot Band also participated in a number of outside album projects with producer Brian Ahern, including sessions for Jonathan Edwards, Rodney Crowell, Mary Kay Place, and Jesse Winchester. James remembers the dilemma he faced on the title track to Winchester's *Nothing But A Breeze:* "Brian wanted me to play bottleneck on my Tele, but it's hard to do because of the arch in the round neck. I didn't have a dobro bar with me, so I asked around and somebody there had a Zippo lighter. I laid the Tele on my lap like a dobro, and played the solo with the Zippo for a slide. It was pretty neat."

Understandably, Elvis' death in 1977 came as a crushing blow to Burton. Rather than sink to inactivity, however, he dived headlong into more sessions work. One of his first projects was with John Denver on an album entitled *I Want To Live* which led to yet another tour offer. "Just before Elvis died I was called to play on a John Denver television special," he recounts. "During the taping, John asked if I would consider going out on a European tour. I said I was working with Elvis, but if scheduling permitted, I would be glad to go. Elvis died in August of 1977, and very shortly I was contacted about John's album. I went in to do the sessions, and John said, 'I want to talk to you about a band.' I hired Glenn D and Emory, and that's how it started. I've been with him for seven years."

Now James' rock and roll shoes have run full circle with his recent onstage association with Jerry Lee Lewis. Suddenly he's rocking with the abandon of a 16-year-old at his first sock hop gig. Burton revels in the new excitement. "I've never had a rehearsal with this band," he points out. "Basically, I went in cold turkey, and it's great. The arrangements aren't locked in, and sometimes it's hard to figure out what Jerry Lee will do next. Instead of a complete solo he might play half, and then bring me in for the last half or something. Or he'll look at Kenny Lovelace [Lewis' guitarist for 19 years] and me and say, 'Let me hear some twin guitars,' [*laughs*] so away we go. It keeps the music exciting. It's good to change things around. When the spotlight falls on you, you say, 'Wow, what do I do now?' "

---

### A SELECTED JAMES BURTON DISCOGRAPHY

**Solo album:** *Guitar Sounds Of James Burton*, A&M, AML554293. **With Merle Haggard:** *Workin' Man Blues*, Capitol, 2503. **With Ricky Nelson:** *Ricky Nelson*, Liberty, LXB-9960; *Ricky Nelson's Greatest Hits*, Rhino, RNLP 215; *The Decca Years*, MCA, 1517. **With Elvis Presley** (on RCA): *This Is Elvis*, CPL2-4031; *Recorded Live On Stage In Memphis*, CPL1-0606; *From Memphis To Vegas*, 6020; *Greatest Hits-Volume One*, AHL1-2347, *Aloha From Hawaii Via Satellite*, CPD2-2642; *Elvis As Recorded At Madison Square Garden*, AFL1-4776. **With Jerry Lee Lewis:** *Jerry Lee Lewis*, Elektra, 6E-184. **With Buffalo Springfield:** *Buffalo Springfield Again*, Atco, 83-226. **With Judy Collins:** *Who Knows Where The Time Goes*, Elektra, EKS-74033. **James Burton and Ralph Mooney:** *Cornpickin' And Slick Slidin'*, Capitol (France; available from Down Home Music, 10341 San Pablo Ave., El Cerrito, CA 94530), 1550751. **With Emmylou Harris:** *Pieces Of The Sky*, Warner Bros., 2284; *Elite Hotel*, Reprise, 2236. **With Gram Parsons** (on Warner Bros.): *GP*, MS2123; *Grievous Angel*, MS 2171. **With John Denver:** *I Want To Live*, RCA, AFL1-2521.

# MAYBELLE CARTER

By Doug Green

**M**AYBELLE CARTER WAS A LEGEND, AND IT SEEMED that she would go on forever, like the impassive Appalachia from which she came. But she had been in failing health for several years—especially since the death of her longtime husband, Ezra J. Carter, in 1975—and she died suddenly of natural causes on October 23, 1978, leaving country music—and indeed all of American music—without one of its most influential guitarists.

Mother Maybelle, as she came to be known, was the creator of the "Carter lick" on the guitar—the playing of the melody with the thumb while brushing the strings for rhythm. This style had a profound effect on guitarists of her own generation and those that followed. She also incorporated hammer-ons, pull-offs, slides and other folk-type embellishments into her style.

Less than three months after the death of Mother Maybelle, Sara Carter Bayes, the last surviving member of the original Carter Family, passed away in her home in Lodi, California. Born in Wise County, Virginia, on July 21, 1898, Sara, like her sister-in-law Maybelle, learned to play the guitar and autoharp at an early age, although she never attained the proficiency and creativity that made Maybelle's playing revolutionary.

Where Maybelle came up with her innovative lick is a matter of conjecture. The guitar was still a relatively new instrument to the Virginia mountains where she grew up, yet she played it as a teenager. Some have credited Leslie Riddles, a black guitarist and blues singer from nearby Kingsport, Tennessee, who did in fact subtly influence the Carter Family's music and performance in later years, but he was not there when Maybelle began playing the instrument.

The information provided in Maybelle's 1949 song folio is oblique: "She started playing the autoharp at the ripe old age of four. When the newness wore off four years later, she took to

plunking the banjo and pretty soon the plunking changed into good banjo playing. About five years later she laid down the banjo in favor of a guitar." In 1961 she told historian Bill Malone that she "learned from her brothers"; although both brothers were musicians, neither had Maybelle's talent.

However shrouded in mystery, the origin of her style may lie with the simplest of explanations: She was a young musician with an instrument that was relatively new to her area. She spent a great deal of time with it, and mainly for her own pleasure she developed an effective way to play melody on the guitar, probably adapting her technique from the banjo.

If the Carter lick does not seem terribly revolutionary today, one must place it in the context of the times: Maybelle was a competent guitarist who had already developed this style when she married Ezra on March 23, 1926, at age 16. Other than on Nick Lucas recordings, the guitar was not heard much in popular music, either onstage or on 78s. It would take country singer Jimmie Rodgers' supple bass runs and Maybelle's deceptively simple lead playing to expose the guitar via record.

In recorded country music, the guitar was usually used as a rhythm instrument; it was fuller—though often less expressive—than the banjo when used to accompany a fiddle, singer, or string band. Though Riley Puckett, an early country performer, demonstrated many flashes of brilliance in his bizarre, erratic guitar playing, it was the stylings of Jimmie Rodgers and Maybelle Carter that suggested the instrument's new potential in country music.

Mother Maybelle was born Maybelle Addington on May 10, 1909, in Nicklesville, a small town in the Poor Valley of mountainous southwest Virginia. She was courted and wed by Ezra Carter, and through him she was introduced to his older brother, A.P. Carter, a cheerful though somewhat haunted man who fiddled a bit and sang. He married Sara Dougherty on June 15,

# AND THE CARTER FAMILY

The Carter Family at Hiltons (formerly Maces Spring) in 1976: Maybelle on autoharp, Sara on guitar, and Sarah's daughter Janette at rear.

wood Flower." When the songs were not in the proper key for singing, the solution was simple: Maybelle either capoed up to the proper fret, or, reversing direction, simply tuned the guitar down—at times as much as five frets, allowing her to finger in *C* while actually playing in *G*. Like her approach to music, her approach to innovation was direct, straightforward, and simple.

The distinctive characteristic of the Carter Family guitar sound involved Maybelle's right-hand picking technique: melody executed with a thumb lead in the bass; rhythm filled in on the treble strings with brush strokes (the "Church Lick") executed by one or more fingers (usually the second, since it is the longest); and melody and rhythm enlivened with bass runs, hammer-ons, and pull-offs.

The original Carter Family lineup consisted of Maybelle's brother-in-law A.P. Carter (left), Maybelle (center) on guitar, and A.P.'s wife Sara on autoharp.

1915. A distant cousin of Maybelle's, Sara possessed a stunning voice: deep and clear. She had learned to play banjo, guitar, and autoharp, and she frequently performed with A.P. A Carter family legend has it that when A.P. first saw Sara she was playing the autoharp and singing "Engine 143."

It seemed natural that A.P., Sara, and Maybelle would get together to play. A.P. sang bass, and he had a massive collection of traditional folk tunes he'd gathered in his years as a carpenter and tree salesman, and Sara and Maybelle harmonized well, though somewhat stiffly by contemporary standards. They began to harbor aspirations of a professional career, and in late July 1927, they drove 25 miles from their homes in Maces Spring, Virginia, to the town of Bristol, which was divided in half by the Virginia-Tennessee state line. The trip took them eight hours, but it was worth the hardship. There Ralph Peer, a talent scout, was auditioning for Victor Records. If he liked what he heard, he'd record a musician on the spot.

Peer heard many singers, musicians, and bands during the week he spent in Bristol, but he liked the tubercular railroader Jimmie Rodgers and the Carter Family best of all. On August 1, the Carters made their first recordings in the upper story of a house at 410 State Street. By August 4, they had completed six sides: "Bury Me Under A Weeping Willow," "The Poor Orphan Child," "The Storms Are On The Ocean," "Little Log Cabin By The Sea," "Single Girl, Married Girl," and "Wandering Boy." Maybelle used a Stella guitar for her earliest sessions, replacing it in 1929 with a Gibson L-5 that she was to use for the rest of her career.

Between 1927 and 1934 the Carter Family recorded most of their best-known songs for Victor, including "Foggy Mountain Top," "My Clinch Mountain Home," "Forsaken Lovers," "Thinking Of My Blue Eyes," "Lulu Walls," "Sweet Fern," and the song that was to become the anthem for country guitarists, "Wild-

Besides using the capo, Maybelle often tuned her guitar down one to one-and-a-half steps, assumedly to retain the *C*-chord forms with which she felt most comfortable when changing keys to match A.P.'s bass and Sara's low-alto vocal ranges.

The piece most often associated with the Carter name is "Wildwood Flower," first recorded at Camden, New Jersey, May 9, 1928. This selection proved to be the group's biggest seller— over a million sales in 78s alone.

The Carter Family's career was spotty. Though they were known all over the United States by the late '20s, they did not travel much, and their influence was largely felt on record. In 1932 Ralph Peer united them with Jimmie Rodgers for a recording session in Louisville, Kentucky. Included among these sides are two duets by Jimmie and Sara, "The Wonderful City" and "Why There's A Tear In My Eye," the only sacred song Rodgers ever recorded. "We recorded with Jimmie Rodgers not more than a year before he died," Maybelle later recalled. "In fact, he wasn't able to play his guitar very much, he was that sick, so I played for him and he sang. I had to play like him, you know, so everybody would think it was him. But it was me."

Ever hardworking, the Carter Family recorded 20 new songs for Victor in December 1934, each of which was done in one take. In 1935 they moved to the American Record Company (ARC). They recorded "Lonesome Valley," "Single Girl, Married Girl," "Sunnyside," and many of their earlier hits for ARC before moving on to the newly-formed, energetic Decca label in June 1936. Many Carter Family buffs consider the three years spent with Decca to be the family's finest period. They were writing as well as preserving genuine Appalachian ballads, and Maybelle's guitar playing was at its peak: In addition to her Carter lick, Maybelle had learned to fingerpick as well, and she had also learned to coax lead lines from an autoharp. The material they recorded ranged from spirituals ("Honey In The Rock") to blues ("Coal Miner's Blues") and railroading songs ("Reckless Motorman").

In 1938 the entire family moved to Del Rio, Texas, to play a twice-daily show over the powerful Mexican border radio stations, XEG, XENT, and XERA. At the same time it could be said that the Carters became less and more of a family. A.P. and Sara had divorced a few years earlier, though they still recorded together, and in 1939 Sara married Coy Bayes. A.P. and Sara's children, Joe and Janette, became a frequent part of radio and stage shows, as did Ezra and Maybelle's daughters, Helen, Anita, and June.

The Carter Family recorded a set of sessions for Columbia in 1940. On October 14, 1941, they journeyed to New York City to record for Victor; it was their final session. In 14 years of recording, they had produced nearly 300 sides.

The family finally disbanded in 1943 while they were working at the WBT radio station in Charlotte, North Carolina. Coy Bayes took Sara with him to California; she had been the least driven and least compelled performer of the trio, and left music without any apparent reservations. A.P. returned to Maces Spring to open a little country store—which still stands, although the area is now named Hiltons. He drifted in and out of music, often performing and occasionally recording with his son and daughter, until his death in 1960.

But Maybelle had more than her talent; she had an ambition the others had lacked. With her three daughters she formed an act called The Carter Sisters And Mother Maybelle, first joining *The Old Dominion Barn Dance* show on WRVA radio in Richmond, Virginia, and then later moving to the *Grand Ole Opry* show in 1949. The group recorded with Victor and Columbia.

Oddly enough, Maybelle's role was diminished in the new group she nominally headed. Helen's accordion playing, June's boisterous humor, and Anita's lovely solo voice were all main features of the act. Maybelle added a bit of harmony, a few measures of her once-unique guitar playing, a couple of solo "heart songs," and some autoharp flourishes. Mother Maybelle felt her guitar playing to be so out of step when they joined the *Grand Ole Opry* that she brought along a lead guitarist whose more modern style was, she felt, better suited to the times. His name was Chet Atkins.

The Carter Sisters And Mother Maybelle was a popular bread-and-butter country act for years. A number of widely-spaced events in the last 15 years of Maybelle's life helped rescue her contributions from the obscurity to which she had relegated herself. One was her appearance at the 1963 Newport Folk Festival, where her influence on the guitar playing of folksinger Woody Guthrie, and through him to Bob Dylan, Jack Elliot, Joan Baez, and other folk singers and country artists was recognized and lauded. Here a new generation was introduced to her music.

In 1967 Maybelle and Sara were professionally reunited in an appearance at the Newport Folk Festival, after which they made *An Historic Reunion*, their first recording together in over 25 years.

June Carter married country singer Johnny Cash during the '60s, and the Carter Sisters And Mother Maybelle became a firm fixture on his touring show and TV series. Another major event in Maybelle's career was the election of the original Carter Family to the Country Music Hall Of Fame in 1970, an acknowledgement of her pioneering role from her peers. In 1973 she joined with the Nitty Gritty Dirt Band and a host of country stars for the recording of the LP *Will The Circle Be Unbroken*.

Joe and Janette, A.P., and Sara's children, began a series of Carter Family reunions in the mid-'70s. It was at these affairs that Sara made her last appearances. Though frail, she still played her O-28 Martin guitar simply and straightforwardly. The years did not seem to have affected the quality of her voice; even though it had grown deeper with time, it was still supple and strong—characteristics that Sara herself embodied. Her death, at the age of 80, came in the early morning hours of January 8, 1979.

During the mid-'70s, age began taking its toll on Maybelle; when arthritis stilled the magic of her fingers on the guitar, this quiet, unassuming, stoic woman continued on autoharp. After Ezra's death, however, she appeared less and less frequently with Cash and was in and out of the hospital. She had been off the road a year, in declining health, when she died at age 69.

Suddenly she was gone, and she was missed. Over 50 years ago she began a revolution in guitar playing that is still being felt. Her recorded output is large, and much of her best work can still be heard. By today's standards her guitar work, though lovely, has none of the flash of recent players. But its clean, understated elegance tells volumes about the times and the places that produced one of country music's most important pioneers, and about this shy, reserved woman, one of America's most influential guitarists.

---

### A SELECTED CARTER FAMILY DISCOGRAPHY

**Solo albums:** *Carter Family Album*, Liberty (dist. by United Artists), 7230; *Happiest Days Of All*, Camden, ACL1-0501; *Lonesome Pine Special*, Camden, 2473; *Mid The Green Fields Of Virginia*, Victor, ANL1-1107; *More Golden Gems From The Original Carter Family*, Camden, 2554; *My Old Cottage Home*, Camden, ACL1-0047; *Original And Great Carter Family*, Camden 586; *Precious Memories*, Camden, 9020; *Three Generations*, Columbia, KC-33084; (Sara and Maybelle only) *An Historic Reunion*, Columbia, CL2561; (Maybelle only) *Mother Maybelle Carter*, Columbia, KG 32436. **With others:** Nitty Gritty Dirt Band, *Will The Circle Be Unbroken*, United Artists, 9801; *50 Years Of Country Music*, Camden ADL2-0782; *Stars Of The Grand Ole Opry 1926-1974*, Victor, CPL2-0466; *World's Favorite Hymns*, Columbia, C-32246.

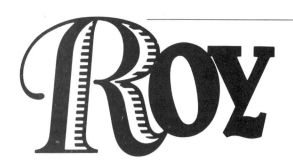

# ROY CLARK

By Jon Sievert

**E**NTERTAINER ROY CLARK IS PROBABLY THE MOST visible guitarist in America today. Nearly 35 million viewers tune in 52 weeks a year to see his pickin' and grinnin' on television's *Hee Haw*. Another 15 million or so see him on the nights when he hosts the *Tonight Show* and almost always sings and plays a song. Then, of course, there are the untold millions who catch him on his numerous TV guest spots on the afternoon talk shows or prime-time variety shows and specials. And last, but hardly least, are the several hundred thousand fans who see him live in concert during the 250 or so dates he does each year, crisscrossing the country and featuring his guitar out front in his multi-faceted act. Not even the most widely-acclaimed guitar

25

legends can match this kind of exposure.

Of course, Roy Clark's high visibility can be attributed to other resources besides his guitar playing. He is an outstanding banjo picker and a masterful comic. And his fine singing voice has aided a very fertile 18-year recording career that has produced a long string of hit records on the country charts and several that have crossed over to the pop category. Roy's music industry awards would probably fill a room. In addition to the gold records, there are the results of his unprecedented sweep of the major country awards in 1974 when he was voted Entertainer Of The Year by both the Country Music Association and the Academy Of Country Music. Also during that same year the American Guild Of Variety Artists selected him Country Music Star Of The Year. Other awards too numerous to mention attest to his stature as a master entertainer.

Clark also holds an armful of awards attributing to his virtuosity on guitar, banjo, fiddle, and several other popular stringed instruments. Readers of *Music City News* have voted him Instrumentalist Of The Year several times, as did the Country Music Association in 1977. *Playboy* readers have chosen him Picker Of The Year twice. And since Chet Atkins ascended to *Guitar Player*'s Gallery of The Greats, Roy appears to have become heir apparent to *GP*'s Best Country Guitarist award in the annual readership poll. He has won the award handily for the last three years and has opened up a lead in this year's poll.

Music came early to Roy Clark. Born to a musical family in Meaherrin, Virginia, on April 15, 1933, he made his public performing debut at age four, singing "Last Night As I Lay On The Prairie." His mother was a pianist. His father, originally a tobacco farmer who moved to Washington, D.C., to accept a government job when Roy was 11, often moonlighted five nights a week playing guitar, banjo, and fiddle. Roy began to beat around on a tenor banjo and then a mandolin at a young age, but it wasn't until he was 14 that he fully tuned in to the sound of a neighbor's guitar and developed an overwhelming passion for playing. That year, for Christmas, he got his first guitar—a Sears Silvertone that cost $14.95. Within two weeks he had mastered open chords and was playing behind his father at a square dance. From then on his father made sure that Roy got around to see the wide variety of musicians playing in the Washington, D.C., area. The city was, and is, a veritable melting pot of people from all over the world and features nearly every kind of music. That appreciation of variety has always been evident in Roy's work and has allowed him to defy strict categorization.

Soon after his first intense learning burst on the guitar, Roy developed the same passion for the 5-string banjo—a passion he soon parlayed into two National Banjo Championships at ages 16 and 17. The second win carried an appearance at Nashville's *Grand Ole Opry*. Through his late teens and early 20s he continued to hone his skills as an instrumentalist/vocalist/humorist, playing bars, dances, and on local TV and radio in the D.C. area. During this period Roy seriously considered professional baseball, and at 18 he actually turned professional boxer, winning 15 straight fights as a light-heavyweight before the 16th bout convinced him to try something else.

In about 1955, a local TV appearance led to a radio job with singer Jimmy Dean, who was then a kingpin on the local Washington scene, but not yet the national star he would

become. The two worked together on radio and TV, and when Dean left for New York, Roy took over the gig with his own special blend of instrumental flash pieces, singing, and humor. In about 1960, with things going very smoothly, Roy decided it was time to make a career decision. Though his job was quite comfortable, he began looking for a way out of town. Along came country singer Wanda Jackson, on her way to the Las Vegas Golden Nugget club, and looking for a guitar player and front man for her band. Roy fit the bill.

Clark stayed with Jackson for a little over a year, long enough to play lead guitar on her biggest hit, "Let's Have A Party." It was also Roy's good fortune that Jackson's manager was a showbiz-savvy man named Jim Halsey, who had previously managed country singer/guitarist Hank Thompson and had been involved as a promoter since age 17. Halsey quickly recognized the superstar potential of Roy's collective talents, which Wanda's show gave him ample opportunity to display. When Jackson dissolved her band, Halsey became Roy's first and, to date, only manager. The two quickly negotiated a recording contract, and *Lightning* [out of print] was soon released by Capitol Records. The album features songs as well as instrumental arrangements of such tunes as "Fingers On Fire" and "Drifter's Polka," played, indeed, at lightning speed.

At the same time Roy began to intensify his televison work. He had always been aware of the potential of the medium, having appeared on it for the first time in 1948 when he sang on *The Hayloft Conservatory Of Musical Interpretation* show—only a few months after he took up the guitar. He had appeared on local variety shows, but his manager began to place him in different settings, such as the dual-comedy role of Cousin Roy and (in drag) Big Mama Halsey on one of the most popular shows in the country, *The Beverly Hillbillies*. His biggest national breakthrough, however, came in January 1963 when he was selected as a guest for the *Tonight Show* during the interim period after Jack Parr left and Johnny Carson took over. His old friend and partner, Jimmy Dean, was the guest host who chose him to appear. His successful guest spot eventually led to his first invitation to host the show himself.

Subsequently, Roy has turned up on just about every variety and celebrity show in existence, including the *Mike Douglas, Merv Griffin, Dinah Shore, Flip Wilson,* and *Hollywood Squares* programs. Guest acting roles included appearances on *The Odd Couple* and *Love, American Style*. And though television was providing widespread exposure, Roy did not neglect his live concerts—hitting the road at a rate of 250 shows a year, thereby providing direct personal contact with his fans.

In 1969, CBS came to him with a pilot for a cornball, country-style version of *Laugh-In* and asked him to co-host it with singer Buck Owens. Though dubious at first, Roy took the challenge and *Hee Haw* very quickly jumped to the top of the summer ratings and won a regular spot in the fall lineup of shows. In 1971, with ratings still very high, CBS decided to cancel the show. Almost immediately it was put into syndication and has since become one of the most popular syndicated shows in history. Since then, Roy's popularity has continued to mushroom with guest spots, commercials, concerts, and a recording career that spans nearly 40 albums (including several consisting totally of guitar instrumentals). He has a nearly unique ability to completely erase the distinctions between country and pop; this talent has allowed him to establish some landmarks for country

**Roy Clark performing on a Gibson Byrdland.**

performers. He was one of the first to headline his own show in the big showrooms along the Las Vegas hotel strip and is certainly the most popular country musician in that town today. He currently plays the Frontier for two shows a night, seven nights a week, 12 weeks a year, to sellout crowds. He was also the first country artist to headline his own show in the Soviet Union, playing to enthusiastic, turn-away crowds in a 21-day, three-city tour in January 1976.

These days Roy continues the workaholic schedule he has always maintained, though now that means his life is planned almost to the hour as much as six months in advance, and his schedule is handed to him on a computer printout. To meet his backbreaking cycle of concerts, television, recording, commercials, and most recently, movies, Roy pilots his Mitsubishi MU-2J turboprop plane in and out of the airports of America en route to his jobs.

A typical Roy Clark show will last 90 minutes to two hours and is pretty much the same wherever he plays, though in Las Vegas a 40-piece orchestra replaces the country band that backs Roy on the road. For the past two years that band has been Rodney Lay And Wild West, which features Lay on bass and vocals, Vernon Sandusky on guitar, and Darrell Price on keyboards. The band is also a separate working entity apart from Roy and has recently begun recording its own album. Mainstays on the show wherever it goes are Buck Trent, Roy's banjo-picking sidekick from *Hee Haw*, 14-year-old banjo whiz Jimmy Henley, Jimmy's father James, who backs on guitar, and a vocal quartet, currently Paradise. The first third to half of the show features individual performances by Wild West, Paradise, and Trent. Then on comes Roy in a custom-made suit and hat, opening with a song and accompanying himself on guitar. The remainder of the show is a pastiche of humor, songs, guitar, and a bit of fiddle. Current guitar instrumental mainstays in the set are "Ghost Riders In The Sky," "Lara's Theme," and his almost-trademark "Malaguena," played on a 12-string Ovation acoustic. Roy's primary guitar was, until very recently, a Gretsch Super Axe. He is now playing a prototype of a Gretsch Roy Clark model.

This interview was conducted in Las Vegas, where Roy was playing the Desert Inn for the first time. Not surprisingly, Roy's audience looked pretty much like the same crowd he drew several weeks later in San Carlos, California—a cross section of the down-home side of America that is really a reflection of the man himself. Though he is probably the highest-paid performer in country music, Roy maintains a strong one-to-one relationship with his audience of devoted fans, signing autographs and establishing a personal contact with each person he meets.

\* \* \* \*

*Y*OU'RE KNOWN AS A MULTI-TALENTED ENTERTAINER. *How much of you is Roy Clark the guitarist?*

Well, I think that is what I am, basically—a guitar player—although I have let it go. I get frustrated because I don't play enough. I see a kid playing six hours a night in a club, and he's got fantastic chops, and I look at him and think, "Where did it go, I used to be able to do that." I could play that way all night long and even faster than I could think at one time. And then it dawned on me that I was playing six hours a night when I was doing that. Now, even here in Las Vegas, which is about the most

I work because we're doing two shows a night, seven nights a week, I am playing upfront leads probably only seven minutes per show—say 15 total minutes a night. That's actual playing, although I'm onstage quite a bit. So, how in the world are you going to keep your chops that way?

*Does your schedule ever leave time for practice?*

I do what I can. I keep a classical guitar at the house and practice on it a little, but that doesn't really take the place of concentrated practice on new things. Even when I was playing six hours a night, I'd go out and jam the rest of the night learning new tunes. Even when you are playing that much, it's important to make sure you are working on different licks and don't get locked into the same old ones. You may really be able to do them great, but when a chance comes for a little challenge, you are not coordinated enough to do it. You may be able to hear it, but not get it out the ends of your fingers. You end up just about a bar behind everything you're trying to play. I've even gone so far as to try to dream up practice devices like banjo and guitar fingerboards. Just a board so I could sit in the airplane and practice. For the banjo, the picking is what I miss most. For the guitar I just need something where I could note the neck and pick just to get the coordination down. You wouldn't even have to hear it or tune it. Just so the strings had tension on them.

*How much practicing did you do when you were first starting to play?*

I was so intrigued with that first guitar that I must have put in eight or nine hours every day. I would get up early and play a couple of hours before school, come home and grab it as soon as I came in the door. Then I would play it until it was time to eat and sometimes they would bring the food up to me. I just sorta locked myself in my room and went at it.

*What kind of things did you practice?*

I had a book called *Smith's 300 Chords For Guitar* and one called *Smith's Favorite Tunes* [both out of print]. The chord book was the best of its time and is still good because it goes right through basic chords and movable altered chords. I started playing out of them, and if I had a problem, I didn't have to wait until the next week to ask a teacher about it. I just waited until my dad got home from work, and he'd straighten me out and I'd go on to something else.

*Did you get a lot of encouragement from your dad?*

Yeah, he was great. All the time I was growing up and he was playing jobs, he never mentioned anything to me about playing. He never said, "You ought to learn to play," or "Here, you can have this guitar and I'll buy you something if you learn to play." He left it up to me, and when I decided that I wanted to play, I got all the help and encouragement I wanted.

*How long did you keep your Silvertone?*

Quite a while. I learned a lot on that guitar. It had an amazingly good tone, and the action wasn't too bad. As it got older, the action got higher because there wasn't any truss rod in the neck, and it started to warp. So I started playing it like a Dobro.

*What was your first good guitar?*

I got a used Martin D-18 around 1948. My dad traded an old shotgun, a fishing pole, a banjo head, and about 20 bucks for it. I guess it was about ten years old then, and he still has it. He sent it back to Martin and had it completely rebuilt. I didn't have a case for it—I carried it around in a pillowcase.

*When did you take up the banjo intensely?*

Roy Clark's multi-instrumental virtuosity runs the gamut.

I guess around age 15. When I started playing guitar, I became really aware of all the different sounds and things going on. That was about the time that [bluegrass banjo legend] Earl Scruggs was really hot. We used to listen to him on the *Grand Ole Opry* radio show on Saturday nights, and I would visualize him as having 14 fingers. There was no way you could figure out how he was getting all this pickin' out of one instrument. All the banjo players I had ever seen played with the Grandpa Jones frailin' style. So I traded on old [Gibson] F-4 mandolin I had for an old Washburn 5-string without a resonator and started pickin' at it. I got a lot of help from a cousin of Earl's named Smitty Irvin and a friend named Buster Austin. They really got me started, so I began using the banjo and the guitar. Then I bought another mandolin and a fiddle and started playing them, too. I would just buy an instrument and go and find somebody who played it and just bug him until he showed me something on it.

*Were there a lot of people around to ask?*

At the time Washington, D.C., was just loaded with musicians. I guess most of them had migrated there to go to work for the government. That was a big attraction. There were great guitar players everywhere you looked. There must have been 2,000 clubs there, and every one of them had a band.

*What kind of material were you doing?*

All kinds of things. A lot of [legendary country singer] Hank Williams, because that was around the heart of his career. As far as instrumental things, I did anything and everything that came out. [Guitarist] Arthur Smith was big with the "Guitar Boogie" and "Thing Is On Fire," and I did all of his stuff. I did some early things of Chet Atkins', but I was into flatpickin', so it was a little hard for me. I would fingerpick, but I was more into the Arthur Smith things. There was another great guitar player around named Al Alexander who wrote a tune on my first album. I think it was he and Arthur Smith who really got me thinking about speed.

*It sounds like you weren't pinned into one idiom even then.*

I've been fascinated by all music since I can remember, and

D.C. offered such amazing variety. It was the greatest place to get started because people from all over the world were there. Instead of just playing one type of music and saying, "This is what I do," I tried to please all of them. I learned anything that came up and was popular.

*Did you sit down and work them out yourself?*

Yeah, but I could never copy note-for-note. I probably didn't have the ability to. I'd hear it my way and work it out like that. I would learn enough of the melody from the record, but I never had the dedication or discipline to just stick in there and learn to do it note-for-note.

*Did you get yourself into performing situations almost from the start?*

That's about the way it happened. I'd just sorta get into performing situations with my dad playing and all. I was having so much fun playing I wasn't thinking about becoming a star or being successful or whatever. Oh, I might have dreamed about it or something, but I didn't know anything about how that happened, so I just played. The guys in the band would say: "We need somebody to sing. We don't want to do it. Get Roy, he'll do it." I didn't know any better, and my dad would say, "Get up there, you can do it." And I'd get up and sing and people would applaud. So it just sorta started building that way. I sang on the old Dumont network back in 1948, when TV was still in its infancy.

*When did you decide to make a career out of music?*

Well, it kind of came gradually because there were so many things that I was wanting to do. There was boxing and baseball, both of which I was really serious about. But music was always there. I was always playing, and I was about 25 before realizing that I'd spent so much time in music and that I'd better get my act together and see if I had what it takes to build a career. I was playing the clubs, making $200 or $300 dollars a week with no obligations, skimming right through life and hollering "Ya Hoo" a lot. I started realizing that it wasn't going to be that way forever.

*When did you go electric?*

The first thing I did was put a DeArmond pickup on that Martin, and that really blew my mind. I got into picking, and the guys I was playing with couldn't hold me back. I just wanted to pick, and they said, "Hey, you're supposed to be playing rhythm." And I'd say: "Yeah, but let me play one. Let me get out here in the front and grin a lot." So I used that for a while and then my dad found another guitarist to play with us named Bill Harrell. He had a National full-size electric that he played, and he also owned a King Recorder which my dad bought for me. That was my first real electric guitar.

*What do you do when you go into the studio to record?*

Panic, first. And then just sit down and start getting into it. I don't go in often enough, and when you're onstage you just play, and if you blow a note its gone. The technique gets sloppy because even if you're recording the same tunes you're playing onstage, there are a lot of things you just don't hear. When you go into a studio and start picking and play it back, you hear all kinds of noises, creaks, grinds, and groans coming out of the guitar, and you suddenly realize that you are really going to have to get in there and work at it to get it clean again.

*How much do you prepare before you go in to record?*

Not at all. That's the way my recording career has been from the start. I've never dedicated myself and devoted the time to it. We've just walked in when we've had three days off and cut the record, and the albums sound exactly like that. Next year is going to be the first year that we are starting to try some creative things in recording. I want to take some time off and really put together an album that I've always wanted to do. Basically it will be an instrumental album featuring some really hot guitar pieces in the vein of my earlier things. Something I can point to and say, this is really what I'm capable of doing. Instead, now I play something and say, "Well, the engineers did a good job and it's well-mastered and it's not bad sounding, but I know I can do better than that."

*Do you have any records you really like?*

None that I would honestly say contain my best work all the way through. I listen back to something and wonder why in the world I did it that way—where was my mind when I did that? I'm sure at the moment it seemed like I really wanted to play that, but that's the kind of thing you can avoid by taking your time and going over your music for like a six-month period. You come back a week later and listen, and if it still sounds good, you keep it. If not, you dump it and try again.

*How do you think time has affected your playing?*

I must say that I am really subdued and settled compared to what I used to be. Success will do that to you, I guess. It turns your thinking around; you don't have that freedom, that pure gut feeling of just getting out and *flailing* it. You have a tendency to hold back and be more reserved, which takes away from your performance. I used to do things where I didn't know what I was doing; now I have an idea what I'm doing, but I'm afraid to do it. I hold back, because I think it's tacky or doesn't mean anything anymore. Good guitar players used to come down and watch our shows when they got off work just to see this kid up there who was just so abandoned on the guitar. It would be good to play with that freedom again.

---

### A SELECTED ROY CLARK DISCOGRAPHY

**Solo albums:** (On Capitol): *Greatest!*, SM-369; *Guitar Spectacular*, SM-2425; *Lightning Fingers Of Roy Clark*, ST-1780; *So Much To Remember*, SM-11412. (On Dot): *Best Of Roy Clark*, 25986; *Roy Clark Country*, 25997; *Family Album*, 26018; *Live!*, 26005; *Come Live With Me*, 26010; *Do You Believe This?*, 25895; *I Never Picked Cotton*, 25980; *Incredible Roy Clark*, 25990; *Magnificent Sanctuary Band*, 25993; *Other Side Of Roy Clark*, 25977; *Superpicker*, 26008; *Urban Suburban*, 25863; *Yesterday When I Was Young*, 25953. (On ABC/Dot): *In Concert*, DOSD-2054; *Family & Friends*, DOSD-2005; *Greatest Hits*, DOSD-2030; *Classic Clark*, DOSD-2010; *Country Comes To Carnegie Hall*, 2087; *The Entertainer*, DOSD-2001; *Heart To Heart*, DOSD-2041; *Hookin' It*, 2099; *Labor Of Love*, 1053; *My Music & Me*, 2072; *Pair Of Fives*, 2015. (On Word [4800 W. Waco Dr., Waco, TX 76703]): *Roy Clark Sings Gospel*, 8654; *Greatest Gospel Songs*, 8698. (On MCA): *Best Of*, 27015; *Roy Clark In Concert*, 37132; *Roy Clark's Greatest Hits, Vol. 1*, 27050.

# FLOYD CRAMER

By Bob Doerschuk

**H**IS NAME IS FLOYD CRAMER, AND HE IS ONE OF THE most influential pianists in the music business. His tinkling, sentimental style is echoed in literally every modern country and western tune that carries a piano line, and with the exploding popularity of that genre, that means a lot of keyboard players are following in Cramer's footsteps.

Born in 1934 in Shreveport, Louisiana, Cramer has been playing since the age of five, and began recording in 1952 on Abbott Records. In 1955, he entered the stratosphere of country music with his debut on Nashville's *Grand Ole Opry*. Within a few years, he became a top session man in the Nashville studios, playing with a long list of popular performers, including Jim Reeves ("He'll Have To Go"), Don Gibson ("Sea Of Heartbreak"), Jimmy Dean ("Big Bad John"), and Elvis Presley (a number of hits, from "Heartbreak Hotel" to "It's Now Or Never").

Cramer's first hit single—"Last Date," recorded in the '50s—was also his last hit single, although some of his later releases, including "On The Rebound," "Flip Flop Bop," and "San Antonio Rose," have earned respectable sales. His effort now goes mainly into concert appearances, where his low-key, country-boyish personality and commercial, easy-listening selections usually win over his audiences.

The crowd that turned out for his performance at the Wolf Trap outdoor theater in Vienna, Virginia, was downright enraptured as soon as Cramer walked out onstage. They quietly hummed along with his simple, fluid arrangements of "The Entertainer," "Both Sides Now," "Blue Eyes Crying In The Rain," "Sunny," and other pop standards, and gave him a send-off as warm as the Virginia evening air.

Before the concert, Cramer discussed his musical and personal history backstage.

\* \* \* \*

**W**ERE YOU RAISED, LIKE MANY OF TODAY'S COUNTRY *musicians, on the airwaves of the* Grand Ole Opry*?*
Really, I was raised in a small town in Arkansas, although I was born in Louisiana, and there were no other musicians in the area. But of course I listened to the radio, and my parents bought me a piano when I was small. They wanted me to take lessons, and I didn't like to take lessons at all; I wanted to just play tunes instead. The fact the piano was there was a big influence; when I had nothing else to do, I played the piano. Eventually, when I was 13 or 14 years old, I got more interested in playing. The more interested I got, the more I played, so by the time I got out of high school, I'd made up my mind that I wanted to be in the music business. So I went to Shreveport and started to work on KWKH with the Louisiana Hayride.

*That's the same program where Elvis got his start.*
Right. In fact, he came there after I joined the show, and I worked some tours with him in Texas. We also did some movie things together, like *Blue Hawaii* and *Girl Happy*.

*What kind of music did you follow when you began playing?*
I played music I heard in church. I used to follow quartet music, and also country music.

*Did you do technical exercises when you were learning to play?*
Well, mostly it was by ear, but I did take a few lessons earlier, before I got out of high school. I didn't like those exercises. I know I should have worked at it more—now I realize that. But I'm still in the process of learning; I think all musicians are.

*Do you do exercises now?*
Sometimes, but basically I just work at new tunes I hear.

*Could you describe your bent note technique?*
Well, technically, it's just like a slur or a grace note. You just strike the note below the note you want to hit, then slide up to the right one, while playing a harmony note above it. It's like making an intentional mistake, then recovering. This is the same device that steel guitar players use, only they use pedals to slide more smoothly to the right pitch.

*You have refused to endorse any one brand of piano. Why?*
I've been approached to do that by a number of companies, but I just don't want to get involved in endorsing this brand or that.

*Is there in fact a make of piano you prefer to play?*
In the studios, I usually play a Baldwin or a Steinway—the

Steinways most often, I guess, mainly because they're the most available to me. They're both good, and so are a lot of other pianos besides them.

*You recorded an organ album called* Floyd Cramer Gets Organized [*out of print*].

Well, that was really half an album—half piano and half organ—and I did another organ album later. The organ is not one of my favorite instruments. The touch is different, and I prefer the piano touch. I just never played an organ much. If you could get some unusual sounds on it, I'd say "Yeah, I like it," but I'll stick with the piano for now.

*Have you explored other kinds of keyboards?*

I've done some things on the electric piano, but I really haven't gotten into a lot of the other things—the synthesizers and stuff like that.

*Do you see country music using these kinds of instruments in the future?*

They can use them best in the background, I would say.

*What country pianists were you aware of when you were starting out?*

One recording pianist I knew of back then was Moon Mulligan, and Owen Bradley was doing some things—they used to call him "Half Moon." He was a producer in Nashville, and he played on some of his own productions. There weren't really a lot of country background pianists at that time. What there was was this kind of limited, Lefty Frizzell style—he had a piano on all his hits, playing just a plinking, honky-tonk type background. So it just eventually evolved, and they started using more piano.

*These days in country music, how important is reading music?*

In country music, I would say it isn't that important. It would help, of course, When I was really busy in the studios doing two or three sessions a day, some of the artists would come in with string arrangements or horn arrangements, and naturally, they'd have the parts written out. So in cases like that, a knowledge of music helps.

*Do you do much studio work any more?*

No. I've cut out a lot because of the traveling and concerts we do.

*How did you break into the tight-knit studio crowd in Nashville?*

Well, when I lived in Shreveport, I came to Nashville on several trips to record with Webb Pierce, and I met Fred Rose of Acuff-Rose there, and Owen Bradley and Chet Atkins, who was an assistant A&R man then. This was in 1954. I'd been in Shreveport for four years, and I'd worked the road, traveling. I'd gotten married in 1954, so in '55, I said, "I'm not getting anywhere. I'm playing, I'm making a living, but that's not enough; I want to do more." So, after meeting these people in Nashville, I decided, "Well, I'm just gonna move, and take a chance. I may have to come to Nashville and work the road again, but at least I'll be where everybody's wanting to go," and

**Floyd Cramer is the originator of the "bent note" or "pedal sound" piano lick which imitated the phrasing of the pedal steel guitar.**

where all the people from the Hayride had already gone. I did work the road when I came to Nashville. I worked with Marty Robbins and did some things with Jim Reeves until it got to the point where, if I'd leave town, I'd blow a recording session because somebody would call me. So I said, "Well, I'm just not gonna work the road anymore, and if it doesn't work out, I'll just leave Nashville and maybe go back to Louisiana." So I just stayed in town and kept doing the sessions, and it eventually got bigger and bigger.

*On Jimmy Dean's "Big Bad John," you produced an anvil sound. Did you do that on a keyboard instrument?*

No. It was just a big piece of iron, like a weight, that was in the studio. We had a coat rack that was back behind the piano against the wall, so I got a coat hanger and hung that steel thing up and hit it with a hammer. That particular song didn't sound to me like it needed a piano, because of the arrangement we were doing.

*What do you think of the new directions country music seems to be taking—the "progressive country" style, for instance?*

Well, it's expanding, of course; that's pretty obvious. I think it's a great direction, because it's getting to where there's no limit. A country artist can be a top hit, so I'm very happy with what's going on.

*Why do you think country music is becoming so popular?*

It's broadened itself. The songs themselves have a wider scope. Hank Williams songs, for instance, are international—the lyrics and the melodies are something that people can hum, if they want to. Also, they're written about true, down-to-earth feelings that really touch people.

*Country music is not technically a challenging music. Do you think this is a major drawback?*

No. You don't have to play 90 notes a second to play country music, or to play any kind of music, and make it sound good, unless you just want to do a jazz thing, and then that's fine.

---

**A SELECTED FLOYD CRAMER DISCOGRAPHY**

**Solo albums** (On Victor): *Almost Persuaded*, AYL1-3900; *Great Country Hits*, AYL1-4008; *Piano Masterpieces*, AYL1-3745; *This Is*, VPS-6031. *Million Seller Country Piano Hits*, Alshire, 5107. *Floyd Cramer Country*, RCA, APL1-1541.

---

# CHARLIE DANIELS

By Jim Hatlo

**C**HANCES ARE, YOU ALREADY KNOW HOW THE STORY came out. Johnny outplayed the devil to cinch the gold fiddle—and in the bargain helped the Charlie Daniels Band collect for its Epic album *Million Mile Reflections*, a double-platinum certification, a Grammy award for Best Country Performance By A Group in 1979, Instrumentalist Of The Year, and Best Instrumental Group Of The Year awards. Not a bad haul for an afternoon's work.

gia" from *Million Mile Reflections* remains the biggest fiddle hit in the history of southern rock; in fact, it is probably the biggest fiddle hit in the history of rock and roll, period. A concert video

version still gets airplay on Music TV. It's not surprising that the record is the favorite fiddle disc of its narrator, co-author, and principal performer, Charlie Daniels.

"I like what I played on that," says Daniels, who is not much given to admiring his own work. "I had seven fiddles on it at one point, all overdubbed, to get that ominous sort of sound." Daniels established himself as rock and roll's best-known fiddler in 1975, slippin' and slidin' through "The South's Gonna Do It Again," a hit single that became the national anthem of southern rock. But "The Devil Went Down To Georgia" made Daniels and the fiddle as much an American folk institution as

Rocky Balboa and his right cross or Indiana Jones and his whip.

Daniels started his career as a guitarist. He always opens his shows on guitar, a Gibson red-sunburst Les Paul. But today when he ducks offstage mid-set and then reappears with his black Barcus-Berry fiddle under his chin, the crowds come unglued. "I'd agree that there's something about the fiddle that sets off an audience," he says. "The fiddle is kind of a good-time instrument. People expect a good time when they see it."

This year a lot of people paid to have a good time watching Daniels play the fiddle. By the end of 1983, the Charlie Daniels Band will have logged more than 200 days on the road. "We're probably working more dates now than we have at any time since '75 or '76," says Daniels. "I love the live performances. We won't always do as many dates as we're doing this year; but we're a hard-working band, and we always have been. The longest we've ever been home is about four and a half months, and that was three years ago when I broke my arm in three places and it was in a sling. That was the only reason we weren't out there."

Daniels and his troupe are confirmed road warriors, which accounts for more of the spoils in the CDB trophy case: Academy of Country Music awards for Best Touring Group of 1980 and of 1981, respectively: and *Performance Magazine*'s Road Crew Of The Year award for 1979. But even from the first, a mixture of tenacious drive and exuberant showmanship has characterized Charlie Daniels' career.

Charlie started learning guitar on a borrowed instrument when he was 15, in his hometown of Wilmington, North Carolina. "This friend of mine, Russell Palmer, who's now a mortician in Sanford, North Carolina, had an old Stella that his daddy had given him," Charlie recalls. "He'd gotten a book and learned a couple of chords on it, then just threw it in the closet or something. One day he happened to take it out when I was over there. I'd always wanted to learn how to play, so I got him to show me two chords. I believe I borrowed his guitar that same night."

It was a night Charlie's parents didn't soon forget. They arrived home from an evening out, walked into the house—and were greeted by Charlie springing out of a closet, guitar in hand, to perform his first concert. All two chords' worth.

A year and a half later Charlie began fiddling. "I was playing guitar with another guitar picker," Charlie says, "so we figured we needed a different instrument. After a year of guitar I started messing with mandolin. Since the fingering on a fiddle is the same as the fingering on a mandolin, except the fiddle doesn't have any frets, in a little while I got to fooling around with fiddle, too."

What were his earliest influences? "All bluegrass," he says. "Whoever happened to be playing with the bands I really liked. But Benny Martin has always been one of my very favorite fiddlers. He's got a unique style. If you listen to bluegrass—the way Bill Monroe plays it, which is what I think of as bluegrass in its pristine form—there's a lot of blues in it. If you really listen to Monroe, you'll hear a lot of blues licks on the mandolin and on the fiddle. Especially from the fiddle player he's got, Kenny Baker, who I think is the best bluegrass fiddler in the world. But to me, Benny Martin's style didn't lean as much in the direction of the blues as the other fiddlers' styles did. He had a more melodic touch in anything he'd play—a lot of double stops and pretty, melodic things very few other bluegrass players used. I

liked that a lot."

Charlie's first band was a bluegrass group, the Misty Mountain Boys. "We did stuff by Flatt And Scruggs, Bill Monroe, Reno And Smiley, the Lonesome Pines Fiddlers, the Stanley Brothers—all standard bluegrass," he says. "Then and now, to my way of thinking, the best instrumentation for a bluegrass band is all acoustic instruments: guitar, doghouse [upright] bass, 5-string banjo, fiddle, and mandolin. Bill Monroe has always had the best bluegrass band. We copied—tried to copy—the music of any band that had that particular instrumentation, or something very much like it."

Daniels played square dances and local shows with the Misty Mountain Boys until rock and roll began muscling in on the mid-'50s record charts. Though Charlie's interest was piqued by the new music, he didn't exactly rush out and buy an electric guitar; actually he co-signed an installment contract for a friend who wanted to buy an amplifier. When the friend left town, Charlie was left with the amp.

He decided that he might as well go the whole route, so he bought an electric guitar to go with it. Soon he was picking rockabilly guitar in local clubs. By 1958 he was playing music full-time.

Charlie got his first taste of popularity in 1959 with a single called "Jaguar" on the Epic label. The producer was a man named Bob Johnston. Daniels renamed his group the Jaguars in an effort to capitalize on the success of the record, but the venture's real—and unforseen—payoff was to come nine years later. During much of the '60s, Daniels paid his dues working a wearying succession of clubs and honky-tonks. "We played every mudhole in this country," he said later. "Places nobody even *heard* of."

Then, late in 1968, Bob Johnston was in Nashville producing a session for an artist who had come down from relative seclusion in Woodstock, New York, to cut an album in Music City. The artist's name was Bob Dylan. The album was *Nashville Skyline.*

Daniels, who had made some inroads into the Nashville studio scene, asked Johnston to get him on as a sideman for the session. Johnston agreed to try, with the understanding that Charlie would come in for one number only—to play electric *bass*—and then make way for an established studio bassist. But Dylan liked what he heard from Charlie, and told Johnston to keep Daniels in the studio. "I guess I was just *real* hungry," Charlie later told an interviewer. "I said, 'Well, here it is, rough, wrong, or raw.' And that just happened to be what Dylan was looking for."

*Nashville Skyline* got mixed reviews from the critics, some of whom hailed it as an extension of Dylan's art to the displaced white hillbillies in the North, others of whom scorned it as a blatant, calculated grab for a share of the expanding country music market. The public ignored the intellectualizing long enough for *Nashville Skyline* to hit # 3 on the charts. Dylan was sufficiently pleased with it to record two more albums in Nashville the following year, *Self-Portrait* and *New Morning.* He hired Charlie Daniels to play on both of them.

The Dylan sessions confirmed Charlie as an in-demand Nashville sideman. Charlie's late-'60s studio activity also brought him face-to-face with his bluegrass roots. On one session he found himself playing backup guitar for Flatt And Scruggs. After Flatt And Scruggs went their separate ways in 1969,

**Charlie Daniels' "The Devil Went Down To Georgia" was the biggest fiddle hit in the history of southern rock.**

Charlie played fiddle for Scruggs on some *Grand Ole Opry* appearances. The former Misty Mountain Boy was coming up in the world.

Daniels organized the Charlie Daniels Band in 1971. Two more years of hard touring passed before the group scored its first national hit, "Uneasy Rider," a 1973 single in the talking-blues tradition that recounted the adventures of a long-haired country boy stranded in a redneck bar. The Top Ten single came from the band's Kama Sutra LP *Honey In The Rock* [out of print], which never got past # 164 on the national charts. But after "Uneasy Rider," people knew who the Charlie Daniels Band was.

Its 1974 album *Fire On The Mountain* climbed to # 38 on the charts, and the following year the band scored its first fiddle hit with "The South's Gonna Do It Again," from the LP *Nightrider*. The 1976 Epic release *Saddle Tramp* went gold.

As of 1983 the CDB could claim two gold albums (*Saddle Tramp* and 1982's *Windows*); one platinum album (1980's *Full Moon*, which included the hit "In America," a southern-style call to the colors); and the double platinum *Million Mile Reflections*. You can come up with a second double platinum LP if you lump the original Kama Sutra sales figures for *Fire On The Mountain* with the sales of the LP's re-release by epic.

A track record like that is money in the bank in the here-to-day, in-the-oldies-bin-tomorrow world of the music business. It didn't evolve from a carefully mapped out marketing/packaging scheme, but it didn't happen by accident, either. Much of Daniels' success in the '70s comes directly from his years on the club circuit during the '60s, and so does the wide variety of styles reflected in his music. He simply learned, firsthand in the trenches, what it was that people wanted to hear.

"If you listen to any one of our albums, you'll pick out a lot of different influences," Charlie says. "That's not conscious, that's just the way my mind operates. Where that came from, basically, is working in the beer joints years ago. I played clubs for about 12 years. Music changes a lot, and if you're playing in a copy band—and this was especially true at the time we were doing it—people want to hear Tony Bennett, they want to hear the Beatles, they want to hear a little jazz, a little 'Desafinado,' and a touch of this, that, and the other thing. All kinds of styles. I think the best training ground, and the best *proving* ground, for musicians to get a basic background in music is in the clubs. I don't think anybody can do better than that. Now, when we sit down and write, a lot of those styles that we played through the years just kind of come into our original music."

Different instruments that Charlie has played through the years have come into his music at various times, too. Mandolin made an early appearance on a couple of cuts from *Te John, Grease, And Wolfman*, a '70s release of "vintage" tracks dating from the boogie-band period before the official formation of the CDB. Charlie plays mandolin on "I'll Try Again" and "Tomorrow's Gonna Be Another Day." He also plays acoustic steel-string guitar on "Black Autumn."

Though he never plays acoustic guitar onstage ("It's just easier to deal with the electric"), he has used acoustics on a number of his albums. One of the most interesting such cuts is "Rainbow Ride," which closes *Million Mile Reflections*. The laid-back opening section of the 7:24-minute song is accompan-

**Charlie Daniels flatpicks his fiddle during a freewheeling "Orange Blossom Special."**

ied solely by fingerpicked nylon-string guitar.

"I like the nylon-string sound for certain things," Charlie says. "When I first went to Nashville in '67, it was the folky type era where there was a lot of fingerpicking on gut- [nylon-] string guitars going on. I did quite a bit of that during that time. Besides, the gut-string guitars are very easy on your fingers; they're good to sit around with. I do a lot of writing on a gut-string, especially the soft stuff. A guitar's sound can set a mood for you, and the gut-string puts me in a mood for writing in a certain fashion."

Almost all of Daniels' writing is done on some type of guitar. At his home near Nashville, where he raises quarter horses when he isn't on the road, guitars are virtually part of the furniture. "I've got a slew of guitars, even though there are only about three that I play regularly," he says. "The rest of them sit around the house. I try to keep them wherever I'm going to be. I've got guitars upstairs in the bedroom, guitars downstairs—so that whenever I want one, I'm just a few seconds away from picking one up." He even has a half-size acoustic that was built for him a year ago by luthier/repairman Randy Wood, which conveniently fits beneath the seat of his touring bus.

Charlie plays his guitars with a mixture of flatpicking and fingerpicking techniques. Flatpicking, he favors a Fender medium pick for both acoustic and electric work. He usually holds the pick conventionally, between the thumb and the first (index) finger, but sometimes—on tremolo passages, for instance—he holds it between the thumb and the third finger.

He uses a thumbpick for his fingerpicking, generally playing with thumb and two fingers. "I cut the tip of my ring finger off in an accident in '55," he explains. "But it doesn't cause me any problems. If I ever need three fingers with the thumb, I use my little [fourth] finger."

Charlie adds fingerpicks when he switches to banjo, which he uses more frequently today than he did in the band's formative years (its first significant appearance on a CDB album came in "Cumberland Mountain Number Nine" from *Saddle Tramp*). He traces his interest in the instrument back to the early days of Flatt And Scruggs.

"I'm 46, and I go pretty far back on the banjo," he says, "back to people like Stringbean [Dave "Stringbean" Akeman] and Uncle Dave Macon, and the drop-thumb style. But when Earl Scruggs came along, with his three-finger picking, I got excited. Flatt And Scruggs played out of Raleigh, North Carolina, on WPTM for a while. That's where I heard a lot of my first banjo picking. When Lester and Earl came there, interest in banjo in our part of the country went way up. There used to be a saying that you could shake a bush in North Carolina and five banjo players would come running out. But I just wanted to figure out that style.

"I remember sitting in bed one night, taking the banjo and playing real slow. I got to leading more with my index finger, more like Don Reno than like Earl Scruggs. Afterward, I just kept fooling with the banjo through the years. It's never been my primary instrument; it's always been kind of a sideline with me.

But I enjoy picking it."

The Charlie Daniels Band's operation has been refined for maximum efficiency and smoothness, with one objective in mind: giving each audience its money's worth. "That's the name of the game," says Charlie. "People don't pay money to come and listen to something they don't want to hear. They deserve to have a good time. If the audience enjoys itself, it's a successful show." To Daniels, that is the bottom line whether the band is in a club or a stadium. He makes no distinction between venues.

"I can't speak 100 percent for the rest of the band," he says, "but I think they feel the same way. When I walk on a stage, it just becomes a stage with a crowd of people out front. It doesn't make any difference where it is. We can't afford to let it make a difference. Tonight we may be indoors at a small city club, tomorrow night we may be outdoors at a state fair. But when I start a show, it's my job to do, for that day, the very best I can no matter where it is. Maybe the next day I can do better. Maybe I'll do worse, or maybe I'll do the same; but I do what I have to do at the time."

That attitude has a lot to do with the band's consistently successful tours. A key factor behind the CDB's equally successful recording output is Daniels' philosophy about staying on top of contemporary musical trends.

He doesn't.

The former copy-band leader has found his musical niche, and he stays with it: "It sounds like a helluva pompous statement to make, and I really don't mean it that way at all, but we pay very little attention to what anybody else is doing, or any kinds of trends or fads. Of course, we try to keep up with the studio sounds, the modern equipment. But I decided a long time ago that if you align yourself with something like the 'in' thing, the 'happening' thing, you go out with it. As far as our style of music is concerned, I believe it's very little affected by what else is going on. I want it to be us. We'll be around a lot longer that way."

The unity of style comes in part from a unity of personnel. Turnover in the Charlie Daniels Band is essentially nonexistent. Keyboards player Joel "Taz" DiGregorio began working with Daniels in the late '60s and signed on permanently in 1970. Drummer Fred Edwards likewise has been with the band for more than ten years. The greenest members are Crain and bassist Charlie Hayward: They have only been around since 1975.

"The newest member of the road crew—speaking of the inner circle, the ones on our payroll—probably has been with us for seven or eight years," says Daniels. "You get to looking back, and you realize that a lot of these kids grew up with us. We've got guys who are in their thirties, married and paying mortgages now, with a couple of kids, who were single and in their twenties when they came with us."

Again, that solidarity is as much a product of Charlie's experience as it is of good fortune. As a bandleader, he learned to look for specific qualities in his sidemen.

"Talent and personality is what it boils down to," he says. "I want a guy who can pick, but I've got to have a guy who can get along with everybody. All this beautiful family-type thing we've built up over the last ten years wouldn't have happened if the wrong people had been in it. We don't like moaning and arguing and whinning and fussing—it's a waste of time. I don't have time for that. I haven't got time for hard drugs. I don't like to talk to people who are drunk. And if you're not interested in doing what I want to do, then I don't want you in this outfit. I don't care how good you can play, I don't care if you're an electronics wizard; it don't make me no never mind. If you can't get with the program, I don't want you. *We* don't want you.

"People want to know how to get ahead in the world. *Get along* with people. I don't mean you have to take a bunch of junk; you have to make people respect you. But folks love to be around people who aren't bitching and complaining all the time. I don't—I won't—be around people who do that. My life is too short to spend listening to somebody bitch about something I can't do a thing about, or to spend *worrying* about something I can't do a thing about. There are enough things that I *can* do something about, like playing a damn good set of music, and having the best road crew in the business."

Given the right attitude, how does a musician make it through the smoke and noise of the beer joints to achieve the kind of platinum-plated success that the Charlie Daniels Band enjoys?

"You've got to *want* to do it. That's the only way you'll ever do anything, really," Daniels replies. "I'm not knocking unions, but you can't depend on unions, you can't depend on the government—you can't depend on anybody but the Lord and yourself, in that order. You have to sit down and look in the mirror and say, 'What am I worth to somebody? What am I really worth? Do I work hard, or am I the first one in line to punch out on the time clock?'

"If you're going to do something, be the best s.o.b. that ever did that—or as close to it as you can get. You do that by concentrating on it, by living it, eating it, breathing it, sleeping it. Don't get up in the competition of this business if you're soft, and if you're not going to say, 'I am committing myself to this; I don't give a damn how long it takes. If I have to work twice as hard as anybody ever has, I'll *be* here.' If you can't give it that kind of commitment, save yourself some trouble and don't try.

"And you have to enjoy the *act* of doing it, the act of going up and playing music for those people—not that you get paid for it, or the showbusiness aura of the thing. For me, the biggest thing in my day is standing on that stage, playing my guitar, playing my fiddle, playing my banjo, singing my songs—that's it.

"If you can't get interested enough in music to feel that way—you're not going to make it."

---

### A SELECTED CHARLIE DANIELS DISCOGRAPHY

**With the Charlie Daniels Band** (on Epic): *Te John, Grease And Wolfman*, PE34665; *Uneasy Rider*, PE34369; *Fire On The Mountain*, JE34365; *Nightrider*, PE34002; *Saddle Tramp*, PE34150; *High Lonesome*, PE34377; *Midnight Wind*, PE34970; *Million Mile Reflections*, JE35751; *Full Moon*, FE36571; *Windows*, FE37694; *A Decade Of Hits*, FE38795; *Banded Together*, PE36177.
**With Bob Dylan** (on Columbia): *Nashville Skyline*, 9825; *Self-Portrait*, 30050; *New Morning*, 0290.

**By Dennis E. Hensley**

**D**ON EVERLY, ONE HALF OF THE FAMOUS EVERLY Brothers, first learned guitar from his father, Ike Everly (also a major influence on Merle Travis). At 17, Don came to Nashville as a songwriter for Athens Music Company, and in 1956 he and his brother Phil joined the *Grand Ole Opry* as vocalists. In the late '50s and early '60s, the Everlys earned gold record after gold record for such rock and roll classics as "Bye Bye Love," "Wake Up, Little Susie," "Bird Dog," "'Till I Kissed You," "All I Have To Do Is Dream," and their biggest hit, "Cathy's Clown," all of which were written by Don.

\* \* \* \*

*C*AN YOU TELL US ABOUT SOME OF THE ARTISTS THAT *first influenced you?*

The Delmore Brothers and the Bales Brothers influenced the style of singing Phil and I did. My father and my two uncles were the original Everly Brothers when they sang as a trio on radio, and they were the ones Phil and I copied in singing style and even in playing style on guitar.

*Did you try to preserve that sound?*

Yes, we did. Phil and I released a special album entitled *Songs Our Daddy Taught Us.* On it, we were the only vocalists— no chorus or backup or extra harmony singers—and the only instruments on the album were our two rhythm guitars. It was a clean album, and it projected the original sound of country music. Unfortunately, it's out of print today.

*Your father appeared on the old* Johnny Cash Show, *didn't he?*

That's right. He and Mother Maybelle Carter sang together, and then they played kind of a unique guitar duet: my dad did the left-hand fingering while Mother Maybelle plucked the right-hand action.

*What was your father's style of playing?*

My dad, my uncles, and artists like Mother Maybelle all were early radio performers, long before electric instruments. They used a right-hand style of plucking which offered loud volume and a built-in harmony. That style of picking was adaptable to the banjo and autoharp, too. It's not dead today; Grandpa Jones

still does it on banjo, and Earl Scruggs on guitar.

*How many guitars do you own?*

At present, 15. I have one Martin, but all of the others are Gibson models. My father played a Gibson and taught me to play on a Gibson, so, besides appreciating their quality, I'm sentimentally linked to them. As a kid I was interested in things other than music, so sometimes my dad paid me 25¢ an hour to practice the guitar. It paid off for him, I guess.

*What types of strings and picks do you prefer?*

Either Martin or Gibson light-gauge strings. I use standard sets; I don't substitute or modify the packaged sets. I use a nylon pick of medium size and thickness, with a hole in the middle. Since I play a lot of rhythm, I like a flexible, but controllable, plectrum.

*Do you play anything besides the guitar?*

Harmonica playing is my hobby. I used to fingerpick a 5-string banjo, but not anymore. Playing other instruments is a big help to me as a songwriter. If I can hear and distinguish various instruments in my mind as I compose, my material is always better, more mature, more polished.

*Do you play lead guitar on any of your records?*

Frankly, no. In fact, I only played rhythm on about half of our records. When I began recording in the early '50s, we had 2-track studios. The band would cut the instrumental track, and then Phil and I would overdub the vocal track. Naturally, in the early part of our career we were expected to work on the instrumental cut first and then sing later. In time, however, with 16-track studios, everything got sophisticated, and we never played guitar in a session.

*Is there a place for phase-shifters, echo chambers, and fuzztones in your style of country music?*

I'm a traditionalist at heart, but I'm always open to new ideas. In the '50s, Chet Atkins devised a wah-wah by running a volume control through a tonal foot pedal. He demonstrated it for Phil and me, and we agreed to use it on "Till I Kissed You." The song was a hit. Chet and I have been close friends for 20 years. I wrote the liner notes for his *Teensville* album [out of print].

*Why did you and Phil break up your act?*

For several years Phil and I wanted to experiment in musical

expressions on our own, but the record companies and booking agents kept pressuring us to stay together. Finally, we just called it quits. Now we're both happy. In late 1976 Phil won the top BMI songwriter's award for "When Will I Be Loved?" which Linda Ronstadt had a monster hit with. And me, well, I've got a successful album out called *Brother Jukebox*, and I'm busy as a songwriter, too. We both are happy and successful and, most of all, free!

[*Ed. Note: Don and Phil Everly began working together again in 1983.*]

---

### A SELECTED DON EVERLY DISCOGRAPHY

**Solo albums:** *Brother Jukebox*, Hickory Records, AH 44003. **With The Everly Brothers** (compact disc): *Cadence Classics—Their 20 Greatest Hits*, Rhino, RNCD-5258. (LPs): *Everly Brothers*, Rhino, RNLP 211; *Reunion Concert*, Passport, PB 11001; *Songs Our Daddy Taught Us*, Rhino, RNLP 212; *Original Classics*, Arista, AL9-8207; *Stories We Could Tell*, RCA, LSP-4250; *EB84*, Mercury, 822431-1; *Born Yesterday*, Mercury, 826142-1.

# LESTER FLATT

**By Doug Green**

Early in the morning on May 11, 1979, Lester Flatt entered the cardiac care unit at Baptist Hospital in Nashville, Tennessee, suffering from severe chest pains. Not quite eight hours later he died of heart failure, succumbing at last to the string of major illnesses with which he struggled valiantly over the past few years. So ended the life of one of the three most influential men in the evolution of bluegrass music.

Lester Raymond Flatt was born June 19, 1914, in Overton County, near Sparta, Tennessee. He was one of nine children of a sharecropping farmer and fiddler. Married at 17, Lester went to work in a mill in Covington, Virginia, where he formed a band called the Harmonizers. He made his radio debut when the group played over a station — WDJB — in Roanoke, inia. He later went to work with the Happy-Go-Lucky Boys before an opportunity came to play full-time with Charlie Monroe and his Kentucky Pardners.

Although by that point the Monroe brothers, Charlie and Bill, had been separated for a couple of years, Charlie still felt that a mandolin was an essential part of the Kentucky Pardners' sound. Lester was hired as a mandolinist and tenor singer. His wife Gladys was hired as a singer and guitarist, using the stage name of Bobbie Jean. Flatt later claimed that after leaving Charlie he never picked up the mandolin; but he did a creditable job on the instrument. His mandolin playing is preserved on *Charlie Monroe On The Noonday Jamboree — 1944*.

Later in 1944, Lester quit the Kentucky Pardners and returned to Sparta, getting into the timber business for a few months. Then he received a telegram from Bill Monroe, at that point one of the hottest and most exciting acts on the *Grand Ole Opry*. Lester did not hesitate to accept a job as rhythm guitarist for Monroe's Blue Grass Boys.

He was then 30 years old, and during his four years with Monroe he blossomed into a superb singer, guitarist, and songwriter, virtually defining all those roles in the style of music that has come to be called bluegrass. His singing was high, though unstrained, and distinctive; his guitar playing was economical and straight to the point. It was punctuated by the ascending lick that came to be called "the Flatt run" in his honor. It would become one of the hallmarks of bluegrass. His song-

writing — much of it done in collaboration with Monroe —displayed a flair, perhaps even a genius, for evocative simplicity. Some of the many classics coming from that era were "Sweetheart You Done Me Wrong," "Little Cabin Home On The Hill," and "Will You Be Loving Another Man."

In 1945, Earl Scruggs brought his unique and exciting banjo style to the Blue Grass Boys, and Bill Monroe suddenly found himself heading the most dynamic band in country music: Monroe and Scruggs, the premier instrumentalists of their time; Chubby Wise, a superb fiddler; and Lester Flatt, playing solid rhythm, singing true and with feeling, and writing more and better material all the time.

It was too good to last forever. Weary of the constant grind of the road, Scruggs quit in 1948. Two weeks later so did Flatt; and as he was working out his notice, so did Cedric Rainwater, the bass player. Rainwater was actually the man who made the suggestion that he, Flatt, and Scruggs form a band of their own. That they did within weeks, adding singer/guitarist Mac Wiseman (himself now a bluegrass legend) and fiddler Jim Shumate to a group they called Lester Flatt, Earl Scruggs, And The Foggy Mountain Boys.

As with the Blue Grass Boys of 1945-48, the Foggy Mountain Boys of 1948-53 were a band marked by tremendous creative energy. Scruggs, only 19 when he joined Monroe, was still bringing his faultlessly tasteful banjo style to perfection, while Flatt continued to write song after song—such classics as "If I Should Wander Back Tonight," "Little Girl Of Mine In Tennessee," "I'll Never Shed Another Tear," "Cabin On The Hill," "Blue Ridge Mountain Home," "Cabin In Caroline," and many others.

In 1953 Flatt and Scruggs signed with longtime sponsor Martha White Mills. The theme song for their product (flour) became better-known nationwide than the product itself; Flatt and Scruggs moved to Nashville and became Opry members in 1955.

Their music took a mellower turn in the years that followed, but their reputation continued to grow. They became darlings of the folk revival of the '60s, which took them to every corner of the country. At the same time, through radio — and later, television—shows, and through hit records like *The Ballad Of*

*Jed Clampett* (the first bluegrass record to go to #1 on the *Billboard* charts), they strengthened their appeal to their bread-and-butter country audience while gaining national attention as well.

The partnership of Flatt and Scruggs came to an unhappy end in 1969, with each wishing to do different things in music. Scruggs and his sons continued with the progressive bluegrass that they pursue to this day. Flatt returned to a traditional sound. It was a sound without the earlier fire and intensity, but it was warm and endearing. With his band—which he called the Nashville Grass—he spent another decade on the road, on the Opry, and on radio and television.

Though the Nashville Grass had fluctuating personnel, it was a consistently fine band. The last four or five years were somewhat difficult for Lester Flatt. His body began to give out, though his desire to perform remained. He had suffered heart problems as early as the mid-'60s, and he underwent five hours

of open-heart surgery in Nashville in July, 1975. With admirable determination, he kept his band together and continued to appear; but he became increasingly more frail. Pneumonia and flu hospitalized him for three weeks early in 1978. Late that year he suffered a cerebral hemorrhage, and though for some months he appeared well on the road to recovery, the cardiac seizure he suffered in May was more than his weakened body could stand.

Some 250 mourners attended his funeral in Hendersonville, Tennessee, including John Hartford, Roy Acuff, Grandpa and Ramona Jones, and Ernest Tubb, among others. On May 14, he was buried in the Tennessee hills near Sparta.

An extremely influential performer in bluegrass, country, and, indeed, all of American music, he remained modest about his success and his fame. But history will not overlook his contributions as a pioneer of bluegrass music, and his imprint on the music itself will endure for as long as it is played.

---

### A SELECTED LESTER FLATT DISCOGRAPHY

**Solo albums** (on Victor): *Best Of Lester Flatt*, APL1-0578; *Lester Flatt, Live Bluegrass Festival*, APL1-0588; *Foggy Mountain Breakdown*, ANL1-1202; *Nashville's Greatest Instrumentalists*, ANL1-2181; *Stars Of The Grand Ole Opry, 1926-1974*, CPL2-0466. *Flatt Gospel*, Canaan (4800 W. Waco Dr., Waco, TX 76703), 9775; *Lester Raymond Flatt*, Flying Fish, 015; *Tennessee Jubilee*, Flying Fish, 012. **With Flatt & Scruggs** (on Columbia): *Changin' Times*, CS09596; *Country's Greatest Hits, Vol. 1*, CG-9; *Fabulous Sound Of Flatt & Scruggs*, CG-30; *Flatt & Scruggs At Carnegie Hall*, CS-8845; *Greatest Hits*, CS-9370. (On Rounder): *The Golden Era*, Special Series 05; *Don't Get Above Your Raisin'*, Special Series 08. *The Original Sound*, Mercury, MG 20773. **With Bill Monroe:** *The Original Bluegrass Band*, Rounder, Special Series 06. **With Charlie Monroe:** *Charlie Monroe On The Noonday Jamboree-1944*, Country Records (Box 191, Floyd, VA 24091), 538.

# HANK GARLAND

**By Rich Kienzle**

N ASHVILLE CATS," JOHN SEBASTIAN ADMIRINGLY SANG
in his 1967 composition, "play clean as country water, play wild
as mountain dew, been playin' since they's babies," and "get
work before they're two." Allowing for artistic license on the last
phrase, those descriptions fit Hank Garland particularly well.
Along with Chet Atkins, Harold Bradley, and Grady Martin, Hank
was among the first true guitar virtuosos to emerge from the
Nashville studios—a player who helped define the standards by
which other Nashville session guitarists are judged.

Garland epitomized the image of the Nashville picker: the
guitarist able to walk into a studio, tune up, hear a run-through
of the songs to be recorded, and invent a creative and sympathetic backing on the spot; the consummate musician who
would leave the last session of the day for a night of jamming in
a Printer's Alley nightclub; the inveterate experimenter interested in the latest guitar model and addicted to trying out new
sounds, licks, and devices; the person for whom the instrument
was not just an end in itself, but a means to the end of creating
music.

Hank's influence extended far beyond the studios of Nashville. His 1960 *Jazz Winds From A New Direction* had a considerable effect on players throughout the country. A young
Pittsburg R&B guitarist named George Benson was taken by it,
as was another young musician from Mississippi who was into
rock and blues, Bucky Barrett. Above all, the LP gave Nashville
musicians new admiration and stature in the jazz world. It was
almost as if Garland had smothered the "hillbilly" stereotypes
with chorus upon chorus of brilliant, bop-flavored jazz. Before
Hank Garland, the very idea of a steel guitarist such as Buddy
Emmons recording with a jazz group—as he did in 1963 with
his *Steel Guitar Jazz* album—or of mainstream jazz bassist Ray
Brown and drummer Shelly Manne working with country
mandolinists Jethro Burns and Tiny Moore, would have been all
but unthinkable.

Hank Garland's professional career spanned only 15 years.
In 1961, at the age of 30, his dream of becoming "the best guitar
player in the world" was shattered in a violent auto accident
near Nashville. After lingering near death, he began to recover,
but the price paid was devastatingly high. Severe brain damage

claimed most of his motor functions and coordination, and his
dreams of greater music to come seemed to have evaporated.
Shortly thereafter he left Nashville, never to return to the studios
where he made his reputation as a country and jazz sideman on
recordings by Elvis Presley, Rusty Draper, Jim Reeves, Don
Gibson, Webb Pierce, Patsy Cline, Brenda Lee, Charlie Rich, Patti
Page, Jerry Lee Lewis, and numerous others.

This wasn't the end of the Hank Garland legend. Drawing
upon vast determination and courage, he began relearning the
guitar from scratch, encouraged by his family, particularly his
brother Bill. It would be two years after the accident until he
regained any command of the instrument, and 13 more before
he returned to Nashville for a brief appearance at the 1976 Fan
Fair Reunion Show—where his rendition of his 1949 composition "Sugarfoot Rag" left moist eyes among performers and
audience members. They could see and hear that while Hank
Garland might not be returning to the Nashville studios, he had
certainly returned from one of the most uncertain and harrow-
ing journeys any musician could ever make.

\* \* \* \*

Walter Louis Garland was born November 11, 1930, in
Cowpens, South Carolina, a small town just northeast of Spartanburg, not far from the North Carolina border. It was an area
dominated by hard-core country music, which had quite an
impact upon young Hank. Chet Atkins, who worked closely with
Garland through the years, recalls that "Hank said his first
inspiration was the Carter Family. He heard Maybelle picking
the 'Wildwood Flower' when he was a little kid, and he dreamed
that night he was playing it and he couldn't wait, of course, to get
a guitar." Garland's father bought him a used Encore steel-string
when Hank was six, and young Garland began taking lessons
from one Mr. Fowler, who taught him basic chords and
positions.

Early on, Hank was attracted to another young guitarist, who
was beginning to make his mark as a musician. Arthur Smith was
just 17 when he began playing over radio station WSBA in
Spartanburg, and Hank listened closely to him. Smith's electric

lines captivated Garland to the point that the younger musician attempted to electrify his acoustic. Atkins remembers Hank's account of this event: "He told me he hooked an electric cord to the strings and plugged it in the wall and almost burned the guitar up."

As World War II began, Hank was heading into adolescence as a true guitar addict. By the time he was in his teens he was proficient enough to join Shorty Painter's band, a local group that gave him his first taste of performing experience. Garland remembers getting his first electric guitar during his time, although he isn't sure if it was an arch-top Gibson or Epiphone. He did, however, have a De Armond pickup on it , and ran it through a small Gibson amplifier.

His first real break as a professional musician came quite by chance. He had gone downtown to Alexander's Music Store in Spartanburg to buy a string, and while there he was introduced to *Grand Ole Opry* member Paul Howard. Howard was passing through with his western swing-styled Georgia Cotton Pickers group, and after handshakes were exchanged someone quickly produced a guitar and amp. Garland picked a little, and Howard—who played a major role in ending the Opry's long-standing ban on electric guitars—was impressed. He offered Garland a job with the Cotton Pickers in Nashville, and told him he would call in two weeks to finalize the deal. It was 1945, and Hank was only 15 years old.

Garland went home ecstatic and explained it all to his parents, who had some initial reservations because of their son's age and the fact that he would have to leave school. But Hank's pleading over the next two weeks softened them, and when Howard finally called telling him to come to Nashville's Tulane Hotel, they reluctantly assented. When Hank arrived at the Tulane, however, Howard didn't remember him. Hank was crushed, but went on to ask Howard if he could play on the Opry that night anyhow. The bandleader agreed, and that evening Garland was featured on a boogie-woogie instrumental that brought the audience at the Ryman Auditorium to its feet. Backstage after the performance Howard dubbed Hank the "Baby Cotton Picker" and told him, "Kid, you have a job here as long as I got one."

For the next eight weeks he worked on the road and on the Opry with the Cotton Pickers, but because of extraneous circumstances his initial stay with the group was cut short: At 15 Garland wasn't old enough to join the Musicians Union, and child-labor laws banned anyone that age from working full-time. Crestfallen, Hank returned home to Cowpens, his only consolation being Howard's promise to recall him to Nashville when Garland turned 16. On November 11, 1946, Hank got his call from Howard, and a short time later he was back in Nashville with the Cotton Pickers.

Chet Atkins was in Nashville for the first time in 1946, working as a sideman with Red Foley on the Opry. He recalls with laughter and great affection his first meeting Garland there: "He was a little old, fat, red-faced punk, and he hadn't gotten all of his height yet. He was playing choruses that he heard on Bob Wills records done by Jimmy Wyble. And he rushed an awful lot; he'd pick up tempo." Veteran Nashville session guitarist Harold Bradley, who met Garland around the same time through Ernest Tubb's lead player, Billy Byrd, has a similar recollection. "Hank was very fast," he says. "He was rough, but very fast, and he had a lot of phenomenal technique."

Garland's association with Billy Byrd subsequently changed Hank's entire musical direction. Though he played spare, simple leads behind Tubb, Byrd was also a fine jazz guitarist who had grown up jamming Charlie Christian tunes with Bradley. Hank moved into an apartment in Byrd's home and spent his spare moments learning the rudiments of jazz. "Billy showed me how to use my little finger," Garland says. "He'd say, 'Use the damn thing; stick it up on the string there and use it!' " Bradley, who also sat in on many of those sessions, adds, "We taught him songs and jazz licks and just a whole bunch of improvisations. We showed him a lot of the things we knew, and he just went on by us—just got into the jazz thing real heavy."

But one didn't make a living playing jazz guitar in those days around Nashville, so early in 1947 Hank left Howard and the Cotton Pickers when steel guitarist Bob Foster recruited him for a new band being led by singer Cowboy Copas. Copas had just departed from Pee Wee King's Golden West Cowboys after scoring successes with King recordings such as "Fillipino Baby." Hank gained experience doing some of Copas' earliest sessions. According to Dr. Charles K. Wolfe, a professor of English at Middle Tennessee State University at Murfreesboro who is currently working on a bibliography of country music for the Smithsonian, recording session books during the late '40s and '50s are very unclear as to just who worked on what songs, but all the available data points to Hank playing on Copas tunes such as "Don't Let Your Deal Go Down," "Honky Tonkin'," and "Down In Nashville Tennessee."

Another tune which Hank almost certainly worked on was singer Autry Inman's 1948 recording of "You Better Leave Them Guys Alone," where his guitar solo echoes both Les Paul and Django Reinhardt. "I started listening to Django," Hank says, "after Chet told me he was the greatest guitar player in the world." Atkins also remembers hearing Garland on a record for the first time in the late '40s: "I was in Knoxville, and I heard this chorus. I don't recall the artist now, but I remember that then I thought it was the greatest guitar chorus I'd ever heard, so I checked around and found out it was Hank who played it."

It's little wonder that Hank had so much Django in his early guitar work. For a time, he and his friend Bob Moore, who is a longtime Nashville studio bassist, roomed together in a boarding house while Garland was playing with Copas. Moore remembers, "I used to get up every morning to go do a radio show at 5:30 with Lester Flatt and Earl Scruggs. When my alarm would go off, Hank would get up and be practicing even before I finished my breakfast. I'd go do the show and another at noon, then I'd come home. There was Hank, still listening to Django Reinhardt."

Garland spent nearly three years with the Copas band, gaining a reputation for his increasingly masterful guitar work. "He was one of those guys who you could play a lick for, and he'd come back like an echo," says Atkins. "He had such a good ear. Sometimes I'd pick something with fingers that he couldn't just to irritate him. He didn't play fingerstyle, but he could have if he'd wanted." Hank today recalls that episode with laughter, admitting that "whatever anybody else played, if they played it through one time, I had it." Photos show that throughout his tenure with Copas, Garland primarily used a blonde Epiphone Zephyr Deluxe, but by the end of the decade he had switched over to Gibson guitars.

Nashville, too, was undergoing some radical changes at the

**Prior to a tragic 1961 accident, Hank Garland was one of Nashville's leading session guitarists. He is pictured here playing his favorite guitar, a Gibson L-5 that was made for him.**

time. Until then the Opry was its sole connection with country music. Most country recording sessions were usually done in other cities or with portable equipment in Nashville, and a few were held in radio station studios. Then in 1947 Castle Studios opened in the Tulane Hotel, signaling the beginning of the recording industry there. It also created a new role for local musicians. Although many singers perferred either to use their touring groups or to borrow someone else's group, there was a small enclave of players who made themselves available for sessions—something that until then hadn't been done much in country music. But it was an inevitable by-product of the studio industry, one that became increasingly important in Nashville.

Sometime during 1949 Garland left Copas and began freelancing in the studios. Just how this took place isn't certain.

Harold Bradley remembers Hank coming into a Decca session he was working on with his brother Owen and producer Paul Cohen. "Hank entered the studio," Bradley says, "and since Cohen and my brother liked him, they put him on the session." Cohen also favored a song Hank had written as a fingering exercise, "Sugarfoot Rag." Cohen thought enough of it to record an instrumental version by Garland. Later, lyrics were added by one George Vaughan, and Red Foley recorded this version on November 10, 1949, with Hank doing the now-famous guitar intro and solo. Two days prior to that date, Foley had cut "Chattanoogie Shoe Shine Boy," and the two tunes were paired on a single released early in 1950. Garland got label credit for "Sugarfoot," something quite rare for a sideman, and since "Chattanoogie" became a million-seller, many listeners also heard "Sugarfoot Rag"—which itself was #5 on the *Cash Box* country charts for a time. The song earned Garland the nickname "Sugarfoot," and got him a series of recordings.

By the late '40s and early '50s, Hank, Grady Martin, Harold Bradley, and Chet Atkins were the main guitarists in Nashville. During those days the studios were loose, and the musicians free to contribute their own ideas to songs. Bradley remembers Garland going even further than that: "He had a very good imagination for not only coming up with ideas, but also with arrangements." And Chet Atkins says that this ability was typical for Hank throughout his studio career: "Hank was very outspoken, and he had a lot of ideas. He didn't take any talk from any producer. If they said something smart to him, his face would get real red and he'd say something back. But he was such a good musician that everyone had a terrible amount of respect for him, so nobody stepped on his toes. He could only help you: He was so good, he could never hurt you."

Garland did a number of early Nashville sessions, including a notable one with singer Eddie Hill in 1952. The song, "The Hot Guitar," featured Hank, Chet, and Jerry Byrd imitating other guitarists as well as themselves. The flipside cut, "Steamboat Stomp," was done with just Hank, a steel guitarist, and a rhythm section. Having begun as a routine western-swing number, the song found Garland taking an incredible bebop guitar break in the middle which turned the tune inside out. Hank's jazz talents were crystalizing. Having already assimilated elements of Django, Christian, and Barney Kessel, he now showed signs of Barry Galbraith and Tal Farlow influences in his playing.

In 1955, Elvis Presley's Sun recordings began stirring up the South. Changes were on the way as rockabilly began grabbing a surprisingly large audience. One of the harbingers of change was in a September 1955 Decca recording where Garland did a session with boogie-woogie pianist and singer Roy Hall. At the time of the recording, rockabilly wasn't terribly compatible with jazz guitar playing, and Garland knew it. "Hank told me what he did to get ready for that," Bradley says. "He turned on radio station WLAC, which back then was playing R&B, to get a lot of ideas before he came in to do that one. He knew it was going to be a funkier style of music than we were accustomed to playing." At that September 15 session Hank and Hall recorded a tune titled "Whole Lotta Shakin' Goin' On" [*Rare Rockabilly*], and Hank's blues licks were good. It would be nearly two years before pianist Jerry Lee Lewis transformed the same song into a rock and roll classic.

But even those sporadic sessions didn't prepare Nashville for the onslaught that followed Elvis' burst upon the national

**Drawing upon vast determination and courage, Hank began relearning the guitar from scratch when he regained control of his motor functions.**

scene after his first RCA records were released in 1956. Though some of his singles sound country by today's standards, they weren't originally perceived that way. As rock and roll spread across America many radio stations turned away from country, causing some young country singers to drop their fiddlers and steel guitarists in favor of the loudest drummer they could find. Finally, country record sales and personal appearances by artists began to slip, and Nashville was in trouble. "They ran the fiddle players and steel players back into the woods," says Bradley. "Some of them were not able to survive a wait of two to three years before they would get hired again."

Hank Garland, however, was one of the lucky musicians. After the intital trauma wore off, some Nashville producers started to persuade as many country singers as possible to record rock and roll-flavored records. Everyone from Carl Smith and Red Foley to Little Jimmy Dickens, Webb Pierce, Johnny Horton, and Marty Robbins jumped on the bandwagon—some of them reluctantly. The musicians, obviously, also had to adapt. Garland recalls having to use lighter gauge strings, and adds, "I had to turn another knob on the amplifier to make the sound more tinny." These records varied in quality, and reached their peak in 1957 and 1958.

By the late '50s the pop-influenced "Nashville Sound" began to coalesce, and once again Hank Garland was one of its prime movers, able to add nearly any type of accompaniment. While the vocal choruses and softer sounds received some criticism from country purists, these changes nevertheless helped country music recover from the mid-'50s rock and roll barrage. Hank, Harold, and Grady often worked together on sessions, each taking solos according to their respective specialties: Grady doing funkier tunes, Harold playing pop-oriented material, and Hank handling fast numbers. Garland played on a number of hit records during this time, including Ferlin Husky's "Gone," Jim Reeves' "He'll Have To Go" [*Legendary Performer*], Don Gibson's "Sea Of Heartbreak" and "Just One Time" (both with Chet Atkins), the Wilburn Brothers "A Woman's Intuition," Kitty Wells' "Jealousy," and Webb Pierce's "I Ain't Never" and "Tupelo County Jail"—the latter featuring Hank picking some gutsy, bass-string runs.

Garland's versatility and ability to work up song arrangements may have helped to bring him and Elvis Presley together in the studio for the first time on June 10 and 11, 1958, while Elvis was on leave from the Army. Although Scotty Moore had played regularly with Elvis since 1954, he was now working with him on a per-job basis. Elvis was beginning to expand his musical range, adding more pop-oriented numbers to his repertoire. Though most of his tunes still rocked, it was obvious that he was trying to appeal to a wider audience. So Garland got the call on a number of sessions with Elvis from 1958 to 1961, playing on songs such as "I Got Stung," "A Fool Such As I," "Big Hunk 'O Love," "Stuck On You" (which had Hank on 6-string bass), "It's Now Or Never," "Are You Lonesome Tonight," "Surrender," "I Feel So Bad," and "Little Sister." He also picked guitar on Elvis' *His Hand In Mine* LP. Harold Bradley remembers Hank using an early Gibson ES-355-TD—SV with "the first Vari-tone switch we'd ever seen" on many of the rock and roll sessions, deviating from his Gibsons only on the "Little Sister" cut. Bradley comments: "I started advertising Fender, and Hank borrowed my Jazzmaster to play on the song because he didn't have a guitar with the sound he wanted to get."

Hank also did some concerts with Presley, among them Elvis' March 25, 1961, Benefit show in Honolulu—which was Presley's last live performance for eight years. Garland was featured predominently, and when Elvis introduced the band, everyone got a routine intro while Hank was referred to as "one of the finest guitar players anywhere in the country today." In addition, Garland continued flexing his country-jazz muscles. This is clearly evident in his work with jazz great Johnny Smith

and Harold Bradley on Don Gibson's *Gibson, Guitars, And Girls* LP, which was recorded around 1960.

On October 27, 1960, with Grady Martin sitting in the producer's chair subbing for Law, Hank recorded *Jazz Winds From A New Direction* with Burton, Dave Brubeck drummer Joe Morello, and bassist Joe Benjamin. They played six songs that day, including bop standards such as "Move," as well as "Riot-Chous," "Relaxin'," and "Always." The LP turned many heads, including those of jazz aficionados who couldn't believe that such a great guitarist could come from Nashville. All during this time Hank was still picking up direction, listening intently to Wes Montgomery and others. His fingerstyle chops were improving, and it looked like Garland was finally entering the world of jazz guitar on his own terms.

Unfortunately, this was not to be. In the summer of 1961 while traveling in his car near Springfield, Tennessee, Garland was involved in an auto accident. When he regained consciousness at the hospital, the doctors attending him had determined that he had sustained severe brain damage. With his talents thus impaired and lacking the ability to coordinate his hands, it seemed indeed that Hank Garland's career was over.

The loss of ability to play would have sent most guitarists into a deep depression, but Hank decided to fight back. He practiced for two years after the accident, studying and working scales and arpeggios while fighting to regain control over his instrument. After two more years he'd gotten some of his command back, and his advice to similarly afflicted guitarists is succinct: "Don't give up."

Hank Garland's records are still appreciated by guitar buffs all over the world. Today, Hank advises rock and country guitarists interested in jazz to work on scales for speed and to "start out slow and build up and go faster if you can." He still plays with a rehearsal group around Spartanburg, and says, "I think the current scene seems better than before. There are more kinds of music and more ways to go." And in Nashville, where he inspired people such as Harold Bradley, Leon Rhodes, and Bucky Barrett, his influence continues. Harold Bradley best sums up Hank Garland's career as a guitarist: "We haven't had another one come down the pike who plays the lines that he played. We've got some guys who play fast, but they don't play the lines and they don't have the feeling, the soul."

---

**A SELECTED HANK GARLAND DISCOGRAPHY**

**Solo albums** (on Columbia): *The Velvet Guitar Of Hank Garland* (out of print); *Jazz Winds From A New Direction*, JCS-8372; *Unforgettable Guitar* (out of print). **With Elvis Presley** (on RCA): *Original 50 Gold Award Hits, Volume 1*, LPM-6401; *Something For Everybody*, LSP-2371; *Elvis Is Back!*, LSP-2231; *Elvis Aron Presley*, CPL8-3699; *His Hand In Mine*, LSP-2328.v**With others:** Jim Reeves, *A Legendary Performer*, RCA, CPL1-1891; Patti Page, *Patti Page Sings Country & Western Golden Hits*, Mercury, MG 20615; Justin Tubb, *Country Boy In Love*, Decca (out of print); Grady Martin, *Country Western Dance-O-Rama*, Decca (out of print); Jerry Lee Lewis, *Original Golden Hits, Volume 2*, Sun, LP-103; Charlie Rich, *Lonely Weekends*, Sun, LP-110; Don Gibson, *Gibson, Guitars, And Girls*, RCA (out of print); Owen Bradley, *The Big Guitar*, Decca (out of print); Red Foley, *The Red Foley Story*, MCA, 117; Patsy Cline, *Country Hall Of Fame*, British MCA, CDL-8077; Webb Pierce, *The Best Of Webb Pierce*, MCA 2-4089; Webb Pierce, *Western Express*, German MCA/Coral, 801-445-370; Autry Inman, *Boogie With A Bullet*, Dutch Redita, LP-109; Tommy Jackson, *Square Dance Tonight*, Dot (out of print); Tommy Jackson, *Do Si Do*, Dot (out of print); the Nashville All-Stars, *After The Riot At Newport*, RCA, LPM-2302. **Anthologies:** *CBS Rockabilly Classics, Vols. 1, 2, & 3*, British CBS, 82401, 82993, and 83911; *Mercury Rockabillies*, British Phillips, 6336, 257; *Victor Rock 'N Rollers*, British RCA, PL42809; *MCA Rare Rockabilly, Vols. 1, 3, & 4*, British MCA, MCFM 2697, 2833, and 3035. [*Ed. Note: All British, Dutch, and German LPs listed are available from Down Home Music, 10341 San Pablo Ave., El Cerrito, CA 94530.*]

# EMMYLOU HARRIS

By Jas Obrecht

COUNTRY SINGER EMMYLOU HARRIS' PRISTINE VOICE carries the tenderest of ballads and up-tempo country rock equally well, and she has accompanied herself on acoustic guitar since she first began performing over a decade ago. After playing around the East and recording a poorly-handled album for Prestige Records during the late '60s, Emmylou formed a band in Washington, D.C., and came to the attention of the Flying Burrito Brothers. In 1972 country singer Gram Parsons recruited Emmylou to sing on his *GP* album, which also featured Elvis Presley's main backup musicians, guitarist James Burton and pianist Glen D. Hardin. The following year she embarked on a tour with Gram and the Fallen Angel Band. After Gram's death in September 1973, Emmylou played around Washington, D.C., until she was signed by Warner Brothers. In 1975 *Pieces Of The Sky* was released, featuring Burton and Hardin. Three more albums have followed, *Elite Hotel, Luxury Liner*, and *Quarter Moon In A Ten Cent Town*. In addition to writing, arranging, and recording music, Emmylou tours extensively with her group, the Hot Band, whose members have included some of the best players around—Burton, Hardin, guitarist Albert Lee, pedal steel guitarist Hank De Vito, and bassist Emory Gordy, to name a few.

\* \* \* \*

*WHAT ABOUT YOUR EARLY MUSICAL BACKGROUND— when did you first start playing guitar?*

I got a guitar when I was 16. It was a Kay that my grandfather bought in a pawnshop in Birmingham, Alabama, and I would just sit around and read guitar books and try to figure out what to do. That was my first guitar; then about three years later I saved $150.00 and bought a Gibson J-50, and it has been a succession of old Gibsons ever since.

*What made you go with Gibsons?*

No premeditation there—I've just always run into ones that were good. I have a couple of J-200s that I use onstage. My main one, which used to belong to Joe Walsh, is an early-'50s model with a factory pickup in it. It plays just great and has a good feel to it. It turns out that by using a microphone inside we could get

a really good sound out of it, better than with just the pickup. In 1976 Albert Lee found another J-200 in a store in Nashville that was spray-painted black—it looked like it had been to Earl Sheib's. It was very tacky, but it looked good and played well, so I bought it. It didn't have a factory pickup in it, so we put in a DiMarzio.

*Who were your early influences?*

I guess I was into [folksingers] Joan Baez, Judy Collins, Tom Rush, and Ian And Sylvia. Pete Seeger was sort of a spiritual influence, and I was a five-year subscriber to *Sing Out!* magazine.

*Where were your early performances?*

When I was going to the University of North Carolina in Greensboro I started playing a little club called The Red Door. In fact, it was just a bar, and they had a jukebox they would unplug for three shows a night. So I'd have one microphone and stand up and play, and other people would be there to play and we'd alternate. We'd make about ten dollars a night. I met a 12-string guitarist named Mike Williams, and we got an Ian And Sylvia-type duo going. We played country music, some Beatles' songs, and originals. I learned a good bit from him because he would tune my J-50 like a high-strung, and we would actually work out parts. [*Ed. Note: "High-strung" refers to any of several alternative tunings in which one or more strings are replaced with lighter gauges tuned an octave higher.*]

*How did you come to record with Jubilee Records?*

I was in New York at the time—around 1969—and the guy who was managing me then told me that he couldn't get me a record deal with anyone but Jubilee. After I had signed I found out that he had signed Jubilee to produce me also, which was something I didn't know about. I couldn't get out of the contract, so I figured I might as well go in and do an album. We went and did three three-hour sessions, and that was the *Gliding Bird* [out of print] album.

*What happened from there?*

Well, I was in New York and singing at Gerdes Folk City, opening for a lot of acts. The album died, which was to be expected, and then I didn't do much of anything. I worked as a waitress and in a bookstore, and I played some local TV shows. I

48

became pregnant, and after my daughter was born in 1970 I left New York and went to Nashville for a short period of time. Eventually I went back to Washington, D.C., to join my parents and sort of regroup and figure out what I was going to do. While I was there I met Bill and Taffy Danoff, who are now with the Starland Vocal Band, and I discovered there was work to do in clubs and that you could actually make a living there singing, which I had never been able to do at that time. For a year I worked in clubs, playing guitar and singing. I had an acoustic lead player named Gary Mule, who is a very fine guitarist. And I had a bass player, Tom Guidera, who was later in my first country band. The three of us played six nights a week wherever we could work.

*How did you meet the Flying Burrito Brothers?*

I was working with my trio at a little place on Pennsylvania Avenue called Tammany Hall, and we were just down the street from the Cellar Door, which has national talent, and the Flying Burrito Brothers were playing there. They came down to where I was performing, and I sang "It Wasn't God Who Made Honky-tonk Angels." They said, "Why don't you come and sit in, because we are thinking about having a girl in the group." So when I finished work I would go down there and we would do a few songs. Chris Hillman was in the Burrito Brothers then. After they finished their week at that club they had a show in Baltimore, and sometime during that week they decided to break up. I don't really know what happened, but apparently Gram Parsons showed up for the show in Baltimore, and he told Chris Hillman that he wanted to do an album with a girl in order to get the high tenor parts. Chris told him about me, and Gram came down and sat in at my show one night. There were three people in the audience, and I did a few songs. Gram said, "Sounds great, I'll be in touch with you," and a year later he was. In August 1972 I went out to L.A. to record *GP* with Gram, and then in early 1973 my little folk trio split up so I could go on the road with Gram.

*At this point were you definitely into country?*

Yeah, I always did a little bit of country, but it was my association with Gram that sort of plunged me over the deep end. He was a very, very strong influence on my music. He was the one single influence on what I am doing today, and he gave me a direction that I hadn't realized before.

*What happened after Gram's death?*

I stayed in Washington and formed my own band. I tried to get a country band similar to the Fallen Angels, but I had to choose from local musicians in the area. I was lucky—I got Tom, my old bass player who had converted to country music on his own while he was playing with a rock band, and he helped me form the Angel Band. I got a good steel player, a good guitar player, and a drummer, and we rehearsed for a couple of weeks in an outbuilding of one of the band members. The place had no heat, so we had to invest in some insulating material, and we all went over one day and fixed the place up and brought in some space heaters. We practiced there and then opened at The Red Fox, a bluegrass club in Bethesda, Maryland. We then started working pretty steadily—maybe four or five nights a week—and we played D.C. for the rest of 1973. Eddie Tickner, who had been my manager since I had started working for Gram, brought some people from Warner Brothers to hear me, and I signed with the label.

*How did you assemble the players for your Hot Band?*

It was really Gram who had assembled that band. He was the

Emmylou "always did a little of country," but her association with Gram Parsons plunged her over the deep end.

one who said: "I am going to do a country record, and I'm going to do it right. I'm going to get hot players who know country, and the best players are Glen D Hardin, James Burton, [drummer] Ronnie Tutt, and Emory Gordy." Warner Brothers said, "Look, we would like to propose that you get a hot band, and we'll fund it for you." So I figured what have I got to lose—all I could do is ask them. We had done sessions with these players for *Pieces Of The Sky*. Ronnie Tutt couldn't do it, but I was able to get Glen D, James, and Emory. And then I really lucked into Hank De Vito and [drummer] John Ware—John happened to come in and he liked what he heard and joined the band. Hank showed up at rehearsal one day with a steel and played great. *Voila*, we had a hot band. I've got a whole new band now, practically, but every time I have had to replace a member I have had just incredible luck. When James left, Albert Lee picked up the ball and ran with it. James is like a poet—he plays things on that guitar that are so simple, and I just don't think there is anyone comparable to him. At the same time, there's Albert Lee, who in his own right is just as good and has a unique style all his own. Working with the two has been quite a trip. In fact, this whole bunch of musicians are inspiring, to say the least.

*What is the difference between playing with James Burton and Albert Lee?*

The first year I played with James I was so in awe of the whole thing that a lot of times I looked on the Hot Band as a vehicle to put the spotlight on James and to say, "Hey, everybody, I hope you realize who you are getting to hear." There were a lot of people coming to see the band who'd go, "Wow, James Burton!" I regret that I never got to see Elvis in Las Vegas on the last date he did with Glen D and James, because Glen D and James played incredibly well together. They have a certain magic—it is like some people who can sing together, effortlessly—because they have the certain same feel for phrase and texture that comes not only from working together, but also from just the way they naturally play. James and Glen D always had that. It was something that I was aware of, but never got to sit back from an audience viewpoint and watch. With Albert Lee, we really got even hotter. He put the "Luxury Liner" edge to the band, whereas James provided the "Las Vegas" edge. Their styles are very, very different, but it's hard to explain. When James plays Las Vegas-style, there's a certain roll in his style—almost a geometrical ellipse kind of thing. Albert is a real straightforwrd, driving player. At the same time, they are both extremely tasteful players—just great, both of them. I have a guitar player with me now, Frank Reckard, who I'm really pleased with. He embodies almost both styles; he gets the texture James gets, and he can really drive out, like Albert. I now have a very good fiddle and mandolin player in my band, Ricky Skaggs. So I've been extremely lucky. I have been able to play with some of the best players around, and just the fact that I can keep time with them means that I have learned something in the past few years, at least as far as my guitar playing is concerned.

*How do you think you've changed since* Pieces Of The Sky?

Well, I suppose that I am a little more confident in what I am doing. I take a little more active part in things; I am not as afraid to speak up if I have an idea. I got into all this with a lot of ideas anyway, but now I can voice them better. I don't ever really think back about how I have changed—maybe I haven't changed at all. But as far as working with the band, this has been a really big piece of my life for the last few years. In fact, it has almost been the chief thing in my life, because I have spent more time on the road than I have doing anything else.

*Do you perform songs on the road before you record them?*

Yes. I pretty much line them up and get a feel for them, and then we work them up at a rehearsal if we have time. This band has had very few rehearsals, and usually we work up arrangements and play them on the road. We did that with songs like "Pancho & Lefty," "C'est La Vie," and "I'll Be Your San Antone Rose" [all on *Luxury Liner*]. We did these in our show before we recorded them because I was tired of the material we were doing and I wanted something new. But I always like to have at least three or four songs at a session that have no previous arrangements, just something my producer Brian Ahern and I have worked on. We work up an arrangement and throw it out to the band to see what they come up with. "Making Believe" [*Luxury Liner*] and "One Of These Days" [*Elite Hotel*] were some of these. A lot of times these songs end up being really magic because of the spontaneity they elicit. Just a bass line and a little guitar hook or something can elevate the song into a whole other level. That's the recording experience; when it's at its best for me is when I find myself in the middle of all these people that are adding the perfect final touches to the songs and making the arrangements really work.

*How would you describe your playing technique?*

Let's see, my producer calls it "creative rhythm guitar." Basically I just play with the feel that I sing to. I use an open strum, and I don't do any other stops and chunky beats and stuff like that. I use a large triangular medium-gauge pick that has rounded corners; this shape is most comfortable for me. I have always used medium-gauge strings, usually D'Angelicos. I like mediums because they are not as hard to play as heavies, and they don't go out of tune as much as lights.

*What other guitars do you own besides your stage J-200s?*

I have a Gibson J-50 that I use for most of my studio work, and a Gibson SJN, which was one of my first guitars. I also have a New York Martin, and I just gave away my Martin D-28 to a friend. I also have a tiny Gibson that Jerry Jeff Walker gave me—I don't know what model it is. Recently I bought a Fender Mustang electric guitar, which is sort of a joke at this point. I want to try to learn how to play it, even if it's only in the privacy of my music room. It's a couple of years old, and has a nice little dynamic vibrato on it. They threw in a Mosrite strap and a sharkskin case, and I'm ready to rock!

*What advice would you give young performers?*

I think that if you are learning to sing, it's good to learn to play an instrument—piano or guitar; it is always a good thing. It helps you develop your own phrasing style, and if you are able to pick guitar and keep time, it's probably going to help your singing. I don't know whether my singing influences the feel, or the playing influences my singing—to me they are really interwoven.

---

### A SELECTED EMMYLOU HARRIS DISCOGRAPHY

**Solo:** (on Warner Bros.) *Blue Kentucky Girl*, BSK-3318; *Cimarron*, BSK-3603; *Last Date*, 1-23740; *Light Of The Stable*, BSK-3484; *Profile (Best Of Emmylou Harris)*, BSK-3258; *Profile II (Best Of Emmylou Harris)*, 1-25161; *Quarter Moon In A Ten Cent Town*, BSK-3141; *White Shoes*, 1-23961; *Luxury Liner*, BSK-3115. (On Reprise) *Elite Hotel*, MSK-2286; *Pieces Of The Sky*, MSK-2284. **With Linda Ronstadt:** *Get Closer*, Asylum, 60185-1. **With Linda Ronstadt and Dolly Parton:** *Trio*, Warner Bros., WB-25491. **With George Jones:** *Ladies' Choice*, Epic, FE-39272. **With Waylon Jennings:** *Waylon & Company*, Victor, AHL1-4826. **With John Anderson:** *You & I: Classic Country Duets*, Warner Bros., 1-25171.

# WAYLON JENNINGS

By Frank Joseph

**C**OUNTRY SINGER/BANDLEADER WAYLON JENNINGS demanded and won total artistic control over his records from his current label, RCA/Nashville, in 1973. One major point granted, breaking a long-held Nashville taboo, was that Jennings' road band, the Waylors, would be permitted to accompany him in the studio. In addition to the Waylors' importance in realizing Jennings' concepts, this fundamental right directly affected Waylon as a guitar player. Though he had been playing lead onstage with the Waylors since their inception in the early '60s, for the first time outside of his initial Nashville recordings Waylon's staccato-tipped Telecaster began being featured on his studio efforts. Although unintended, Jennings' revolt against the "Nashville sound," with its homogenized arrangements and hurried assembly-line recording sessions, shook the country music industry to its core and won him his unwanted "outlaw" tag. "I didn't want to destroy it. I just didn't want to be part of it," he remarked to anyone who would listen. To Jennings, the stand for artistic freedom meant only that he was finally able to execute his music his own way.

Beginning with 1973's *Lonesome, On'ry And Mean* and *Honky Tonk Heroes* LPs, Jennings went on to fashion a lean, muscular brand of country that displays both history and integrity. His music is also characterized by its innovation and diversity—especially in the way he has used the guitar to create reverberating walls of sound, from the acoustic blues-based *This Time* to the crackling country twang of *It's Only Rock And Roll*.

Over the past decade Waylon has increasingly relied on his own sinewy lead playing for many of his hits—"I'm A Ramblin' Man," "Are You Sure Hank Done It This Way," "I've Always Been Crazy," "Luckenbach, Texas" [all on *Greatest Hits*], "Theme From The Dukes Of Hazzard" [*Music Man*], and his two recent chart-toppers from *It's Only Rock And Roll*, "Lucille" and "Breakin' Down." In the process, Jennings has become one of country music's biggest superstars, with a large rock following enamored by his hard driving, guitar-dominated sound.

"It all comes from electric rhythms," Waylon is quick to explain about both his music and guitar approach. As an example, he cites his former mentor and friend, the late rock and roll titan Buddy Holly. Like the rhythmically oriented Holly,

Jennings is an accomplished soloist, and like two other guitarist/bandleaders whose music he admires—Muddy Waters and Rolling Stone Keith Richards—Jennings has astutely blended his individualistic 6-string approach with other hand-picked players. Due in part to his superb voice, his callous '60s producers, and his reticence concerning his playing, Jennings' considerable talents as a guitarist have until recently been overshadowed.

Born June 15, 1937, in Littlefield, Texas, Waylon recalls, "As far back as I can remember, I was intrigued by guitar. I can remember when I was three, trying to get out of this jumper swing and reaching for my daddy's guitar—an old Gene Autry with a cowboy on a horse rearin' up. In fact, I can't remember when I didn't want to play guitar and sing." By ten he was doing both, having been given a nylon-string Stella by his parents. With his mother (who also played) showing him basic *C, F,* and *G* chords and his father teaching him "Spanish Fandango," American-style, Waylon was on his way. At 12 he was confident enough to enter local talent shows.

The Jennings family moved to nearby Lubbock, where Waylon secured a DJ job to reportedly become America's youngest disc jockey. At 13 he organized his first band, the Texas Longhorns, drawing heavily from two of his earliest and most enduring heroes—Ernest Tubb and Hank Williams. By the early '50s Waylon was making guest appearances on local radio station KLLL's *Sunday Dance Party*. It was there that he met two other area singers and guitarists who influenced his formative years—Buddy Holly and the multi-talented Sonny Curtis.

In 1956 Curtis supplied some of the lead work for Buddy's first records (made for Decca in Nashville) before going on to a successful career as a songwriter and guitarist. Currently, along with his solo LPs, Curtis sings and plays guitar with Buddy's excellent former band, the Crickets, who tour as a part of Jennings' road show. But before all this happened, Sonny remembers joining guitars with Waylon to back up local singers. At that point in 1954 and '55, Jennings was starting to develop his lead playing. Looking back, Waylon credits Curtis as an early inspiration: "Sonny's a great artist and a great musician, and I learned a lot of guitar from him."

At that time Waylon was also learning a lot of guitar from Buddy Holly. Starting in the mid-'50s and continuing up until Holly's death in February 1959, the two jammed whenever circumstances would allow. If anything, their friendship grew stronger after Buddy achieved stardom, and often Waylon played guitars lent by Buddy, including Fender Stratocasters and acoustic J-200 and J-45 Gibsons (the latter was used by Waylon to back a local singer who recorded one of his early compositions).

Today Waylon is understandably tired of necromanic inquiries concerning his realtionship with Buddy, but he is the first to offer that Buddy's music and guitar approach have greatly shaped his concepts. Like Buddy, Waylon is a master electric rhythm player: His powerfully churning, syncopated chording defines the "Waylon sound." But while Jennings' lead playing is based on Buddy's lead/rhythm concept, Jennings has added his own string bending, blues phrasing, and pedal steel techniques for a uniquely personal, instantly recognizable style. It is a tribute to Waylon's creativity that he has incorporated Holly's spirit—what he calls "Buddy's energy"—as a beginning, rather than an ending, for his own efforts.

And it is a tribute to Holly's genius that he was the first to recognize Jennings' talent. By the summer of 1958 Buddy wanted to produce and record new talent at Norman Petty's studio in Clovis, New Mexico, where Buddy and the Crickets had made rock and roll history over the previous 18 months. His friend Waylon was a logical choice, and that September Waylon

cut his first 45, "Jole Blon" (Brunswick), with Buddy producing and playing guitar and King Curtis blowing saxophone. For Waylon, the single was unsuccessful, and for Buddy it marked the last Clovis session. Tragically, Holly died four months later in a plane crash, and it is here that Jennings became inexorably linked to Buddy's destiny. In October Holly had amicably parted with the Crickets—drummer J.I. Allison and bassist Joe B. Mauldin. According to Jennings and others close to Holly, the split was only to be temporary. In the interim, Buddy hired Waylon to play electric bass (an instrument he had never played) on his quickly arranged final tour. As it turned out, Jennings himself narrowly avoided the ill-fated flight.

Now plagued by the morbid curiosity of Holly cultists, Waylon is adamant on the details concerning his association with Buddy: He was never a Cricket. Jennings was the first to understand that he could not have replaced the excellent Mauldin in Buddy's music. He emphasizes, "I wasn't Buddy's bass player. I was his protege." This statement is not one of arrogance. It is Jennings' attempt to set the record straight and close the door on needless questions about a painful experience. However, Waylon openly and freely refers to Buddy's influence when discussing his music and guitar playing. Finally, while his stature as a country artist may have obscured it, Waylon's expert reliance on rocking "electric rhythms" has made him one of Holly's grand successors.

Following Buddy's death, a shaken Jennings returned to Lubbock, resuming a DJ job before eventually pursuing music again. In the early '60s, now a full-time lead guitarist, Waylon relocated in Phoenix, Arizona, where he formed the Waylors. Based at JD's, a Phoenix club, Jennings had become a regional attraction by 1964 with his hot electric sound and unusual repertoire, which included Bob Dylan material.

In 1965 A&M Records signed Waylon and issued his first studio album, *Folk Country*. Later that year, at the urging of singer Bobby Bare, Chet Atkins signed Waylon to RCA.

Atkins, now a close friend and Waylon's most sympathetic '60s producer, was at the mixing console when Jennings cut his first Nashville record, "Stop The World," a fine country rocker spiced by Waylon's piercing guitar solo. However, for the remainder of the decade Jennings was marketed in the dubious "folk/country" category as he encountered rigid restraints of the Nashville sound. Regardless, he cut some driving electric sides and raised a few Music City eyebrows by becoming perhaps the first country artist to record Beatles and Rolling Stones compositions, notably "Norwegian Wood" and "Honky Tonk Woman." Waylon's finest '60s output can be heard on two RCA compilations: *Only Daddy That'll Walk The Line*, with Jennings supplying much of the lead work, and *Heartaches By The Number*, which features James Burton's brilliant guitar. In 1970 Jennings further surprised Music Row by winning a Grammy for his version of "MacArthur Park" from *Are You Ready For The Country*.

While it appeared that Waylon was on the verge of becoming a front-line country artist in the traditional Nashville mold, he didn't quite see it that way. In particular, he was extremely unhappy with the hurried record sessions, an industry-wide practice he was forced to work under. He felt that some studio pickers, who regularly backed four different artists a day, too often had their heads buried in chord charts, unaware of the performer. At that point Jennings was hanging out at Tompall Glaser's studio, picking and writing with Willie Nelson and other like-minded country artists. In 1972 Jennings began renegotiating his contract, and RCA had the foresight to meet his conditions. Waylon's stand cannot be overestimated. Without it, it is highly unlikely that some top-flight artists would have ever been permitted to showcase their fine road guitarists on records.

Since 1972 Waylon has risen to international stardom. Founded on his distinct 6-string and the Waylors' superb accompaniment, Jennings has furnished some of the most guitar-dominated music in a heavily guitar-oriented idiom. Rarely given to interviews, Waylon agreed to talk to *Guitar Player*, genuinely surprised at the interest in his guitar and its function in his music.

\*    \*    \*    \*

*Y*OUR INSISTENCE ON RECORDING WITH THE WAYLORS *opened the studio door for many road pickers, such as members of Willie Nelson's and Ricky Skaggs' bands. When did you first want to use the Waylors in the studio?*

Back in the '60s I wanted to use my road band for my records, but that was just something that didn't happen here in Nashville. And that's no disrespect to the session players; they're great and they've proven that. But I work in a different way, and I have to do things my own way. And that doesn't mean I'm necessarily right, but then that doesn't mean I'm necessarily

wrong, either.

*Back then, were you playing guitar on your records?*

Not too much. Chet Atkins encouraged me, but I had producers like Danny Davis. And Danny is a great believer in writing everything down. So I got a complex about my guitar playing, and I couldn't get comfortable with it.

*How were you able to become comfortable with your playing?*

I'm still not real comfortable. I don't consider myself a great guitar player at all. I play good when I can feel it. But I don't consider myself a hot guitarist.

*When did you begin playing lead onstage?*

That's hard to say, but I have some tapes from a KLLL radio show in 1956 where I was playing lead. You know, I learned to play lead in self-defense [*laughs*]! I found I was paying the lead players more than I was paying myself. Finally, I learned to play in front of people, and there I was doing it.

*Who were your early guitar heroes, the players you tried to learn from?*

Sonny Curtis taught me a lot of guitar, and I learned from Buddy Holly. That was before I went to work for him. I liked what he did. See, I'm a rhythm player—that's what I flash myself as—and I like that because I think rhythm players are really the most important thing in the band. One thing I learned from Buddy's rhythm playing was to use full chords to fill up the sound.

*Did you ever study with a guitar teacher?*

Once my parents arranged lessons for me, and that lasted about two weeks. The teacher was showing me how to work my hand around the neck, which I already knew because I'd been playing for three or four years, and I figured this ain't gonna work. That was it.

*In the June '82* Guitar Player *story on Buddy Holly, you were quoted as saying that you played his Stratocasters on some songs.*

Well, I did play Buddy Holly's some, but I never used them that much. I never liked Stratocasters—they got too many knobs.

*What was the first electric guitar you played?*

I got this little Fender Musicmaster when I was in Arizona. Before that I used a Kay with a pickup I put on and an Alamo amplifier. I started playing a Telecaster in 1964, and the one I got then is the one I got now. It was given to me with a Fender Twin with JBL speakers by my band at JD's for a Christmas present. I now own six or seven old Telecasters, and they're hard to find. But I still play my first one—the '63—for most things, and that's the one I use to record.

*The leather work on the '63 is beautiful. Who did it?*

There was a cleanup man at this club in Arizona called Wild Bill's, and he put it on for me.

*Sonny Curtis and Buddy Holly were taken with blues artists, and they both loved R&B. Your lead playing has a definite blues quality. Your phrasing leaves a lot of space between notes, and you bend strings a good deal.*

That's because I love black music. I think black music and country music are a beat apart: One man singing about a woman he can't keep and the other about a woman he can't get. Back in Texas I used to listen to KWKH in Shreveport, Louisiana, to *Stan The Man And His No-Name Record Jive*. That was before rock and roll, and he'd play Bobby "Blue" Bland and B.B. King. I just love B.B. King; he plays guitar so good I don't even want to talk about him. Another guitar player I really like is Mel Brown, who's a good friend. He plays with Bobby Bland, and he's great. But I'll tell you who I really love—ol' Jimmy Reed. Someday they're going to realize just how great he was.

*How did you develop your string-bending technique?*

I used to deliver ice in what they called "Black Town," and I'd go to a place called the Dew Drop Inn. I met this guy who called himself Chuck Berry, Jr., and he taught me to use a banjo string for the high *E* on the guitar and move the rest of the strings up. That way I could bend the strings, and he's the one who taught me that. That's really when I started playing lead guitar.

*When did you first play lead on your records?*

When I first came to Nashville. It was on a song called "Stop The World And Let Me Off," and right in the middle of the break I realized I was playing guitar in front of Chet Atkins. And I got nervous—it's kind of tough getting in the man's territory. But not long ago he asked me to play guitar on one of his records [as yet unreleased]. I was still nervous, but it was fun.

*Your tone has changed since the '60s, especially for solos. Your single-note playing has a twanging, staccato ping or pop. How do you create this unique sound?*

Instead of picking the strings, I pull them a good bit with my fingers. I can play a little Chet Atkins style with my fingers, and I use my fingernails a lot to *pull* the strings to get the sound you're talking about.

*Beginning with* Honky Tonk Heroes, *you and the Waylors have presented a guitar-dominated sound on record and onstage. How did that evolve?*

It's just something I've always wanted. I love guitar sounds, and you can't get me enough guitar sounds. I'll go into the studio and overdub six or seven guitar parts. But really, it all comes from electric rhythms.

*Do you work out solos before recording them?*

No, I never practice a solo first. In fact, I purposely don't learn the songs we're going to do until I get there with the band because I get bored real quick, and I'll start messing with melodies that are good. For my leads, everything I do is off the top of my head. If I were to learn it letter-perfect, which I can't do anyway, I'd never use it. I never play the same solo twice. I'll be in the studio and they'll say, "Play what you did a little while ago on so and so." And I'll say, "Did you record it?" Because I never know what the hell I did!

*You were one of the first country guitarists to use a phase shifter on many tunes. What is the appeal of this effect?*

It gives me more highs for my leads, and it fills up the sound, though it can get a little buzzy in the head if you don't watch it. And it's real good for rhythm patterns.

*How do you record your guitar?*

I usually go directly through the board. That way I get much more control over the sound I want. It's the same thing I get from an amp, but it's just one less generation. Plus I can still use my phase shifter.

*A couple of your albums—*This Time, *in particular—are based on steel-string guitar. What acoustic guitars do you use?*

My favorite acoustic—the one I record with—belonged to Chet Atkins. I saw it hanging on his office wall, and I just picked it up. And when you hold it and play it, you can just feel it. Well, I really liked that guitar and Jessi [Colter], my wife, went and talked Chet out of it and gave it to me for my birthday. It's handmade with the name Star on the head, but that's all I know about it. [*Ed. Note: The Star acoustic was built by luthier Hascal Haile, 605 4th Street Blvd., Tompkinsville, KY 42167.*]

*How has your guitar playing grown over the years?*

I don't know if it has. I've listened to things I did in 1964 and 1965, and sometimes I think I was playing better then because I was playing [in clubs] every night. But if anything, I think my feel has gotten better.

*On some of your later albums you play all the lead, and on others you split the solos with other guitarists. Why is that?*

I use other guitar players because I can't think of everything, and I know that.

*What advice would you give aspiring players?*

Basically, I'd tell them that we all need to learn to laugh at ourselves. As long as we can do that, there ain't that much problem. but if we can't do that, then we're in trouble.

---

### A SELECTED WAYLON JENNINGS DISCOGRAPHY

**Solo albums** (on RCA): *Folk Country*, LPM 3523; *Leavin' Town*, LPM 3620; *Waylon Sings Ol' Harlan*, LPM 3660; *Nashville Rebel*, LPM 3736; *Love Of The Common People*, LPM 3825; *Hanging On*, LPM 3918; *Only The Greatest*, LPM 4023; *Jewels*, LPM 4085; *Just To Satisfy You*, LSP 4137; *Country Folk*, LSP 4180; *Waylon*, LSP 4260; *Singer Of Sad Songs*, LSP 4418; *The Taker*, LSP 4487; *Cedartown, Georgia*, LSP 4567; *Good Hearted Woman*, LSP 4647; *Ladies Love Outlaws*, LSP 4751; *Lonesome, On'ry And Mean*, LSP 4854; *This Time*, APL1-0539; *Honky Tonk Heroes*, APL1-0240; *Only Daddy That'll Walk The Line*, ACL1-0306; *Are You Ready For The Country*, APL1-1816; *What Goes Around Comes Around*, AHL1-3493; *Dreaming My Dreams*, AYL1-4072; *I've Always Been Crazy*, AYL1-4164; *Music Man*, AYL1-4250; *Ol' Waylon*, APL1-2317; *The Outlaws*, APL1-1321; *Ramblin' Man*, AYL1-4073; *Waylon Live*, AYL1-4163; *Black On Black*, AHL1-4247; *It's Only Rock And Roll*, AHL1-4673; *Best Of Waylon Jennings*, AFL1-4341; *Waylon—Greatest Hits*, AHL1-3378. (On other labels): *Waylon Jennings At DJ's*, Sound Ltd. (available in import shops), 1001; *Waylon Jennings*, Vocalion, 731; *Don't Think Twice*, A&M, S-4238; *Country Style Of Waylon Jennings*, A&M, AMLB 1006; *The One And Only Waylon*, Camden, CAS 2183; *Heartaches By The Number*, Camden; CAS 2556; *Ruby, Don't Take Your Love To Town*, Camden, CAS 2608; *Banded Together*, Epic, PE-36177, *Wanted! The Outlaws*, RCA AOL1-1321, **With Willie Nelson:** *Will The Wolf Survive*, MCA, 5688; *Waylon & Willie*, RCA, AFL1-2686; *WWII*, RCA, AFL 1-4455. **With Jessi Colter:** *A Country Star Is Born*, RCA, 433; *Leather And Lace*, RCA, AAL1-3931. **With others:** Johnny Cash, *I Would Like To See You Again*, Columbia, KC-35313; George Jones, *George Jones And Friends*, Epic, 35544. **Soundtracks:** *Mackintosh & TJ*, RCA, APL1-1520; *Ned Kelly*, United Artists, LKA0-300; *The Pursuit Of D.B. Cooper*, Polydor, PDI-6344. **Anthologies:** *White Mansions*, A&M, SP-6004; *60 Years Of Country Music*, RCA, CPL2-4351.

# DOUG KERSHAW

By Mark Humphrey

**D**OUG KERSHAW SIZES UP THE MIDNIGHT CROWD AT Hollywood's Palomino Club and then tells his band in a stage whisper that borders on a bellow, "Goddammit, let's get them boys woke up!" His fiddle screams like a bayou wildcat; he cuts loose with a blood-curdling "Aaiiiyyyeeeeee!" and proceeds to stomp and shimmy across the stage, a swampland dervish. His bow flashes like a strobe light during a methedrine-pace "Devil's Dream," and his chiseled features, framed by long black hair, can't help but remind one of Niccoló Paganini, the violinist/showman who so astonished Europe in the 1830s that he was accused of *being* the Devil's dream (how, other than by a Faustian pact, could his virtuosic speed and agility be accounted for?). No one has yet suggested that Kershaw, one of America's best-known and most-recorded fiddlers, is in league with the Prince of Darkness; but there is indeed something hell-bent about the ferocity of his fiddling.

In part, it is the result of his Cajun background. A rough-hewn, defiantly unassimilated people, Louisiana's French-speaking Acadians work hard and play harder, taking native pride in their prodigious capacities for drink and music-making. The fiddle and accordion are the key instruments in Cajun music, and Doug's ear was turned early by the fiddling of Rufus Thibodeaux and the legendary Harry Choates. (Choates, who lived the Cajun life to the hilt, died of alcohol detoxification in a Dallas jail.) Despite the influence, Kershaw is the first to point out that his style is far removed from traditional Acadian music. "I've developed a feel, a sound, and a way of playing," he says, "but it's no particular style. I've heard them all, and over the years I've combined several—blues, bluegrass, country, and rock and roll. It's all combined with my feeling. My music isn't traditional Cajun music, but *I'm* Cajun, and my music has a Cajun interpretation." In fact, Doug is proud to be called that most popular sobriquet for an Acadian "Coon ass," of which he says, "It's a lovin' term, if it's said right."

("Coon ass" is thought to derive from old French, meaning "prostitute" or "unclean woman." More popularly, it is thought to refer to traits a Cajun has in common with the raccoon; tenacity and adaptibility. As one Cajun said, "A coon ass is someone who eats anything that don't eat him first.")

Kershaw's French background is matched by a Napoleonic ego that unabashedly takes his native genius for granted. When asked how he compares his fiddling to that of other stylists, he bats not an eye and replies, "It's the other way around. They're compared to *me*." Even so, it's hard not to like this man who obviously relishes his role, which is part barroom rowdy, and part demonic string wizard cast from the Paganini mold.

Doug began life in 1936 on a houseboat off Tiel Ridge, an island on the Louisiana Gulf Coast. Jack and Rita Kershaw and their four sons eked out a meager living from hunting and trapping, and music was one of their few pleasures. "My mother and my dad both were musical," Doug recalls. His earliest musical recollections are of the *fais do do*, which he explains: "A *fais do do* was a house dance where everybody gathered once a week and everybody played music. The kids were all in one room, and the wives took turns taking care of them. They'd try to put them to sleep, and they'd sing *fais do do* to the melody of whatever song was playing. *Fais do do* means 'go to sleep.'"

Surrounded by music, Doug took to the fiddle at age five. "Uncle Abel made my first fiddle from a cigar box," he recalls. "The strings were wire from a screen window. 'Course, Mama ran out of the screens while I was learning." Family tragedy forced Doug to use his precocious talent to help support his mother and brothers when his father committed suicide (Doug was seven at the time). "I was trying to make a living after my dad died," he says. "I was shining shoes in Lake Arthur, and was getting whipped every day by these little black boys who already had the territory staked out. So when I brought my fiddle, it got up a crowd. I'd say I'd play if the people would let me shine their shoes. Every time they let me shine a pair of shoes, I'd play another song. I made $10.20 that first day—that was good money back then."

By the time he was nine, Doug was appearing at the aptly-named Bucket Of Blood, the sort of place of which every performer's nightmares are made. "There was chicken wire around the bandstand," he recalls. "Fights every night, and people throwing beer bottles. It was normal to me then, but now I know it was *rough*."

His brother Pee Wee had a band, the Continental Playboys,

and Doug joined them when he was 11. Doug's younger brother Rustly also joined, and the two of them were to be professional partners for nearly 20 years. "We played all over south Louisiana and the fringe of Texas," says Doug, and the Kershaw brothers widened their audience by appearing on Lake Charles' KPLC-TV in 1953. "We opened it, the first show on there," he says. "We had Fridays, and Jimmy Newman had Wednesdays. We were the Bewley Gang. It was a weekly show, sponsored by Bewley Flour. Mama washed our shirts every week; we always wore the same shirts."

The influence of television and a broader, more diverse audience had its effect on Kershaw's music. "I switched from playing strictly French music to playing country and rock around '53, when we started doing the television show. Country was big then, and rock was just starting. I'd take ten French songs, ten country songs, and ten rock and roll, and play four hours of dance music. Then we started making records and developing styles." Doug stuck out with Rusty, and together they recorded the Crowley-based Feature label. Feature was owned by Jay Miller, who recorded some of the best blues, Cajun, and rockabilly music Louisiana had to offer, and whom Doug recalls none too fondly. Miller received composer's credits for "Diggy Liggy Lo," but Kershaw disputes Miller's authorship. Doug alleges that several early Kershaw originals wound up under someone else's name.

Despite the pitfalls, Rusty And Doug (as they were billed back then) were on their way. They appeared on the famous *Louisiana Hayride*, of which Doug recalls, "[Elvis] Presley and I started there the same night. We were the only ones who held our own with them. He was tough! I wasn't there too long, because we went from there to West Virginia, and then from there to the *Grand Ole Opry*, and then from there to hell and back."

The Opry appearances in 1957 were a special treat for the Kershaw brothers; Doug had come a long way from fiddling for shoe shines in Lake Arthur. "We got a great reception on the Opry," he recalls. "Unfortunately, we were interrupted by the Army in '58." The interruption was brief, however, and by 1960 they were back in Nashville, recording for the Hickory label (they had signed with Hickory in 1955). Their greatest success came in 1961, when Rusty and Doug recorded "Diggy Liggy Lo" and "Louisiana Man." The latter record sold 3.5 million copies, and the song has been recorded over 850 times. Rusty and Doug rode the crest of those hits for a while, then in 1964 came to a parting of the ways. There were a few slack years, and then Doug's solo career took off, thanks again to the good graces of television.

In 1969, Doug shared the stage on the *Johnny Cash Show* with Bob Dylan and Joni Mitchell. The Cash appearance brought the "Ragin' Cajun" to millions who might otherwise never have heard him, especially those who tuned in to catch a rare appearance by the then-reclusive Dylan. Doug's once slicked-back hair now fell in long strands to his shoulders, and the fringed cowboy attire of his Opry days was replaced by velvet Edwardian suits and frilly shirts. *Newsweek* described him as " . . . thrashing around like an angry body twisting as if it had a tail to lash." Doug was soon playing rock festivals, appearing on the same bill with the Doors and the Byrds.

The novelty of Doug's gumbo of Cajun boogie, rock and roll, and country eventually wore thin on the rock circuit, however, and today he says he's come home to the country: "Hell, let's face it, I lean towards country music, and the country field *likes* me. This is where I'm aiming now. The rest will take care of itself."

The thing Doug takes care of best is what has paid his rent for over three decades, namely, playing his fiddle. "I can't even explain how easy it is for me," he says. "I don't know how to explain my technique, it just came naturally. I've never practiced in 20 years. I don't have to. I know the instrument." His technique is nothing if not unorthodox—the fiddle held almost at arm's length as he gyrates across the stage.

"I'm a singer first, and I always played background for myself, so I didn't know I wasn't supposed to do that," he says. "I started playing with a full-sized fiddle, with my arm fully extended. As I grew, I kept the arm extended and the fiddle kept going down! It's just an extension of my body, the fiddle."

When pressed for explanations of his technique, Doug can only say, "Oh, jeez, I don't know how to tell you that. I play on three, even on four strings at once. I use 'em all." Four strings at once? How? "How?" he replies with a chuckle. "Very well! It's chords sliding, like a pedal steel almost. I push hard, and I play with a very loose bow. If I had three bows, I'd show you a lot of stuff!"

His bow generally is placed over the bottom of the fingerboard. Doug's bowing motion comes more from the wrist than the elbow, and he adds, only half-joking, "A lot of it comes from my knees." Though many country fiddlers use alternate tunings for effects, Doug says, "I can cross-tune if I want to, but I don't have to. I don't use cross-tunings."

And what about his frantic stage presence? Did that evolve from dancing while he played for shoe-shine money on the streets of Lake Arthur? "It came out of just enjoying it," he says. "I have no explanation for it." His wife, Pamela, adds, "I think a lot of the dancing has to do with his fighting the wire," (*i.e.,* the cord from the fiddle to the amp). Doug laughs and says, "It's true! Very possible."

Although Doug has used a cordless box, a unit that substitutes short-range radio signals for a patch cord, he actually prefers to work with the trailing wire. "I've used the box for gigs like the Superdome [New Orleans] or the Astrodome [Houston], where I have to ride in to the stage on a golf cart," he says, "but jumping the wire is part of my act now."

Since his music is heavily amplified, it would seem natural that Doug might discard the "classic" fiddle for a streamlined solidbody electric, but he has resisted the temptation. "Fender and others have given me solidbody electric fiddles," he says, "but I find them awkward. I still like the feel of the acoustic instrument in my hands."

Asked which of his albums he considers the best examples of his fiddle style, Doug replies, "*Cajun Way, Mama Kershaw's Boy, Spanish Moss,* and *Alive & Pickin'.* Ideas for his solos come on the spur of the moment, he says, not from the general repertoire of Cajun fiddle licks. "I make 'em up as I go," he explains. "If one works for a song, I'll use it again." He chuckles. "I'll play it 'til I get it right."

In addition to the fiddle, Doug plays a variety of other instruments, including accordion and guitar. "That's where I get all my sounds and ideas from, the guitar," he says. "I write all my songs on the guitar."

As with his fiddle technique, Doug takes his guitar style for granted. "It's just my kind of picking," he says matter-of-factly. "It feels better for writing songs." Do other Cajuns play that way? "I don't know," he shrugs. "It's just me."

Doug's other great talent is songwriting, which he has done consistently throughout his career. "After I wrote 'Louisiana Man,'" he recalls, "I wrote quite a few songs pertaining to my family and what I knew. Anymore, I don't have to experience a situation to write about it. I've been hurt, I've been loved, I've been everything, so I pretty well know how it feels."

One of his songs, "Cajun Joe (The Bully Of The Bayou)," concerns a tough who would "fight anything, a beast or a man, in bayou waters or on dry land." He gets his comeuppance, though, from a little guy "120 pounds soaking wet." The song owed its plot to Kershaw family history. "The story comes from a thing I heard about my grandfather," Doug recalls. "This one guy called KoKo David, man, he was tough. My grandfather was about six-foot-three but kind of chicken, and his dream was to beat one of those damn bullies up. So he went up to KoKo David in a saloon. KoKok was drunk. My grandfather said, 'KoKo, what's the matter?' He said, 'Well, Albert, I just can't find nobody to fight with no more.' Albert said, 'Hey, I've got an idea! We'll go outside, and you lie down and I'll straddle you and pretend I'm beating on you. And the first s.o.b. who comes along and separates us, you get up and beat the hell out of him.' KoKo said, 'You got a deal!' They went out there, he lay down, Grandpa put his knees on KoKo's arms—and he beat the hell out of him!"

Coming from such colorful stock, Kershaw has a rich legacy to pass on to the next generation. "I have two little ones," he says proudly. "Tyler, who's now 3½, and Zachary, who's 5. He's already wanting to do it," Doug says, and no doubt Zachary will have something better than a cigar box to play when he's ready to begin. "He's my future partner."

What advice would Doug have for Zachary and other aspiring fiddlers? "There's no end to what you can do with the instrument," he says. "no end." Doug should know, since the "Devil's box" has brought him from a houseboat on Tiel Ridge Island to Nashville and Hollywood. "Don't kid yourself just because it has four strings and it's small. There's nothing you can't do with it if you put your mind to it."

---

### A SELECTED DOUG KERSHAW DISCOGRAPHY

**Solo albums:** *Kershaw (Genus Cambarus)*, Hickory (2510 Franklin Rd., Nashville, TN 37204), LPS-163; *Wichita Wildcat*, CBS, Q16035; *Instant Hero*, Scotti Brothers (dist. by CBS), FZ37428. (On Warner Bros.): *Cajun Way*, 1820; *Devil's Elbow*, BS 2649; *Ragin' Cajun*, BS 2910; *Mama Kershaw's Boy*, BS 2793; *Swamp Grass*, BS 2581; *Spanish Moss*, 1861; *Flip, Flop & Fly*, BS 3025; *Louisiana Man*, BSK 3166; *Doug Kershaw*, WS, 1906; *Alive & Pickin'*, BS 2851; *Douglas James Kershaw*, BS 2725. **With Rusty Kershaw:** *Louisiana Man, Rusty & Doug*, Acuff-Rose (out-of-print), LP 103.

# ALBERT LEE

**By Steve Fishell and Tom Wheeler**

STACCATO HOTLICKS BURST FROM THE STAGE, CHASing the vocal like buckshot shadowing the Roadrunner. The tune is careening headlong around the horn as the lead guitarist maneuvers fearlessly through every curve, somehow calm at 90 miles an hour, punctuating each escalating statement with some new, other-worldly resolution until the song suddenly ends with an impossibly syncopated phrase. The audience roars, except perhaps for a few stunned guitarits who stare in disbelief at Albert Lee. The gaping pickers shake their heads in bewilderment: *How does he do it?*

The most obvious musical hallmark of England's Albert Lee is his taste and precision at high speeds, although he will be the first to tell you with a wide grin that "speed isn't everything, but it helps." One irony of his career is suggested by the lyrics of his song "Country Boy"—*I may look like a city slicker . . . underneath I'm just a cotton picker*—for although he graduated with

honors from Britain's 1960s rock and roll school, he has the reputation of being one of the world's eminent country guitarists.

As an accompanist, Albert differs significantly from the studio multi-stylists who can sound like just about anybody; armed with a Telecaster, he can perfectly embellish music as diverse as Emmylou Harris' modern country or Dave Edmunds' churning rock or even Eric Clapton's funky blues, while always managing to sound exactly like himself.

As Emmylou says, "Albert is conscious of different styles when he's playing due to his early love of country music, the Louvin Brothers, and the Everly Brothers. His playing is hard and metallic but clear and lyrical, with a rock and roll edge. One night onstage during 'Luxury Liner,' at the point where Albert takes off, I turned to Rodney Crowell and said, 'Look at that cave man go.'"

Lee's musicianship is considered state-of-the-art among fellow artists. His right-hand technique employs both the flatpick and several fingers, all at once. And although he holds the pick between the thumb and first finger, he is ever ready to bust out with some right-hand fingering, a 5-string banjo roll, or an occasional pedal steel lick—often but not always with the help of a guitar-mounted pitch-changing device, or pull-string.

Many guitarists have explored the deceptively subtle language of the Fender Telecaster, but few are as fluent or as eloquent as Albert Lee. Like Roy Buchanan or Arlen Roth he is a master of the blistering Tele lick, and like Steve Cropper or James Burton he can mold a disarmingly simple phrase into the perfect fill. He elevates rhythm guitar playing above the common crank-and-bash method to a sophisticated chord-melody style, complete with pianistic boogie bass lines and killer single-note fills. Dave Edmunds' rave-up version of "Sweet Little Lisa" on *Repeat When Necessary* spotlights this refined but gritty rhythm style.

Albert's career has led him to many roles in the record business: band founder and member, sideman, solo artist, studio musician. Since February of '79 he has played side by side with Eric Clapton as a member of Eric's touring and studio band. Aside from Emmylou Harris, Dave Edmunds, and Eric Clapton, a list of other artists with whom he has recorded and/or toured suggests both his versatility and musical prowess: Don Everly, Joe Cocker, Herbie Mann, Eddie Harris, Rosanne Cash, Jackson Browne, Rodney Crowell, Joan Armatrading, and the Crickets.

Albert Lee was born on December 21, 1943, in Herefordshire, England, where his father played English pub music on piano and accordion. At the age of seven Albert took up piano and studied formally for two years, delving into the classics, learning pop tunes, and coming to love rock and roll in part through the music of Jerry Lee Lewis.

In about 1958 he got his hands on his first guitar, a Hofner President acoustic arch-top. Taking an immediate liking to Buddy Holly And The Crickets, he learned all he could from their records. For a time the acoustic guitar served its purpose, but soon Albert longed for an electric like the one on the cover of the *Chirping Crickets* album [out of print], a Fender Stratocaster. He finally scored a Czechoslovakian copy of the Strat called a Grazioso.

Due to an insatiable craving for American country, rock and roll, and rhythm and blues, Albert diligently studied recordings by Jimmy Bryant, Gene Vincent And The Blue Caps (featuring Cliff Gallup on lead guitar), the Louvin Brothers, Ricky Nelson (James Burton on lead), and especially the Everly Brothers. An important milestone was guitarist Hank Garland's masterwork, *Jazz Winds From A New Direction* [Columbia, JCS-8372], the 1960 LP that shattered the barriers between jazz and country.

In 1964 Albert joined fellow Englishmen Chris Farlowe And The Thunderbirds, a seminal R&B/rock and roll band that was somehow overlooked in the U.S. during the British "invasion" of the mid-'60s. He recorded and toured with Farlowe for four years and during this period Albert influenced younger British guitarists, among them Jimmy Page and Steve Howe.

From 1968 to 1970 Albert played throughout England in various club bands, often supporting American country artists on European tours. He then co-founded Heads Hands & Feet, a band whose eclectic sound blended British and American rock and country influences. Their debut album of 1971, *Heads Hands & Feet*, featured Albert's now-classic original version of "Country Boy," a showcase for his dazzling picking style. *Tracks* and *Old Soldiers Never Die* followed. As the last LP's title implies, a sense of frustration had set in over the group's lack of acceptance; they disbanded before its release.

Shortly after the group's demise, its crack rhythm section was signed on as the core of support for what would become Jerry Lee Lewis' *The Session* album. Although sometimes a bit tattered around the edges—due to the "Killer's" penchant for minimal rehearsals and foot-to-the-floor arrangements—the record still crackles with energy, thanks in part to Albert Lee's daredevil rock and roll magic.

In 1973 Lee began occasional touring and recording with the Crickets. A year later, his career took a turn upon his arrival in Los Angeles. Somewhat disappointed in efforts to gain recognition through touring, he pursued the difficult course of L.A. session work. Through his association with the Crickets he met a musical idol, Don Everly of the Everly Brothers, and their friendship remains close to this day.

At the time Don was gigging informally at the Sundance Saloon, a rustic little club in Calabasas, near L.A. Albert accepted Don's invitation to sit in along with pedal steel titan Buddy Emmons. Their reputation as a monster group spread quickly, and their Tuesday-night gigs became legendary. Albert recalls: "I walked in one night and couldn't believe it—there was Emmons sitting there. He used to just nail me to the wall. I had to stop playing sometimes. I couldn't even play rhythm when he'd go into a solo. And he was so unassuming, so quiet, he'd just sit there and hardly utter a word. He'd be so polite: '*Excuse me, I'm going to do a solo now.*' He just killed me—everything he did." The jamming partners later evolved into the studio unit for Everly's *Sunset Towers* LP.

Albert's reputation grew, and his talents led him to more studio and road work. He joined Joe Cocker's 1974 tour of Australia and New Zealand, and his abilities attracted the attention of Cocker's A&M record label. In 1975 he was signed on as a solo artist.

Before the solo album was finished, however, Albert came to another crossroads. An old acquaintance from the Cricket days—veteran session pianist Glen D Hardin—asked him to fill in for James Burton in Emmylou Harris' Hot Band. Burton was committed to Elvis Presley's road group while maintaining his slot with Harris, but when scheduling finally became too hectic for him in the spring of 1976, Albert was asked to become a permanent Hot Bander. *Luxury Liner* was Emmylou's first LP to feature Lee's accompaniment, and its brisk title track amply displayed his amazing agility. The heart-rending "Poncho & Lefty" was underscored by Albert's lyrical sensitivity, while Chuck Berry's "C'est La Vie" was impeccably punctuated with excerpts from his rock and roll vocabulary.

Lee chose this time to complete his postponed solo album, and with the keen assistance of producer Brian Ahern and the Hot Band, *Hiding* was released in 1979. It included Albert's lively vocals, rollicking piano style, and searing guitar work, and although in no way was this stricly a country album, it offered another renditon of "Country Boy." (There is little resemblance to the original: The new version features a snappier rhythm track and was predominatly played on a Telecaster, whereas the original was performed entirely on a nylon-string.) The song's remarkable final solo uses an Echoplex to achieve a boggling avalanche of sixteenth-notes.

Although Albert's solo career led to his departure from the Hot Band in 1978, his guitar work has graced every one of Emmylou Harris' LPs since *Luxury Liner*, including the Grammy award-winning *Blue Kentucky Girl* in 1979. *Evangeline*, released earlier this year [1981], sizzles with more of his solo work on "How High The Moon" and "Oh Atlanta," while the title track is embellished by his lilting, emotional fills. In December 1980 Lee was voted into third place in the Best Country Guitarist category of the annual *Guitar Player* Reader's Poll.

Now Albert is on the road again as a featured member of the Eric Clapton band. He performed on Clapton's live album of last year, *Just One Night*, and has added his touches to Eric's latest studio LP, *Another Ticket*. He recently played a major role in Paul Kennerley's beautiful musical documentary album, *The Legend Of Jesse James*.

Albert has adopted the expression *Posh Rat* for his company.

The term refers to a half-gypsy, and it seems especially appropriate for Albert Lee, who at age 37 shows no signs of forsaking the musician's life on the road.

\* \* \* \*

*M*ANY PEOPLE CONSIDER IT IRONIC THAT A MEMBER OF England's electric guitar scene of the '60s went on to distinguish himself primarily as a country stylist.

Americans think we're really isolated in England, but we're not. It's the same thing that happened to the Beatles—they were exposed to all those records from all different markets and types of music. We get the best of everything over there. If it's good, it filters over. I was lucky enough to pick out some good records.

*Who were your earliest guitar influences?*

The first playing that I really liked was Buddy Holly. As far as technique was concerned, the first records were the early Gene Vincent songs with Cliff Gallup on guitar. He was very influenced by Les Paul and Chet Atkins. Trying to learn his solos really got me to develop more of a jazz technique, using all my fingers and playing scales as opposed to two-fingered walk-ups across the strings. I used to buy everything the Everly Brothers did and also everything by Jerry Lee Lewis, because I always loved to play piano as well.

*Where did you first encounter James Burton's playing—on a Ricky Nelson record?*

Yeah, all of those solos just knocked me out, everything he did, because it was really alien at the time. I thought: "How was he doing *that*? I never knew that anyone could play with an unwound third string. Duane Eddy came over to England in 1960 and did an interview and said, "Well, yeah, all the hot players in the States use thin banjo strings." So then I started using two first strings and throwing away the sixth so that the fifth was on the bottom. That was heavy compared to what I'm using now, but I used to get a great tone out of the Les Paul with

**Albert Lee (right) playing a Phil Kubicki Custom Tele-style with Leo Kottke (left) picking a Fender Telecaster.**

that particular combination of strings.

*On one of the Heads Hands & Feet album jackets there's a photo of you with Jerry Reed. Did he influence your playing?*

Oh yeah, he was a big influence. What he was doing wasn't totally new to me, but he sort of put the stamp of approval on what I was trying to do. I was really into that kind of playing, and when he came along I thought, "Boy, that's where it's at, he's doing it right."

*Chris Farlowe's band was influential in England, yet it never received much recognition in the United States.*

That was a great band. It was so frustrating at the time because we thought we were one of the best. It was hard-driving rock and roll with rhythm and blues, just a small group with guitar, bass, drums, and piano.

*What were your goals when you came to America?*

All the guitar players I knew in England in the early '60s wanted to go to Nashville, but for some reason I wanted to go to L.A. because that's where my two biggest influences were, James Burton and Jimmy Bryant. Also Glen Campbell and the Everly Brothers were there—the kind of music that I liked. I first came to America in '71 or '72 with Heads Hands & Feet.

*And after the breakup of that band, you met up with the Crickets?*

Yes, after the final album. I met the Crickets in London and came over to the States a couple of times with them and recorded in Nashville and Los Angeles. Through them I got to meet a lot of pretty good players and good friends. If I hadn't really been friendly with them, I would have been at a loss in the States. It was during this period that I recorded *The Session* with Jerry Lee Lewis.

*In photos on that album's jacket you're standing behind Jerry Lee in order to watch his hands on the keyboard.*

Yeah, in fact at all times throughout the week there were about four or five cassette players underneath his piano, just getting every lick [*laughs*]. Everybody was totally in awe of him. Boy, I was just in heaven too—I positioned myself right behind him just watching him throughout the entire session.

*Was "the Killer" easy to work with?*

Some people would have found him hard to work with. He worked his own way and that was it. He would bend, but he wouldn't really be dictated to. He would take suggestions, but mainly it had to come from him. He didn't like to run through a song more than three times. Throughout the week he got further and further out there until the last day he didn't even bother to show up. In fact, we were short a couple of tracks, so we did an instrumental of "High School Confidential." But boy, he's unique. He's my piano hero.

*Was your initial status with the Hot Band as a session musician or a full-fledged member?*

They asked me to fill in for James Burton for a couple of weeks. I was really despondent before that. I had just done my album for A&M and they hadn't been too keen on it. I wasn't 100 percent behind it myself. I was just about to leave for England. I didn't know what I was going to do there, but I thought, well, there's nothing in the States. I went to an Emmylou Harris concert in Laguna Beach in southern California, and everyone seemed pleased to see me. I was really surprised. They contacted me pretty soon after that.

*Was it difficult to learn the material?*

I was familiar with most of the stuff because it was fairly

Albert Lee won *Guitar Player*'s Readers Poll five years running in the Country category. He is now a member of their "Gallery Of The Greats."

standard country, and I had Emmylou's albums. Our first gig was some honky-tonk out in San Bernardino. James Burton had called in sick, so I played it cold with no rehearsal. That was probably the best way because they weren't expecting too much. That was fun. We went out on the road, and I think there was a lot of politics going on as to whether or not James was coming back. Finally, I was asked if I wanted to stay. It was a very happy time in my career.

*How did you get together with Eric Clapton?*

I'd known him since the mid-'60s. We used to play around London in similar bands, you know, and we jammed together in clubs. We weren't close friends, just acquaintances in the same circuit. I saw him twice with Cream. We opened for them once with Farlowe. I went onstage with my little 4x10 Bassman and it blew up, so I used Eric's amp, and all the controls were right around 10 [*laughs*].

*How did you meet up with him again?*

It was February of '79. Eric and I got real friendly again working on a [singer] Marc Benno project for A&M in London. He'd been kicking around the idea of getting another guitar player, and my name came up. He asked: "Do you fancy doing it?" It was a difficult decision because my solo album was just about to be released. What should I do—the usual route of playing the Roxy and the Bitter End for a couple of thousand people, or do I go out with Eric and sing a couple of songs and play to 15,000 a night? I chose Eric.

*How do you feel about it in retrospect?*

I still don't know if it was the right thing for my career. It's been great fun with Eric, but I probably would have made more of an impact if I'd gone out on my own and established myself as a front man. I don't know how good it would have been, but at least I would have tried it.

*Are you given a lot of freedom, playing with Eric?*

It varies. It's difficult sometimes because I don't know if I should really put my head down and plow through it and really give him a kick up the arse. That's what he needs sometimes, and that's one reason why I was put into the band. But it's difficult—a fine line whether I'm going to overstep the mark. He's got a very strange sense of humor. He's a lovely guy, but his brain is usually zipping away at 90 miles an hour and if you don't

know him you can be offended at some of the things he says. He's a real good-hearted person deep down. If I do "Country Boy" he'll give me a terribly hard time afterwards [*laughs*].

*Does he play the song with you?*

He used to at one time, but he goes offstage now and has a drink and a cigarette.

*So you don't envision yourself as the consummate sideman for the rest of your career?*

I'd rather have a solo career happening or else be part of a band. It's great working with Eric, but it's something I couldn't do forever, and I'm sure he doesn't expect me to do it forever. I have an identity which I have to establish and I could only go so far with him. I wouldn't like to give in and say I'm going to be a sideman for the rest of my life.

*Among current guitarists, who are some of your favorites?*

I still like Roy Buchanan. I still enjoy Eric, too. He has these moments—it's really weird the way he addresses the guitar. He gives you the impression that he doesn't really know that much. He's very basic, but he'll do these things sometimes that just completely blow you away, and I'm sure he doesn't know how he's doing it half the time. His feeling is so incredible, and he can just lift it way above the everyday humdrum guitar. He's inspiring sometimes. And I really like some of the jazz players—Pat Martino, for example. Al Di Meola is quite dazzling, and Phil Baugh is doing some amazing things. Lenny Breau is great at the one thing that he does; I don't think there is anyone to touch him really. [*Ed. Note: One of guitar's most brilliant voices was stilled on August 12, 1984, when Lenny Breau died in Los Angeles.*]

*What about acoustic guitar players?*

Of the classical artists I think I like Julian Bream the best. He's got a lot of heart in the way he plays. Tony Rice is my favorite steel-string player. He never ceases to be interesting.

*What advice do you have for young guitarists who want to be successful as professional pickers?*

Well, you're asking the wrong person [*laughs*]. I don't think I've ever been successful. I've always just played for myself because I've enjoyed the music. As long as I have a roof over my head and can feed my family while playing music that I enjoy, I'll be happy.

---

### A SELECTED ALBERT LEE DISCOGRAPHY

**Solo albums** *Speechless*, MCA Master Series, 5693. *Hiding*, A&M, SP-4750; *Albert Lee*, Polydor, 1-6348. **With Heads Hands & Feet:** *Heads Hands & Feet*, Capitol, SVBB-680; *Tracks*, Capitol, ST-11051; *Old Soldiers Never Die*, Atco, SD-7025. **With the Everly Brothers:** *Reunion Concert*, Passport, PB 11001; *EB84*, Mercury, 822431-1; *Born Yesterday*, Mercury, 826142-1. **With Emmylou Harris** (on Warner Bros.): *Luxury Liner*, BS-2998; *Quarter Moon In A Ten Cent Town*, BSK-3141; *Blue Kentucky Girl*, BSK-3318; *Roses In The Snow*, BSK-3422; *Light Of The Stable—The Christmas Album*, BSK-3484; *Evangeline*, BSK-3508. **With Rodney Crowell** (on Warner Bros.): *Ain't Livin' Long Like This*, BSK-3228; *What Will The Neighbors Think?*, BSK-3407. **With Eric Clapton:** *Just One Night*, RSO, RS-2-4202; *Another Ticket*, RSO, TX-1-3095. **With Jackson Browne:** *Saturate Before Using*, Asylum, ST-712383; *The Pretender*, Asylum, 7E-1079. **With Others:** Jerry Lee Lewis, *The Session*, Mercury, SRM-2803; *Chris Farlow And The Thunderbirds*, Charly (British import), CR-30021; Don Everly, *Sunset Towers*, Ode, SP-77023; the Crickets, *Remnants*, Vertigo, VEL 1020; Jon Lord with the London Symphony Orchestra, *Gemini Suite*, Capitol, SMAS-870; Lonnie Donegan, *Puttin' On The Style*, United Artists, LA-827; Mary Kay Place, *Tonite At The Capri Lounge*, Columbia, X-598; Jonathan Edwards, *Sailboat*, Warner Bros., BS-3020; Tim Krekel, *Crazy Me*, Capricorn, M5N-0219; Rosanne Cash, *Right Or Wrong*, Columbia, JC-36155; Byron Berline, *Outrageous*, Flying Fish, FF-227, Joe Cocker, *Stingray*, A&M, SP-4574; Marc Benno, *Lost In Austin*, A&M, SP-4767; Dave Edmunds, *Repeat When Necessary*, Swan Song, SS-8507; various artists, *The Legend Of Jesse James*, A&M, SP-3718.

# BARBARA MANDRELL

**By Jim Hatlo and Annemarie Colby**

ENTERTAINER OF THE YEAR. NOT ONCE, BUT TWICE— back to back in 1980 and 1981—that coveted title was conferred upon Barbara Mandrell by the Country Music Association. She was the first artist to achieve that double honor; and those awards anchor a cushy nest of laurels that include the 1979 and 1981 Female Vocalist Of The Year awards from the Academy Of Country Music; a Grammy and a Dove for her 1982 gospel album *He Set My Life To Music*; consecutive People's Choice awards as "Favorite All-Around Female Entertainer" (1982 and 1983); an array of trophies and titles from the recording industry and the country music press; and a long list of network TV credits topped by *Barbara Mandrell And The Mandrell Sisters*— which ran for two successful seasons on NBC.

The thousands of fans who pack her live performances (about 100 shows each year) coast to coast certainly would be content to hear her sing her hits, such as "Woman To Woman," "Sleeping Single In A Double Bed," "Midnight Oil," and "If Loving You Is Wrong (I Don't Want To Be Right)," and leave it at that.

Barbara Mandrell won't let them leave it at that.

"My instruments are an important part of the entertainment at our shows," she says emphatically. "The people enjoy it—and I *want* to do it, because that was my first love."

In fact, Mandrell got her first big break in show business without singing a note. She was discovered by country guitar legend Joe Maphis in 1959 at a music trade show in Chicago, where—all of 11 years old—she was playing as a demo steel guitarist for the Standel amplifier company. Her father, Irby Mandrell (today her manager), owned a music store in southern California, and by the time she met Maphis, Barbara had already learned saxophone and accordion, as well as steel. Later she added dobro, banjo, guitar, mandolin, and electric bass to her repertoire.

For years, the instrumental highlight of a Mandrell concert set has been an extended medley—one edition was captured on *Barbara Mandrell Live*—that features her switching back and forth between pedal steel, banjo, dobro, mandolin, and sax, backed by her band, the Do-Rites (named after one of her early hits, "Do Right Woman, Do Right Man"). "The instrumental part

of the show is real challenging," she says. "When you perform, you're sitting down for friends and neighbors. You're not playing for other musicians. I have found that, generally, what works best is to pick old, familiar tunes. The challenge comes in making a tune a little bit different, a little bit innovative: How can you punch it up, and still keep it something that people are used to hearing? And it's hard to think of things that will make it showy, keep it moving, and still give me a chance to use all the instruments."

Why does she go to all that trouble to include an instrumental mini-set in every concert? "Because," she says, "there wouldn't have been any shows, there wouldn't have been any records, there wouldn't have been any TV, there wouldn't have been any Entertainer of the Year—if it hadn't been for a steel guitar."

There might not have been any steel guitar, either, if it hadn't been for an accordion. Born on Christmas Day, 1948, into a musical family (Irby was a singer/guitarist, Barbara's mother Mary was a music teacher and pianist), Barbara was only five when she asked her mother to teach her how to play accordion. She made her performance debut soon afterward, playing the accordion at her family's church in Houston, Texas. Barbara treated the congregation to "Guitar Rag"—the only song she knew. It was a hit (pressed for an encore, she played it again).

She began studying music seriously at age 11, learning steel guitar under the tutelage of veteran steel player Norman Hamlet, who was then working with country singer Rose Maddox. Barbara had only been playing steel for six months when she made her trip to Chicago as a demo musician, and caught Joe Maphis' attention.

The trip home to California included an unplanned stop-over in Las Vegas, where Barbara was featured as part of Maphis' act at the Showboat Hotel, playing steel and sax. Back on the West Coast, Maphis helped the 11-year-old instrumentalist land a spot as a regular on southern California's top country TV show, *Town Hall Party*. She got her first network exposure within a year, over ABC, appearing on Red Foley's *Five Star Jubilee* out of Springfield, Missouri.

That led to a tour with the Johnny Cash Show, where she

The couple had two children, and Barbara stopped performing so she could raise her family. Then Ken, a pilot, was sent on a tour of duty overseas. Barbara went to stay with her parents, who had relocated in Nashville. One Friday night her father took her to the *Grand Ole Opry.* Midway through the show, she whispered to him, "Daddy, if you've got any faith in me, I'd like to try to get on the other side of the microphone again. I wasn't cut out to be in the audience."

Irby Mandrell arranged for her to sit in with steel player Curly Chalker's trio at a Nashville club. Besides playing steel, Barbara sang a few songs. Within two days' time, she had offers of recording contracts from six different companies. In March 1969 she signed with Columbia Records, and soon had charted a cover of soul singer Otis Redding's "I've Been Loving You Too Long." By 1972 she had become a regular on the *Grand Ole Opry.*

"I believe my instruments gave me the opportunity to prove I could sing," she later told writer/musician Doug Green (now of Riders In The Sky). "Nashville is just full of great singers; you really need to have something that sets you apart. I'm convinced it was my instrumental ability that got me the attention."

\* \* \* \*

*Y*OU'RE ONE OF THE FEW FEMALE COUNTRY STARS *who is a bandleader, in the full sense of the word. How did you make the transition from being a picker to being the boss?*

Being a musician first in my life, before I became a singer, I not only have the utmost respect for musicians, I am very particular. After I started recording for Columbia in 1969, I did about three jobs without a band, just working with pickup groups. I went to my dad and I said, "That's it—I quit if I can't have my own band." I had always been used to good arrangements and showmanship, so I was spoiled in that sense. Not that local bands aren't great; in many cases they are fantastic. But it was no good when nobody in the band knew what I was supposed to be doing, and vice versa. It was so frustrating to me. But it's funny how things worked out, because by that point my two sisters were either 12 and 13, or 13 and 14, and for several months prior to that Louise had started studying hard on the bass and Irlene had started studying hard on drums. So they ended up being my first band—Irlene, Louise, my father, and a young man that we hired to be the lead guitar player.

*You were still playing pedal steel on every song?*

I had a gooseneck mike at the steel so I could sing while I played, and I would do most of the show that way. I had the rods [to the pedals] and everything on the steel lengthened, so that I wasn't standing but I wasn't sitting—I was sort of leaning on a stool. I didn't want to be buried in the band. Here I was, Barbara Mandrell the recording artist; but I was also my own steel player. That was the way the band started out, and it evolved over the years as money would allow. I later hired a steel player, so I could get out front. Then eventually Louise and Irlene went their own ways.

*Who is in the Do-Rites now?*

My band now includes Mike Jones, my steel player, who also plays dobro; he's been with me about 11 years. Lonnie Webb, who plays synthesizer, has been here almost that long. Gary Smith has been my pianist for over five years. Charlie Bundy, my bass player, has been with me about four years. My drummer

shared the stage with Patsy Cline, George Jones, and June Carter. After she came home, her father formed a family band. Barbara played steel, Irby sang and played guitar, and Mary Mandrell played electric bass. Hiring a drummer and a lead guitarist, the Mandrells began working dates up and down the West Coast, then broke into the military club circuit. By the time the group disbanded in the late '60s, they had appeared in 18 different countries.

Playing with the Mandrells provided the impetus for Barbara to learn banjo, dobro, and mandolin. The discipline of working four and five nights a week, playing three and four sets a night, both honed her chops and instilled in her a tough ethic for tenacious showmanship. "When I was about 15," she recalls, "my father said, 'Don't play softball! You might break your finger.' Sure enough, I broke one of my picking fingers playing softball—and we had to work that night. The finger was swollen and purple clear down to the hand, and it was in a splint. My mom knew about it, but we didn't tell Dad. So I took the splint and the tape off, bent the fingerpick so it would fit over the fingertip, and went out that night and picked, because I didn't want Dad knowing. The finger is still a little crooked."

In 1967 Barbara married Ken Dudney, who had been the drummer with the family band before leaving to join the Navy.

Randy Wright, who also records for MCA Records as a vocalist now, has been with me about six years; and Gene Miller, on guitar, banjo, and fiddle, became the newest member of the band when I added a seventh man about two years ago. He also takes care of my acoustic instruments for me.

*So there's a lot of continuity in the band. You don't have much turnover.*

No, there hasn't been much turnover. There was at one time; I went through a lot of players to get the ones I've got.

*How do you put together a band that can work over the long haul without any serious conflicts?*

Personalities are real important. When we audition someone, if we're impressed with their musical talent, before they ever play I talk to them about what we expect, business-wise—because we run our band in a very businesslike way. And we get to know them from talking with them. After we've auditioned someone who we think is good enough to join the band, I have a meeting with the other men, and we vote on it. And it's not the majority that rules; it's the minority. If one man says no, then it's no. They are quite a team, and they have a good thing going.

*That sounds very democratic.*

It's almost like a marriage when you perform under these conditions, and it's important to really care for the people you work with. That's how we do it. After someone does join the band, then they are on a three-month probationary time—and so am I. We feel it takes that long to know whether someone really will work out. They can say after the end of the three months, "I'm sorry, it's been nice, but it's really not right for me." Or I can say it. That way, it's not an embarrassment for either one of us, if we're just not happy.

*You mentioned that Lonny Hayes was the latest musician to come through that screening process. He seems to be featured a lot during your multi-instrumental medley.*

Lonny is an incredible guitar player, but his primary instruments are banjo and fiddle. Guitar comes after them. He plays very little banjo in our show, actually. But he's unbelievable on that instrument; he does things like "Devil's Dream" that are just phenomenal.

*Have you learned any licks from him?*

The only person I really learned banjo from was Dale Sledd [guitarist with the Osborne Brothers, and also a banjo player]. I'm mainly self-taught. Back when I was 14 or 15 and we were working military clubs, we played a little bit of everything. "The Ballad Of Jed Clampett" from *The Beverly Hillbillies* [featuring Earl Scruggs on banjo] was popular on the charts, and we thought, "Wouldn't it be neat if we could do that song?" because we were getting requests for it. So I picked up a banjo, and proceeded to pick out that tune as best I could and for a while that was our whole banjo repertoire.

*Are you doing fewer shows on the road now than you once did?*

I play about 100 dates a year. I used to play 200 dates a year, but at that point in time I didn't do all the other things I do now.

I didn't spend as much time on my recordings; I didn't do television as much, I didn't have so many other projects and interviews and photo sessions.

*You have a reputation as a real trouper. When you're tired, and you'd rather go home and go to bed than go onstage, how do you get yourself up to do a show? How do the musicians in your band get up when they're feeling like it isn't a good night?*

I don't know, I've never thought about how they do it. I just expect it from them, and they give it. I think they probably get up the same way I get up. I have a lot of pride in what I do. I've always believed and practiced that each performance is the single most important thing that I'm doing. I mean, it could be my last. I don't mean to be morbid, but we're not promised anything beyond today. I don't take the attitude, "If I get these shows out of the way, then I can do something else." When it comes time to perform, that's of the utmost importance to me. Sometimes I *am* tired; and sometimes I'm ill. I don't know; I've always been able to get a second, third, or fourth wind, and go. I collapsed once; but that was *after* a show back in the beginning years—one of the three dates before I got my band! [*Laughs.*] I had the flu. I don't think I've ever stopped in the middle of a show. I have gotten sick during a show, running offstage for a second, to the old trash basket in the changing room, and then running back on. That happened in 'Vegas a few times. I don't look it, but I'm tough.

*How often do you put together a new show—about once a year? How long does it take to work up a new act?*

We usually come up with a new show once a year; I have to have a new show ready before I go back on tour to places where I've already played the previous one. I like to have a month to do it, but sometimes I'm lucky to get two and a half weeks. It's really varied the last two or three years, due to television and other commitments. I get real nervous about how much time we have, because our arrangements are anything but simple. There's just a lot to retain in a short period. The show we are doing right now is a good one. In fact, I am really challenged to improve it. That's my big thing in life, though—to better my show every year. And the instruments play a real important part in that; it's always challenging to develop that segment. My show runs almost without exception about an hour and 25 minutes, and I can only do so much with the instruments, because I've got my records to sing. People expect them.

*What is the hardest part of working up a new show?*

Creating what you're going to do. Once you *know* what you're going to do, the learning is okay. But figuring out, "Oh, wouldn't this be a great opener? And then we could segue into"—that's the tough part.

*Is there a favorite venue you have? Is television more interesting than, say, doing live concerts?*

No. They're all interesting. No two things are alike. Recording is very different from live shows, and those are very different from TV. It's putting it all together that makes this business fascinating and exciting.

---

**A SELECTED BARBARA MANDRELL DISCOGRAPHY**

**Solo albums:** *Barbara Mandrell Live*, MCA, 5243. **With Bill Monroe:** *Bill Monroe & Friends*, MCA, 5435.

# JOE MAPHIS

By Rich Kienzle

JOE MAPHIS WAS ONE OF COUNTRY MUSIC'S FIRST "flash" guitarists. Dressed in a custom-tailored Nudie western suit with his double-neck Mosrite slung near his belt buckle, he'd stand onstage popping off machine gun-line guitar licks that galvanized his country audience just as Alvin Lee's super-charged rock riffs spellbound rock fans during the late '60s. In the hands of Maphis, a shopworn fiddle tune such as "Fire On The Mountain" was reborn as "Fire On The Strings," laden with dazzling flatpicking that still sounds fresh.

Joe Maphis played one of the first Mosrite electric guitars ever built, powering it with one of the first three Standell

amplifiers made. A country multi-instrumentalist who became a fixture in Hollywood recording studios, he also played lead guitar on Ricky Nelson's first Imperial recordings, and was responsible for bringing James Burton into Nelson's first tour band. All of these events have been part of the 40-year-old professional career of Joe Maphis.

His guitar, banjo, and fiddle playing have also graced numerous TV show and movie soundtracks, including *Thunder Road* and *God's Little Acre*. Joe added guitar to a multitude of '50s rock classics by artists such as the Four Preps and Wanda Jackson. Pop and country stars, too, often called on Maphis.

Some of these were Johnny Bond, Lefty Frizzell, Kay Starr, Jo Stafford, the Collins Kids, Skeets McDonald, Merle Travis, Nick Venet, and Laura Lee Perkins. Then there were the orchestras of Paul Weston and Nelson Riddle, among others, who used Joe extensively. And don't forget the decade's worth of solo and duet arrangements he recorded on Columbia with his wife, singer Rose Lee.

Maphis pioneered a guitar tone that bears a remarkable resemblance to the "Bakersfield Sound" of Buck Owens and Merle Haggard (Joe lived in southern California when both Owens and Haggard were getting started), and echoes of his work can also be heard on early Ventures' records and on surf instrumentals such as the Chantays' "Pipeline." At the age of 60, still touring and recording, Joe Maphis shows no signs of slowing down.

Otis Wilson "Joe" Maphis was born in Suffolk, Virginia, in 1921, and while still a youngster he and his family moved north to Cumberland, Maryland. Joe's father and uncle were both casual musicians, his father specializing in rhythm guitar, and Joe began playing guitar when he was 11. He also learned piano, tinkling the ivories in a local square-dance group—the Railsplitters—with his dad, uncle, and fiddler Ivan Kearns. The band worked around the region during the Depression years, bringing the Maphis family a little added money during those difficult times. While Joe stuck with piano during most of this period in his life, his interest in guitar also continued.

"I grew up with these boys, the Brown brothers," he says, "and one of them, Dewain, him and I would spend more time with guitars just fooling around when other kids were out playing baseball. The only thing we had to listen to in the way of lead guitar was, I remember, [blind singer/guitarist] Riley Puckett. Riley played some of the first of what us boys then called 'hot hillbilly lead guitar.' There was one record we had of him, and we learned to play it. It seemed like it was called 'Frettin' Rag,' though I might be wrong on that title [*Ed. Note: According to published Riley Puckett discographies, Puckett recorded nothing under that title. But he did record an instrumental, 'Fuzzy Rag,' for Columbia in 1927*]. Of course, the Carter Family—and especially Maybelle Carter—influenced me a lot. Her guitar playing was just so pretty, it wasn't long until I was doin' them old things."

Maphis' interest also expanded beyond guitar and piano. He learned tenor (4-string) banjo, fiddle, bass, and bass fiddle as well. "I was just one of those kids who could pick something up and get a tune out of it," he laughs. But the bulk of his time was spent with the guitar, and though his first instrument was hardly of vintage quality ("Merle Travis and I call 'em 'Sears, Roebuck Sweetgum Specials.'"), Joe began trying something with it that he'd never heard anyone else do: transposing fiddle music to single-string leads.

"Ivan Kearns would play a fiddle tune," he recalls, "and I would want to pick that *so bad*, the way he played the fiddle, that I would just start pickin' out the melody. But nobody would pay any attention to it. If they did, they'd say, 'What's that kid doing? He should be playing rhythm for the fiddle.' But it seemed that whatever Ivan'd play I'd want to learn, and so did Dewain. We'd both just fool with them old hoedowns."

Doing fiddle tunes on guitar, however, required rapid speed to make the notes flow smoothly. Maphis credits the way he built his technique to the nature of fiddle and square-dance

music where he lived: "In Maryland and West Virginia, they square dance fast—faster than they do in some places. So, I would learn to pick in whatever tempo that the fiddler was playing. In my area, I was sort of a whiz—for a kid."

Joe had made up his mind to pursue music full-time by late 1938, and drove south to Fredericksburg, Virginia, to see if he could land a job with Blackie Skiles and the Lazy K Ranch Boys. Skiles played regularly on radio station WFVA, but his songs were somewhat different from the simpler country music that then held sway over so many listeners. Blackie did twin-fiddle western swing and Gene Autry-style tunes with his 6-piece group.

Although Joe wanted to join the Lazy K Ranch Boys, the feeling at first wasn't mutual. "I really wanted a job so bad with that great group," Maphis remembers. "Finally, I just picked up the fiddle and knocked a tune off, went to the guitar and played one, pick up the banjo and played a little, picked up the bass and slapped it. I played everything in the band, and one of the guys said, 'Blackie, we don't *need* him, but we better *hire* him. If we don't [competing bandleader] Jack Richey's gonna get him.'" Skiles agreed, and soon Joe was one of the group's main attractions. At one point in the act, the players in the band would hand Maphis their instruments one by one, and he would play them all. While with the Lazy K Ranch Boys he acquired his first quality guitar, A Martin D-28 herringbone. After that, it wasn't Joe's multi-instrumental talents alone that surprised everyone: "I remember when I first got the job, they were amazed at this guy even *playing* lead on a guitar, because it wasn't done in them days."

In 1939 the group moved south to Richmond, Virginia, to the 50,000-watt WRVA Radio to perform. But, saddled with a large lineup of musicians and still playing western swing in an area where it hadn't yet caught on, the Lazy K Ranch Boys eventually disbanded. Shortly thereafter, Joe joined vocalist Sunshine Sue Workman And Her Rangers—a popular, more traditional country band. Maphis played a number of roles. As "Crazy Joe," he was the group comedian. As "Cousin Joe," he served as guitarist and multi-instrumentalist. The Rangers broadcasted three times a day—in the morning, at noon, and at midnight. One person who caught the midnight show, and first heard Maphis' playing, was Merle Tavis—then a regular on Cincinnati radio station WLW's *Boone County Jamboree*.

Maphis remained at WRVA with the Rangers until early 1942 when the WLW management, having lost many of its performers to conscription during World War II, hired the band and moved them to Cincinnati. After only seven months in the southwestern Ohio city, the Rangers disbanded. Maphis traveled to Chicago, and began picking with the Corncrackers on the WLS *National Barn Dance* radio program.

Early in 1944, Joe was drafted into the Army and trained in ordinance. On his way to the Pacific Theater in a troopship, his musical expertise was discovered. He was subsequently assigned to a Special Services unit in Hawaii, and formed a country band called the Swingbilly Revue. The detachment Maphis belonged to included other talented folks such as comedy writer Carl Reiner, Actor Maurice Evans, and the late game show host Allan Ludden.

Honorably discharged in 1946, Joe brought himself and his D-28 back to WLS briefly, then returned to Richmond where Sunshine Sue was starting the *Old Dominion Barn Dance* over

WRVA Radio. With relative ease he resumed his post with the Rangers. In addition, Maphis formed a second Corncrackers, which included Ray Edenton singing and playing standup bass. Around this same time, Joe made his initial musical efforts with electric guitar. He did his first Decca recording as a sideman with performer "Salty" Holmes on December 12, 1947, in New York, where they cut "Mama Blues" and "John Henry." As far as instruments were concerned during this period, Maphis used the D-28 with Sunshine Sue, and a Gibson Super 400 with a Gibson amp at other times on the *Barn Dance.*

While on the *Barn Dance* he met—and eventually married—Rose Lee, who was a singer on the radio show. By 1951, Joe and Rose Lee Maphis were ready to make a move with their new act, combining Joe's spirited playing with solo and duet vocal performances. Far across the country in L.A., promoter Bert "Foreman" Phillips had acquired several hours of daily TV time over station KECA (now KABC), and had recruited Merle Travis. Merle highly recommended his friend Joe Maphis to Phillips, but added that he thought Joe would be reluctant to leave Richmond. However, another friend of the duet, composer/singer Johnny Bond, knew they were ripe for a move, and told Phillips so. "Rosie and I left on a Wednesday," Joe recalls, "and we were on what I call 'assembly-line television' on Monday." Within weeks, Joe and Rose Lee were regional celebrities.

One year later, the *Town Hall Party*—another Opry-style barn dance television show broadcast on KTTV from the old town hall in Compton, California—had begun, and Joe and Rose Lee moved there with Tex Ritter, Merle Travis, Johnny Bond, and other top country artists. About the same time, the Maphises signed a recording contract with Columbia. The most successful song they had was Joe's composition "Dim Lights, Thick Smoke (And Loud, Loud Music)," which he wrote after doing a show at the Blackboard Club in Bakersfield and hearing a very young Buck Owens playing heavily amplified guitar and singing in the Bill Wood's Band.

One night in 1954, while Joe was gigging in a southern California club, he received a visitor who changed his electric guitar performance forever. "I was out in Norwalk doing a personal appearance at the old Pioneer Room, a honky-tonk," he says, "and this preacher, Reverend Ray Boatright, came in the back door at break time and walked up to me and said, 'Joe Maphis, you don't know me but I'm Reverend Boatright.' I thought, 'My Lord, why's a preacher want to come in a honky-tonk lookin' for me?' He said, 'The only way I could find you was to come in here and get you. I think the Lord'll forgive me, but I got a boy out in the car that's a good friend of mine, and he makes the finest guitar you've ever seen. He wants to meet Joe Maphis. In fact, he wants to build you a guitar.'

"I went out there, and here's this young kid that couldn't come into the club, and had a guitar layin' in the back seat that he made for himself. I looked at it, played it; couldn't hook it up, but it was beautiful. I gave the preacher my address and said, 'Bring this young fellow by the house and we'll talk about a guitar.'" The youngster was Semie Moseley, founder of the Mosrite guitar company. He was all of 18 at the time.

"The only thing I contributed to the instrument," Joe says, "was he wanted to make a double-neck and needed to know whether it should be a mandolin or an octave guitar. I said, 'I'd make an octave guitar—the top neck an octave higher.' It worked out on sessions a lot later on. Up on the top of the peghead—that 'M' that's cut in there—the Mosrite company hadn't been thought of yet. That was my idea. The 'M' stood for 'Maphis.' Of course, later on everyone figured it was for 'Mosrite.' But that head was really designed for me."

Semie presented the instrument to Maphis during a *Town Hall Party* broadcast. "Semie was nervous," Joe remembers. "The way he tells it, he didn't have time to tune it up, check it over, plug it in, or nothin', and all at once [announcer] Jay Stewart says, 'We got a young fellow here that wants to talk to Joe Maphis.' First thing I know he's onstage in front of the camera, handing me a guitar. I took it, plugged it in, and started pickin'. It about scared that boy to death. He was afraid it wasn't going to work. But it did, and I played 'Fire On The Strings.'"

Not only did Joe's guitar attract a great deal of attention, but his instrumental prowess, too, caught the ears of many L.A. producers and artists. "One reason I got a lot of recording work," he says, "was that while people said they didn't watch country music on TV, when it came to Saturday night and the *Town Hall Party,* Beverly Hills would have their eyes on it. A lot of my studio calls came from somebody watching it and seeing me there."

Among those impressed by Joe were guitarist/arranger Jack Marshall and arranger Elmer Bernstein. They both began using Maphis on their sessions, including Marshall's *Thunder Road* and Bernstein's *God's Little Acre* soundtracks. Joe recalls stories told by fellow musicians how, when he was asked if he needed a music stand, said yes, took one, and turned the tray flat to set his coffee and ashtray on it. He remembers the *God's Little Acre* date vividly; "I hesitated to take the job, not readin' music any better than us hillbillies do. I told Mr. Bernstein, 'You know, I don't read that well.' and he said, 'What I want is what you *feel.*' I remember they had 30 or 40 pieces in that orchestra, and after we did a couple of passages they were all complimenting me. I think the pop musicians learned to respect the ability of the country guys, admiring what us country boys were doin' without reading music."

Studio work became an important part of Joe's livelihood by the mid-'50s as he worked with an ever-growing number of country performers and pop singers. As his reputation spread, he got regular calls from producers who needed fiddle, banjo, or guitar, and Joe even recalls working with jazz guiter greats George Van Eps, Barney Kessel, and Howard Roberts over the years. He and Kessel, for instance, jammed on cowboy singer Jimmy Wakely's CBS radio show—Kessel starting out with "After You've Gone" and Maphis responding with "Fire On The Strings." What developed was an all-out guitar duel, both players swapping lightening choruses.

While Joe accomplished a lot of different things in the L.A. studios, occasionally his reputation overshadowed what he actually did—as he relates: "People think I wrote the score to *Thunder Road,* which I didn't." Later in the '50s, he played on the pilot soundtrack for the *Bonanza* TV series, as well as on the regular scores for *The Deputy* and *Riverboat* shows. Again, he was mistakenly credited with writing these. "I get a lot of undue credit for those things," he says. "This happens in our business."

There was one vast body of work, however, for which Joe got virtually no recognition: his work on some of the early rockabilly and rock and roll hits emerging from L.A. during the late '50s and early '60s. It all started with a call Joe received from a *Town Hall Party* fan. "We were filming the *Ranch Party* TV show in 1957," Joe says, "and I got a call from Ozzie Nelson. He said, 'My boy Ricky is starting to sing on our TV show, and we've been watchin' you and wondered if you could come down and play backup guitar for him.' They'd cut the backups, but would substitute younger actors miming the guitar parts on the show." From there, Maphis began working on Ricky's Imperial recording sessions (Barney Kessel had played lead on Ricky's first hit, "I'm Walkin'," on Verve).

Joe played on many of Nelson's 1957 hit singles, including "Be Bop Baby," "Have I Told You Lately That I Love You," "Stood Up," "Waitin' In School," "I'm Confessin'," and his first Imperial album.

It was no surprise to anyone when Joe followed Ricky onstage: "Ozzie was hiring me to back Ricky, and I had my own duties with *Town Hall*. But Ozzie was payin' me the price I'd want for a show on the road. One time I flew to Oakland, California, and another time to the Midwest to play behind Ricky." But the schedule eventually proved too much for Maphis to keep up, so he left Nelson's band and was replaced by fellow *Town Party* guitarist James Burton. The rest is history.

Other rock sessions came Joe's way as his talents were noticed by recording execs such as Imperial's Jimmy Haskell and Capitol's Voyle Gilmore. Maphis recorded with Tommy Sands, and along with the *Town Hall Party* band backed the Four Preps on their hit recordings of "26 Miles" and "Big Man." Joe also worked on some of Wanda Jackson's Capitol rockabilly recordings, including "Let's Have A Party," "Savin' My Love," "Hot Dog! That Made Him Mad," and her rendition of "Silver Threads and Golden Needles."

One duet Maphis backed was Larry and Lorrie—the Collins Kids—which became especially important for Joe. He took Larry, then a teenager, and taught him a great deal, influencing the youngster so much that he even bought a scaled-down double-neck Mosrite. By the late '50s, Maphis was working on most of the Collins Kids' Columbia sessions, adding complex guitar backings. In 1957, Joe and Larry recorded four instrumentals for Columbia, including the incredible "Hurricane"—two minutes of pulsating, exciting guitar work that still sounds hot today. In the latter part of the '50s, Maphis even tried doing a rock record of his own with saxophonist Plas Johnson. "Mitch Miller at Columbia got all excited," he says, "and thought we

had a smash hit." But it never succeeded on the charts.

Joe remained with the *Town Hall Party* until it folded in 1961. By that time, he and Rose Lee had left Columbia for Capitol, and Maphis himself recorded an instrumental LP with Merle Travis. He and Rose Lee moved to Bakersfield in the early '60s, and Joe signed a new record contract with Nashville's Starday label.

Joe and Rose Lee toured the country in a motor home during the mid-'60s, finally moving back to Nashville in 1968. He and his son Jody recorded an LP for Chart, *Guitar-Ration Gap*, that same year, and from there Maphis went on to work with gospel artists on the Sacred and Word labels. In 1973 Semie Mosely again made Maphis a double-neck guitar, which differed somewhat from the original he built years before. "It has two pushbutton switches," he says, "with one being a rhythm switch. If you're singing, you just push the button and the tone'll soften up. When you get ready to pick, you hit it again." The new model also has humbucking pickups as opposed to single-coil units on the 1954 original, which was donated to Nashville's Country Music Hall of Fame in 1973.

Even at the age of 60, Joe continues to tour with Rose Lee in their motor home, playing everything from clubs and bluegrass festivals to military bases. Joe was featured on the TV show *Hee Haw* with his old friend, Grandpa Jones, and in 1980 Maphis was named to the Virginia Music Hall Of Fame. The governor of the state even declared a "Joe Maphis Day." One especially pleasing moment for Joe and Rose Lee occurred at a show where country singer Barbara Mandrell honored the Maphises with a plaque. (It was Joe and Rose Lee who took Barbara to Las Vegas for her first professional engagement when she was 12.) Other things keeping Maphis busy include a recording recently completed with Merle Travis in honor of fiddler Clayton McMichen, as well as a double-record acoustic LP on CMH Records with fellow guitarists Merle Travis and Arthur Smith.

Despite his rich and varied career, there's still one thing Joe Maphis would like to do—an original piece, arranged just for him: "Later, before I pass on, maybe somebody would take the little bit of country guitar I do, put myself in their hands, and just add a little sound behind me. I'd say, 'Hey, you're gonna be my arranger; build me something and I'll pick.'" [*Ed. Note: Joe Maphis passed away on June 27, 1986.*]

---

### A SELECTED JOE MAPHIS DISCOGRAPHY

**Solo albums:** *Fire On The Strings*, Columbia, CL-1005; *Rose Lee Maphis*, Columbia [out of print]; *Joe And Rose Lee Maphis*, Capitol [out of print]; *King Of The Strings*, Starday [out of print]; *Mr. & Mrs. Country Music*, Starday, 286; *Guitar Goes To The Jimmy Dean Show*, Starday [out of print]; *Golden Gospel Guitar*, Starday, 322; *Nashville Guitars*, Nashville, 2091; *Gospel Guitar*, Sacred [out of print]; *Guitar-Ration Gap*, Chart [out of print]; *Grass 'N Jazz*, CMH, 6125; *Dim Lights, Thick Smoke*, CMH, 6224; *Boogie Woogie Flattop Guitar Pickin' Man*, MCH, 6239; *Honky-Tonk Cowboy*, CMH, 6251. **With Merle Travis:** *Merle Travis & Joe Maphis*, Capitol, ST-2102; *Country Guitar Greats*, CMH, 9017. **With Grandpa Jones:** *Grandpa Jones Family Album*, CMH, 9015; *Old-Time Country Music Collection*, CMH, 9010. **With Johnny Bond:** *Bottled In Bond*, Harmony, HL-7353; *That Wild, Wicked But Wonderful West*, Starday, 147; *Hot Rod Lincoln—Three Sheets In The Wind*, Starday, 298; *Famous Hot Rodders I Have Known*, Starday, 345; *Ten Little Bottles*, Starday, 333. **With Ricky Nelson:** *Rick Nelson*, United Artists, UAS-9960; *Ricky*, United Artists, LM-1004. **With Wanda Jackson:** *Pioneers Of Rock*, Capitol Starline, 5120; *Rockin' With Wanda*, Capitol England, 1007. **With the Collins Kids:** *CBS Rockabilly Classics, Vols. 1, 2, 3*, British CBS 82401, 82402, 82403. **With others:** *Town Hall Party*, Columbia, CL-1072; *Truck Stop*, Nashville, NLP-2052; *Imperial Rockabillies, Vols. 1, 3*, British UA, 30103, 30312.

---

# SAM McGEE

By Bob Krueger

S AM McGEE IS A NAME WHICH HAS BEEN CLOSELY ASSO-ciated with the *Grand Ole Opry* since the institution's inception in 1925. McGee, as a member of the Fruit Jar Drinkers, was part of that first Opry broadcast, was included in its first road show, was the first musician to use an electric guitar there, and holds the record for having been the Opry's oldest performer.

Sam, born in Franklin, Tennessee, in 1894, missed the *Grand Ole Opry*'s 50th anniversary by two months when he died in a tractor accident on his tobacco farm, August 21, 1975, at the age of 81.

"Mr. Sam" was one of a handful of pioneers in country music guitar playing. Along with people like Riley Puckett, Mother

**A charter member of the *Grand Ole Opry*, Sam McGee introduced fingerstyle guitar to millions.**

Maybelle Carter, and Merle Travis, he helped develop finger-style guitar in country and folk music. A number of McGee's tunes, including "Buck Dancer's Choice," have become folk standards.

Sam and his brother Kirk (on banjo) weathered time and changing musical tastes on the Opry stage, first playing behind people like Uncle Dave Macon and Fiddlin' Arthur Smith, and continued right on through to the addition of more commercial acts to the Opry which came after World War II, when tradition-alist Judge George D. Hay retired from the Opry.

The folk boom of the late '50s and early '60s brought about a new audience which "rediscovered" the McGee brothers. Until his death, Sam continued to play an occasional college campus or folk festival, in addition to maintaining his regular Saturday night spots on the Opry.

The following interview took place on July 4, 1975.

\*   \*   \*   \*

*W*AS 1923 THE YEAR YOU ACTUALLY STARTED PLAYING *professionally?*

Well, yes, but we been playing longer than that. But profes-sionally—in shows and on the *Grand Ole Opry,* and all that—we didn't start until 1925.

*When you started, did you play backup for Uncle Dave Macon?*

I played for him for 20 years. To my opinion, he was one of the greatest entertainers of all time. People could beat him at playing, but when it came to entertaining a crowd, he was in a class by himself. He was the type of fellow that could talk to an audience, and have them laughing one minute, you might say, and almost crying the next. He played the 5-string banjo. He used to play a fingerpicking style, but after he got up in age he

kind of lost the use of his fingers, and he done this claw-hammer picking you know. We call it "claw-hammer" style.

*Did you first play the* Grand Ole Opry *as a member of the* Fruit Jar Drinkers?

We're playing with the Fruit Jar Drinkers on this program now [the Opry], but that started back in '25, too. I got into the band when one of Grandpappy George Wilkenson's men—he was the head of the Fruit Jar Drinkers—got in sort of bad health and wanted me to take his place, and play guitar for him. I was one of the Fruit Jar Drinkers from then 'til now.

*When you started playing full-time with the Opry, and doing road shows, where would you play?*

Theaters, tent shows, schools, just any place that we got a job. We went out here with Roy Acuff, he had a tent show; and Bill Monroe, he had a tent show, too. In fact, I was on the first show that ever left the *Grand Ole Opry*—DeFord Bailey, and Dr. Humphrey Bates and his bunch. There wasn't many people on the road then; we were the first ones that were booked out of radio station WSM, to a mining town in Virginia.

*Did you stay mostly around the south, or did you play up north at all?*

Sometimes we did, but most of it was in surrounding Tennessee, and Georgia, Alabama, Mississippi, and all like that. Sometimes we'd go off, but somehow or another we never did play up north as much. I played my first date in Oklahoma two years ago, and in California this year, 1975.

*Did you work with a fiddler named Arthur Smith?*

We worked with Arthur for seven years on one program. Kester Metal Mender was the product that we sold—kind of a glue or solder, you know. There were three Arthur Smiths. We called this one "Fiddlin' Arthur," and there was Arthur "Guitar Boogie," and then there was a writer who was Arthur "Q"—he was at Knoxville. We called it Arthur Smith And Sam And Kirk McGee And The Dixieliners. Arthur worked for this railroad line that ran, I believe, from Knoxville to Memphis, and it was called the Dixie line. That was from about 1930 to '37.

*How did you two get together?*

Well, we'd been at the Opry a while when it first started. Arthur Smith was already there too, and we'd play some schools, some auditoriums. Arthur was still with the railroad company, and we'd go pick him up at the section camp—they had camp cars, and he was camped on the railroad. We did that for a long time, and finally it got to where he was making more money at that then he was at the railroad (he was a lineman), and he just went into music altogether.

*Your style of playing—fingerpicking—isn't all that common in country music today. It seems most country guitarists are flatpickers. Was that always the case?*

Well, there was more fingerstyle players, but they was still a little different from me in their style of playing. Most of them used a finger and a thumb, like old-time banjo players that play the 5-string banjo. I use two or three fingers, and thumb.

*Do you use fingerpicks?*

Yes, I use picks on account of they take care of your fingers a little better. I use a thumbpick, and two steel [National] fingerpicks.

*Where did you learn your style?*

Well, mostly just picking it up the way I thought I could do it the easiest and the best. I had seen this white fellow, Tom Hood. He's the first one that I seen that tried to play sort of on my style.

But that started with him. Then I bought a guitar from him—that was way back; I was about eleven years old, I guess. I was living on the farm, five or six miles from where I am now.

*What other instruments do you play?*

I think I could play anything with strings on it if I fooled with it a little bit, but I stick mostly to guitar. What kept me from fooling with the fiddle too much was that my daddy was an old-time fiddler, my uncle was an old-time fiddler and also a 5-string banjo player. It seems it just fell my lot to play with them—to play accompaniment for them. I wish I had played a fiddle; I believe I would have loved it, and would have done it well.

*How does your style differ in sound from the flatpickers?*

What I try to do in fingerpicking style, I try to get my basses and the "air" of the tune, as I go. Run them basses in there with your melody and the tune. What's always been my idea—I don't know whether it would be right or not—but I've always tried to play so it sounds pretty good to me, and then I hope it would sound pretty good to you. That was the only direction I had to go by. I don't read music; I can only cheat. I just go y ear.

*Were there any professional fingerpickers in country music before you?*

No, there really wasn't any. That's been a long time ago, about 70 years ago. Really, there wasn't much music going like there is now. They had a lot of music just from house to house: "We'll play here at your house tonight, and maybe next week we'll play over here at this man's house"—like that. But there wasn't a lot of shows and big programs going on all over the whole country like there are now. It seems like the whole world has just gone for music.

*So when you were growing up, you played mostly at home?*

Yeah. About all we did in the winter time was farming. We had about 160 acres of land up here; in the winter why we just cut wood and things like that, and fiddled and danced. Nothing else to do, you know. We grew tobacco, and corn, and hogs. Once a fellow asked Kirk, "How did you get by?" "Well," he said, "We raised what we ate, and ate what we raised." It didn't take a lot of money then, you know; there was no place to spend it. We got along just fine. Then Uncle Dave played a little school near us, and came home with us, and we played some for him. That's what started him and me together. It amused him that somebody could play a lead on a guitar, because all you ever heard was just chords. There wasn't many guitar pickers back then.

*Who were the first guitar pickers you ever saw?*

Well, where we learned the most about the style was from the black people. My daddy ran a little store, and these section hands would come over from the railroad at noon, and they bought pork and beans, sardines, and all that kind of stuff. Well, after they finished their lunch, they would play guitars. Two of them—great big black men, their name was the Steward brothers—they played real good, and that's where I learned to love the blues tunes. Black people were about the only people that played guitars then. It's a little different than I do, but it's the same kind of picking, using your fingers.

*Do you think country music has been hurt because it's been taken from the back porches and into the large concert halls?*

I can give you an idea: I've had two groups of people come to my house today, and that's what they came for—to play some, and to see me, and to talk with me. A musician's like a big preacher. He shouldn't overshoot his audience. But he can get them to fancy that they won't like it as well if they understand what he's doing. On the one hand they might say, "Well, that looks easy; I think I can do that." But if he makes it too hard for them, they'll say, "Well, I haven't got a chance to ever learn that; I'm not going to fool with it."

*You were one of the first to introduce electric instruments to the Opry.*

I didn't play that but a time or two, until they stopped me. At that time, they wouldn't have electrical instruments on the *Grand Ole Opry*. I think it would be better if they cut out some of it now. About 1926, I was going to learn to play that electric steel [National lap steel]. It was something new then; there just wasn't none of them going through the country. Of course, when they play country music like some of them do now, they're kind of getting away from what old country music used to be. I like the old country style of playing; I think that's what the *Grand Ole Opry* started out to be. In fact, that's what Judge Hay told me when I came in with this electric guitar. I got by with it about two Saturday nights; about the third one, he come in and patted me on the shoulder, "Now, you wouldn't play that on the *Grand Ole Opry*. You know we're going to hold it down to earth." And I said, "Well, thank you, Judge, I won't bring it back any more." He was right about it. I thought I'd have something different, but that isn't what counts.

*Who are some of the guitar players whose work you admire?*

I'm going to play with a fellow the end of this month [July, 1975], with Doc Watson. He still don't play in my style of picking—he plays with a straight pick—but he plays right smart. Burt Hutcherson [of the Crook Brothers, formerly with the Gully Jumpers] used to do 30 minutes of fingerpicking, the finest you ever heard. But, of course, his hands have gotten stiff, and he just can't do it anymore. Chet Atkins is a fine player. I played with him in Knoxville, when he was just starting out. There's Tommy Jones; he's just a young boy. He plays with Archie Campbell. He's a good fingerpicker. Billy Grammer—I like his music fine. We talk together about playing, and I brag on him, and he brags on me. I tell him he's my favorite guitar player down here, and he says, "Well, Mr. Sam, I don't know half as much about a guitar as you do." I think he just says that to make me feel good.

*Do you have much time to practice?*

No, I don't do enough. I'd like to do a little more, try to get a little better. Out here on the farm, nobody's left on 405 acres of ground but me, and, you know, there's plenty to do here. I do a little sideline picking, but most of the work's on the farm, of course.

---

## A SELECTED SAM McGEE DISCOGRAPHY

**Solo albums:** *Grandad Of The Country Guitar Pickers*, Arhoolie, ARH 5012. With Kirk McGee: *Opry Old Timers*, Starday, STR 182.

# BILL MONROE

By Dix Bruce

**B**LUEGRASS MUSIC IS A RECENT ARRIVAL ON THE AMERIcan scene. It was born at the turn of the fourth decade of this century, predating the advent of rock and roll by only ten or 12 years. The face of bluegrass, unlike that of rock and roll, is the image of one man: bluegrass' progenitor and main influence, Bill Monroe. Certainly bluegrass has its roots in the music of the southern Appalachian mountains, and there have been bluegrass innovators since Monroe; but no one can deny that bluegrass music is Bill Monroe's own creation.

There are few non-classical mandolin players alive who do not owe the foundations of their styles to Monroe. While he has inspired the gamut of bluegrass, jazz, and even rock mandolin players, he himself has seldom strayed from tight stylistic parameters of melodic, distinctively rhythmic playing.

The style, form, and themes of Monroe's music are strictly bounded. The basic band is always mandolin, guitar, banjo, string bass, and fiddle. The guitar and bass are rarely featured as lead instruments; with the chop chords of the mandolin, their function is to provide the punch rhythm of the band. The chord progressions are simple, usually limited to two or three changes per tune. The lead instruments—mandolin, fiddle, and banjo—generally trade solos with the vocalists. The beauty of the music lies in what is so elegantly stated within these limitations.

Monroe's instrumental compositions express a range of sound and emotion unequaled by any performer in his field. They have come to comprise a primer of songs that every mandolin player must address. "Rawhide," "Kentucky Mandolin," "Bluegrass Stomp," "Bluegrass Breakdown," and "Wheel Hoss" are all challenging bluegrass mandolin classics. Many echo the fiddle tunes Monroe heard as a child; others are intense, fast pieces that communicate his own energetic musical vision. The songs he writes convey a haunting reality, almost always concerning themselves with some aspect of love—love cherished, rejected, fulfilled, or lost. Some songs reflect Monroe's childhood and culture, "Uncle Pen"—an ode to the man who taught him music—probably being the most famous of these. Some songs deal with the lonely existence of life on the road, others are honest expressions of Monroe's religious beliefs. All of Monroe's songs cut straight to the heart with a simple and beautiful poetic quality.

There is virtually no comic or novelty material, because Monroe is a very serious man who cares deeply about his music. For nearly 40 years, he has been striving to bring that music up from his heart and deliver it to his audience.

It all began on a farm in the hills near Rosine, Kentucky, in 1911, when Bill Monroe was born. He was the youngest of eight children. Throughout his childhood he was exposed to hoedown music and to the blues. He mentions a black guitarist and fiddler, Arnold Schultz, as being one of his main influences. Monroe's uncle Pen Vandiver, a fiddler, further sparked his interest in music, and the fiddle was Monroe's first choice as an instrument. Unfortunately, his brother Birch had already claimed the family's fiddle. Bill's second choice was the guitar, but his brother Charlie had claimed it. That left only the mandolin.

Monroe did get to play guitar somewhat, initially, and would regularly "second" on the guitar for his uncle Pen at local house parties and hoedowns. Monroe says that if things had turned out a little differently, he might have been a blues singer. It was the early cross-influence of the blues and hoedown music that led Monroe to his synthesis of the two styles into bluegrass.

Both of Monroe's parents died before he entered his teens and he went to live with his uncle Pen. At 17 he left Kentucky to follow Charlie and Birch north in search of work. Jobs were scarce, but eventually he found employment in the Chicago area, stacking barrels at the Sinclair oil refinery. At times, he was the only one of the three brothers working and he supported the other two on his small salary.

Bill, Charlie, and Birch had continued with their music after the move north and gradually they began to get scattered jobs as a trio. House party dates led to short road trips for WLS radio's *Barn Dance Tour*, with the brothers also doing some exhibition square dancing. For a while Bill continued at Sinclair, taking time off to do the WLS show, since all three brothers agreed that though music was a more enjoyable way of making a living than refinery work, it was nowhere near as steady. But finally the brothers were performing enough that Bill quit Sinclair altogether. It must certainly have been a difficult step. The country was in the depths of the Depression, and any job was a good job. Being employed was an incredibly lucky situation that one

didn't walk away from. Quitting Sinclair was a gamble; but luckily for Monroe, it paid off.

After some initial touring with the WLS *Barn Dance*, Birch settled into a steady refinery job and left the group. Charlie and Bill continued as a duo, the Monroe Brothers, and through a series of associations with radio stations they gained a following throughout the South and the rural Midwest. Their recordings sold well, but the brothers had difficulty getting along and after six years the act split up. The Monroe Brothers went in entirely different directions. It's generally accepted that Bill found his position as the younger brother to be unworkable; that he longed to prove himself with his own music, independent of Charlie.

Bill immediately set about putting together his special style of music, something through which he could express himself in

an exciting and different way. It was 1939 when the first "Blue Grass Boys" appeared on radio station WSM's *Grand Ole Opry*, and they caused quite a stir. Their music was supercharged, even in its seminal form. Originally a quartet with mandolin, guitar, fiddle, and string bass, the Blue Grass Boys didn't add banjo for two years. That step would finally and completely define the classic bluegrass sound.

Dave "Stringbean" Akeman, who played in the frailing style of Uncle Dave Macon, was Monroe's first banjo player. Also joining the group was an accordionist, Sally Ann Forrester; Monroe later said that he chose to add the accordian because his mother had played the instrument. The accordian was gone from the group by autumn of 1946, however, as was Akeman's banjo when Monroe made his first recording with 22-year-old Earl Scruggs. Scruggs had joined Monroe in December of 1945, and his rapid-fire three-finger banjo picking, unheard of at the time, was the final ingredient in the bluegrass sound. The Blue Grass Boys at that point became the classic Monroe band of Monroe, Lester Flatt on guitar, Scruggs on banjo, and Chubby Wise on fiddle, and Birch Monroe on bass.

The music was at an incredible peak, having jelled both stylistically and commercially. There was nothing else like it. Monroe and his Blue Grass Boys toured constantly, in many cases with their own tent show (featuring performers like Uncle Dave Macon) and an exhibition baseball team, returning to Nashville each week for the *Grand Ole Opry* broadcast. It was the beginning of a movement, and Monroe had no peer as a composer or as a performer. Others were to follow shortly, but Bill Monroe and the Blue Grass Boys, with their lightning playing and exciting singing, were on top.

Many classic bluegrass pieces came from this era. One of the Blue Grass Boys' early signature tunes was a reworking of Jimmie Rodgers' "Mule Skinner Blues" into Monroe's own style. Monroe's tenor voice was high and clear, and it seemed to express a feeling of deep lonesomeness. His mandolin playing had developed significantly by this time, emphasizing strong melody and a syncopated, driving rhythm that pushed the band. A hard worker, he expected his band members to be the same and he must have been a difficult man to work for at times. But his main concern was always the music.

The late '40s were good for Monroe, but times were changing. Lester Flatt and Earl Scruggs left the Blue Grass Boys to form their own bluegrass-style band, and there began a succession of Monroe bands through which passed virtually every great figure in bluegrass music, save its mandolin players. Carter Stanley, Jimmy Martin, Don Reno, Mac Wiseman, and many others were once Blue Grass Boys.

The early '50s saw the start of a difficult period in Monroe's career. Country music in general was having an identity crisis in light of the rock and roll revolution. Though bluegrass had never, since its inception, been mass culture, Monroe had always made a good living. But with rock and roll sweeping the country, and with the advent of television, much of Monroe's economic base was eroded and jobs became harder to secure. Ironically, one of Elvis Presley's early recordings included Monroe's "Blue Moon Of Kentucky" on its B side.

It must have hurt Monroe deeply to see his expanding career suddenly and severely decline. What attention the world did give bluegrass went to Flatt and Scruggs, who had managed to make inroads into other entertainment circles. Monroe did his best to survive musically and financially, withdrawing to his Kentucky farm when jobs were scarce. He resisted all temptations to revamp his music along more popular lines. Through his intense pride, even his stubbornness, he weathered those lean times. The roots of his preservance may have gone back to his childhood when, the youngest of the family and troubled by poor vision, he developed a need to excel, to be successful. Through that he forged a single-minded attitude about himself and his music; he drew upon all his experience and strength of will to achieve his goals, realizing that the music was the most important thing in his life. It has never been otherwise. He has always stayed on top of his music, never changing, never faltering.

The folk revival of the early '60s helped Monroe toward a comeback. It also brought him a new audience of northern college students. On the heels of his renewed interest came the popularization of bluegrass festivals, and Monroe was able to found his own at Bean Blossom, Indiana, in 1967. While Monroe had always been regarded as the father of bluegrass music, his achievements at last became more popularly recognized and he was elected to the Country Music Hall of Fame in 1970.

Today, Monroe continually tours the country and still performs regularly with the *Grand Ole Opry*. Any other artist

**The father of bluegrass onstage at the *Grand Ole Opry*.   Left to right: Kenny Baker, Butch Robins, Bill Monroe, Wayne Lewis.**

who had made such a monumental contribution to his field might be content to rest on his laurels, but Monroe's drive is as strong as ever. He says simply, "The road life—I like it. I like to travel. I like to see the country."

Bill Monroe's music developed steadily from his days with the Monroe Brothers, back in the '30s, on into the mid-'60s. There has always been a great deal of movement within its strict boundaries, especially in Monroe's mandolin playing.

Monroe has always tried, he says, to make the music he plays fit with the group he is in, though in his own style. Because of that, Monroe's playing has covered a great range; at times it has been subdued and at times it has been intense, but it has never been flippant or contrived.

To accent his backup playing, Monroe developed a powerful right-hand rhythm chop with an almost drum-like effect. Using a loose, limber wrist motion he gained incredible speed on his solos. Drawing on a great deal of blues phrasing and noting, he punctuated his leads with an outrageous syncopation of right-hand downstrokes. The result was one of the most distinctive and remarkable mandolin styles of our time.

During the following interview Bill Monroe talks about his playing, his early musical influences, his songwriting and composing, and his long career as a performer.

* * * *

*O*VER THE YEARS, IN TALKING ABOUT HOW YOU *began playing, you've mentioned a guitar player named Arnold Schultz as an early influence. Could you tell us a little about him?*

Arnold Schultz. He was a black man, you know, and he played guitar and was a wonderful guitar man. Played the blues, that was what he played. If he was following a fiddler or somebody with a guitar, he really played a different style. I never heard anybody could play anything the way that Arnold Schultz played it, behind fiddle numbers. He played a wonderful rhythm. He could also play the fiddle, you know, a few fiddle numbers, and he played for some square dances.

*Did you learn songs from him?*

No, sir. I've always loved the blues played on the guitar, and when he would play them I loved the way he could do it. There's other people that could play blues too; there was people around where I was raised who could sing the blues like that.

*Were these black people?*

No, they were white people. They was very few colored people that would come around Rosine, Kentucky, where we lived; but Arnold was a fine man and I always loved to hear him play. There's really no man that you could pinpoint to say that his music is in my music, the way that my music is lined out. It's just like Jimmie Rodgers; I've sung some of his numbers, but they was done blue-grass style, which would override his style. If I was going to do Jimmie Rodgers alone, I would just use the guitar myself and do it the way that he did.

*But you never tried to do that, did you?*

Back in the early days I could have, you know, but mandolin's been my instrument ever since I was a young boy.

*I've never met a bluegrass mandolin player that didn't—at least at first—try to play like you. What is your reaction to everybody trying to copy Bill Monroe exactly?*

Well now, I feel good about it; every man has to start somewhere, and if my music helped him get started, why I'm 100 percent for him to do that. I guess a lot of people learned from that and went on into other kinds of music, and a lot of people still play it the way they learned it.

*Does it flatter you?*

Well, I like it either way. Of course, if they play my music and play it the way I have it lined out, I think it's fine. I thank a lot of them for doing it.

*How did you react in the early '50s when Elvis Presley recorded your song "Blue Moon Of Kentucky"?*

I thought Elvis had a good voice. He apologized to me for the way that he changed "Blue Moon Of Kentucky," he did, there at the *Grand Ole Opry*, when he came there and sung it one Saturday night. The record company told him that he needed a style of his own, and so that's what he was searching for when he recorded "Blue Moon Of Kentucky," and I think he had it right for his new style. So, I told him if it would help him get that then I was 100 percent for him.

*You've said that in the beginning what you were trying to do more than anything was to find your own style on the mandolin.*

That's right, and there's a way that I play that had never been played before by anybody. And the way that I use the chords or anything like that in following a lead instrument was never played the way that I do it.

*Something that's always been remarkable about your playing through the years is the many subtle changes it's undergone. For example, when you played with your brother Charlie you played in a different style. You've said that style was not yet bluegrass.*

That's right. It was a style to match his kind of singing and the kind of singing that we'd do in the early days.

*Were you concentrating less on the mandolin exclusively then and more on the entire sound?*

No, I was searching for things on the mandolin then. But, to fit our kind of singing, what I was playing then was what we needed. The kind of style that I play now wouldn't have matched me and Charlie back in the early days.

*It seems that the one person other than Arnold Schultz whom you emphasize as an early influence is your uncle Pen Vandiver.*

Yes, sir, him being the first fiddler that I ever heard, naturally. He was a good fiddler too. He was hard to beat when it came to playing old-time square dance numbers. He had the most perfect time of any fiddler in the world, and he had a wonderful shuffle, you never see anybody today that can play that kind of shuffle.

*How old were you when you began listening to him and playing with him?*

I would say from around six years old, something like that, on up through to ten and 12 years old, I listened to him close. Then on up through my teens Uncle Pen and I would play for square dances.

*With you on the guitar?*

Yes, sir, just where we could make a little extra money, you see. Back then, that was in the Depression when a dollar really meant something. We did a lot of house parties, and some of them had square dances there at the house. The people would all dance and they would donate 15 cents a set.

*Another early influence in your music was the church. What were your early church experiences?*

I guess, back in the early days, with the Methodist and the Baptist churches, everybody come there to hear the singing and the preaching. They had a Methodist church there at Rosine and a Baptist church. They had a good choir singing there; a good lead singer, and back in them days they had tenor singers and bass singers and alto singers. That was way before baritone singing came around.

*Do songs like "Wicked Path Of Sin" come out of that tradition?*

I would say it might have touched in some way, but through the way I was searching for the bluegrass style of singing gospel I wouldn't take a whole lot from Baptist or Methodist. It's a different gospel altogether from Methodist and Baptist. I don't believe I ever heard a quartet there in church. Bluegrass gospel, I think, is wonderful.

*When you were playing with your brothers, before you played with Charlie as a duo and while you were working for the Sinclair Oil Company, had you played professionally much?*

Well, just back to Uncle Pen and me playing for dances and house parties.

*Did you think much about future economic opportunities with the oil company when you decided to try being a musician?*

It wasn't that I decided to be one or the other. Times was rough back then and musicians didn't have the best chance in the world. Very few radio stations paid anything, you see. It was taking a big chance, leaving a good job and going into music.

*Through playing with Charlie and later, when did your music become bluegrass?*

When me and Charlie broke up, I went to building around myself to form the music that I wanted. Any man that I hired had to play my style or he didn't belong in my group. It went to building from that, doing the numbers that would help us get started in that kind of music.

*What made it "bluegrass"?*

The state of Kentucky gave it the name. That's the state I'm from, and I wanted to use some kind of a name from that state so the people would know it was where I was from. So, I took the name "bluegrass." There's not a prettier name in the world than that.

*As far as the music goes, though, what were the changes that you made? Is is true that in 1938 you got a band together to play your music and rehearsed for a month?*

Well, I went to working on it back in late '38 and on up into '39. You see, it gave whoever was going to play for me a chance to practice and get it right. Maybe if a man was holding down a job or something, he'd like to play and sing but he wasn't ready for a big radio program like the *Grand Ole Opry*. So, I had to rehearse them and get them just the way I wanted them.

*There are many stories about your first appearance on the* Grand Ole Opry—*that people listening couldn't believe it. Did you expect that?*

I knew I was going to go in there and give them everything that I had. I had heard the *Grand Ole Opry* for a long time, and I didn't think that they had anything on me in the way of being better than what I was because I wasn't in their class. I wasn't doing old-time country music, singing, or playing old-time mountain fiddle numbers, whatever you want to call it.

*Did you have a feeling of bringing a new kind of music to these people in particular?*

I had a feeling of bringing it to everybody that I played in front of, whether it was the *Grand Ole Opry* or otherwise. I was going to take that to 'em and they could accept it or not.

*Did it matter to you whether they accepted it?*

Well, I wanted them to accept it, 'cause I knew I had to have them on my side if I was to really put it over and make money at it.

*Over the years you've avoided changing your sound for commercial reasons or any other consideration. How have you been able to keep the Bill Monroe sound so pure?*

It's been hard at times. You might have a fiddle player or a banjo player that wants to put his stuff in it, you see. So, it comes right down to where he either had to play mine or he had to get him another job. And he couldn't win out, because if I didn't want his music, why, he'd have to play mine. I couldn't sell his style on the *Grand Ole Opry*—it had to be mine. So, I had to watch people like that and be sure that they played what I wanted. Record companies never gave me any trouble. I always done what song I wanted to do. They never told me I had to do anything. I think they knew to start with that I wouldn't do it. Now, if they gave me a song that I thought I could do, and it was a good song, why I would do it; but it would be in bluegrass style.

*If you could pick a band that was the greatest Bill Monroe band, who would you pick?*

Well, you know now, if I told you this—if I said I would take somebody by the name of George over somebody by the name of Frank, and they'd all been Blue Grass Boys, it would hurt 'em, you know. Say if you worked for me three years and it was a wonderful group, then you and the rest of the group left and I brought in a new bunch; well, your days would have been fine, but when they come along with theirs, their days would have been fine. So you couldn't say that any group could have beat different groups down through the years. I've tried to keep good clear singers that could sing with me—a lead singer who played a good guitar. I've tried to keep the right kind of banjo player and the right kind of fiddle player. And a good bass, to help me keep time straightened out. But, I think each man with me has had his chance; and when he was with me, he would have been hard to beat. They was all good in their day, and I give every man credit. And here's another thing: You might have the finest guitar player in the world, but he might be a man that really wanted beer and whiskey. The next man that come along might not be hardly that good, but still be a good clean, honest man. You have to figure that out, you see, and see which one would really be the best one for you to work with every day.

*How did you work with musicians in whom you saw potential?*

I'd give a man all the chance in the world, and if I could give him any advice, I would do that too. But as long as he worked hard at it and I seen he was improving, I wouldn't ever bother him.

*I believe it was Don Reno who said you were always fair, that you would work with a man to help him get the music right.*

Speaking about Don Reno, when Don Reno come to me and the Blue Grass Boys, he needed Bill Monroe and the Blue Grass Boys to make Don Reno. But Don Reno helped me a lot. He was a good honest man, a hardworking man. He would drive that banjo hard, and he was a good singer. That's the way that it's gone, down through the years.

*You mention drinking and its destructive effect on music. You're a rare person in music in that you don't drink or smoke.*

Well, I don't think I could have been a drunkard, a beer hog, and have ever led the Blue Grass Boys to where they are today. If I had been, I'd have done been barred from the *Grand Ole Opry* and I'd have probably had no telling how many fights. I don't think you have to drink any kind of a drink to make you a better musician. If you think you have to do that you need to think it over, because I don't think your mind's working real good. I think you need to be sober.

*Could you tell us about some of your experiences with your tent show back in the '40s, when you had people like Uncle Dave Macon and harmonica player DeFord Bailey on the bill with the Blue Grass Boys?*

You talk about the tent show—I had that for years, and that gave us five days of work, Monday through Friday; and then back to the *Grand Ole Opry*, so that made six days. If, say, I went on 15, 20 minutes with me and the Blue Grass Boys, then we'd have some comedy for about 15 minutes, then go back to the blue-grass quartet, then maybe have a good fiddle number, and then DeFord Bailey. So it gave you a fine lineup down through the show.

*Was DeFord Bailey a novelty act?*

No, sir, no. There was no comedy with DeFord. It was strictly the harmonica the way it should be played; "Pan American Blues," "Lost John," "The Evening Prayer Blues," numbers like that. You couldn't beat him. He was fine.

*How about Uncle Dave Macon?*

He was a fine showman. Had a good voice and played a good 5-string banjo in his style, and he done a little comedy down through his show. When he was going over fine, he went along just like a clock working. Everything was perfect.

*You had comedians with some of your early band, but you got away from that later. How did the change come about?*

Well, back in the early days the people was trained all over the whole world for so much comedy in a show, so that's why I carried one comedian. Later on, when Stringbean [Dave "Stringbean" Akeman] would work with me, that would give me two comedians. Two working together, they was really powerful, onstage, you know. They could really get the laughs. And that would break the monotony of going from one number to another. It would let the musicians have a little break. Later on there got to be so many numbers like "Blue Moon Of Kentucky," "Mule Skinner Blues," "Footprints In The Snow," and "Uncle Pen," that the people would pay their money and want to hear; and they would want to hear fiddle numbers, banjo numbers, the quartet. So, by the time you get to all that, you don't have much time for comedy. And I think comedy takes away from a good bluegrass show. Bluegrass is way further up in the world than a lot of people give it credit for being. It tells the truth. A lot of songs are true songs. It gives me a good feeling to hear good bluegrass. And I know that a man, if he's a hard worker in it, is doing his best because he wants to hear it that way and he hopes it'll touch you the same way. That's the way I am with my music; I like to play it for myself, and I hope that it's really getting next to the people who listen, too.

*A lot of the songs you've written are songs about being on the road. Is the road a difficult part of your life?*

Well, I raised two children James and Melissa, and they

**Bill Monroe picks his famed 1923 Gibson F-5 built by Lloyd Loar.**

knew that if I went out and worked five days and made what money I could, that I was coming home to them. They knew that I'd be back there, and that I would want to see them just as much as they would want to see me. And they allowed for all that, you know, so that's the way it went for a long time. The road life, I like it. I like to travel, I like to see different country.

*But you must have seen this country a dozen times!*

I have. I've been down a lot of the roads many, many times. But I still like to travel. That's the way it's been with me. Trips have been hard, but you know a promoter, a booker, he has to do the best he can do. If you're putting on a show here in San Francisco, they'll take the best nights that they can get out of the week for the show here. That's the same way all over the whole

**The face of bluegrass is the image of one man: bluegrass' progenitor and main influence, Bill Monroe.**

country—Friday, Saturday, and Sunday is good.

*Do you ever get bored on the road?*

Oh, not too much. If you go out and stay a week or so, or three weeks, you're glad to get home. But then if you work around home maybe a couple weeks, or months, you like to get back on the road again.

*How do you go about writing songs—say, "Kentucky Mandolin"?*

If I'm writing a number like "Kentucky Mandolin" and I've got it started to where I enjoy the first notes, I search for the notes to tie on to that, to keep it going on the way I want it to where it still sounds good to me. Of course, there's brakes in any number where you might not be crazy about where you're going to take it right then, say, whether you can get to another position in another key. "Kentucky Mandolin" was a number that I was writing when I was here in California years and years ago. Doc Watson was playing it with me and I didn't have a title, so he gives it the title "Kentucky Mandolin."

*Do you change songs any after you get the basic form down?*

No, I stay as close as I can to the way that I write a song. That's the trouble with a lot of musicians; they want to do it their way, and their way ain't the right way. They ought to think about the man that writes the song and try to do it right, try to do it his way. It would be much better for them, because they don't know where they're going with it—a lot of them don't. They're jazzing a song up, putting a lot of wild notes in it to show off more that anything else.

*Are there any mandolin players you particularly like?*

There's a lot of good mandolin players, I guess. Take people like Jim and Jesse [McReynolds]. I always thought Jesse

had a good style for their singing and everything; it's different, and I think he really plays a good mandolin.

*What kind of music do you listen to when you relax?*

I like different kinds of music. Of course, bluegrass is number one. I like blues; or I like jazz, if it's not too wild. I like beautiful gospel singing. I like symphony. I've heard some rock and roll that I like. I sure have always liked Elvis Presley's singing, because he done a lot of gospel songs and had a good quartet behind him. So, there's a lot of good music. I like good fiddle music, but I don't like to see a man that plays a good fiddle let some other kind of style override him and get him into that.

*Was Kenny Baker sort of a swing fiddler before he came to you?*

I think so. But I think Kenny does a wonderful job of playing my music.

*Are there any new mandolins being made that you like?*

They make some mandolins over in Japan that have got wonderful fingerboards and play good. They're new, you know; they haven't had a chance really to get the tone in them. I think a mandolin has to be played a lot to get the tone.

*In a mandolin, do you look for a sound like the sound of the mandolin you have now?*

I hope that any mandolin will have a good sound. A lot's in the man that plays the mandolin. I think you have to be really careful and search for the tone. And, when you get the tone right, everything that the mandolin will stand or take, don't ever ride it, keep it right there.

*Is your mandolin the Bill Monroe mandolin? Is that the one that matches your style?*

Yes, sir, it's been a good mandolin down through the years.

*Are you particular about the picks you use?*

I like a heavy pick. I don't like a real light, thin pick because I don't think you can get a tone out of the mandolin with a thin pick. I let the point wear off, because if it's too sharp, why, you don't get the tone. I've tried tortoiseshell and it's pretty good. I use Gibson bronze strings.

*You sometimes use a different tuning—on "Get Up John," for instance. Are there others that you haven't recorded yet?*

Yes, but it's been so long [laughs] I can't remember how I tune them.

*How do you feel about amplifying the mandolin, either by using an electric instrument or by attaching a pickup to an acoustic one? You've never done that yourself.*

No, sir. I've played other people's mandolins a little bit that was electrified. I guess it's alright, according to what kind of music you're playing, what you're trying to do with it. I think it'd be good to play for dances like that, probably.

*Do you still practice a lot?*

We do. We sing and practice some. We play as we ride the bus, you know. If you're working every night, you get a lot of work right there, and a lot of times you can come up with something new right from the stage that will help your music.

*Does new material come to you when you're up on the stage?*

Sometimes it does, yes sir. I listen for music or where it could go to; where you could start from one note and go into something that would really help a number.

*Do you play set solos? In "Bluegrass Breakdown," for example, you might play the melody in one solo. Are you trying to create new things in that way onstage?*

If it's the "Bluegrass Breakdown," I do the best that I can do with it. I try to play my break as good as I can do it. I don't think it should be changed. It should stay the way it was wrote. With numbers like "Arkansas Traveler," "Katy Hill," I don't think you need to make it do something and ruin the number; and that's what you would do if you tried to put other kinds of music in it. They're for square dancing. You know what time a number should be and if you get out there and make it to where it's 100 miles an hour, you've lost your mind. It could never be right; no way in the world it could be right. It's just like a waltz number. If you go out there and play it so fast nobody could waltz—who wins there? And who loses? The musician does. The dancer, he can't do it, because you've ruined it. Any musician ought to learn timing. Now, that's the main thing in music—and there's a lot of different times. Any young musician

ought to be sure to learn it the right way. There's numbers like the "Orange Blossom Special" where you know it's a show-off number, a selling number just like "Rawhide" or "Black Mountain Rag" or something like that. But you just got a few of them numbers, so get back to the real thing. If you're going to play the "Watson Blues," why, it's an old southern style of blues and you don't need to put hot notes in it. You need to learn where a hot note should go, and not let it override the number to where it's going to hurt it. If you're going to play jazz or if you're going to play round dance music then you can throw every hot note in there that you want. Wouldn't hurt a thing.

*Is the same thing true of singing?*

Well, it works sort of the same way. If you've got a voice that can handle the song right, you stay on the note and follow your melody your voice will have a good chance and will help that song. The people out there will hear what you're doing. When you got to putting extra stuff in it, they know it don't go that way so you're only kidding yourself. If you're going to sing "Blue Moon Of Kentucky," you better hold close to the way it was wrote. Or "Kentucky Waltz," or "Uncle Pen"—that's a true song so you wouldn't want to make a show-off song out of it; you want to let the people hear the fiddle music and every word the way the story goes.

*Of all your songs, are there any you sing better than others?*

I wouldn't think so. On any song I would do my best. I don't ever go out onstage and piddle around with it. I give my throat and my voice a chance. By doing that, you've done your best right there and put some power behind it. That's all you need to do with it.

*Do you enjoy having the audience sing along with you?*

Oh, I love that. That's a great part of a lot of our shows today.

*You once said that you thought of bluegrass as a type of competition between band members. Is that the way you view it today?*

I think that's the way it is. You know you've got competition in bluegrass music. If you play a banjo number the best you can play it, the next man that's out there, he's going to play it hard. You've got people up there like Earl Scruggs and Don Reno to face, and you better come with the best that you've got or you're not going to sell. It's the same thing with the singer. He'd better do it good because there's another man they're going to introduce who's going to come out and sing his best. Same thing about the mandolin, or a quartet, or anything. It's a challenge. It's music that needs a lot of practice. You need to practice every time you get a chance.

---

## A SELECTED BILL MONROE DISCOGRAPHY

**Solo albums** (on MCA): *Bean Blossom*, 2-8002; *Best Of Bill Monroe*, 4-2090; *Bluegrass Instrumentals*, 104; *Bluegrass Memories*, 2315; *Bluegrass Ramble*, 88; *Bluegrass Special*, 97; *Bluegrass Time*, 116; *High, Lonesome Sound Of Bill Monroe*, 110; *I Saw The Light*, 527; *I'll Meet You In Church Sunday Morning*, 226; *Kentucky Blue Grass*, 136; *Mr. Bluegrass*, 82; *Bill Monroe, Country Music Hall Of Fame*, 140; *Bill Monroe's Greatest Hits*, 17; *Bill Monroe Sings Bluegrass, Body And Soul*, 2251; *Road Of Life*, 426; *Uncle Pen*, 500; *Voice From On High*, 131; *Weary Traveler*, 2173; *Bill Monroe And His Blue Grass Boys*, Columbia, CS-1065; *Bluegrass Style*, Coral Records, 20077; *Bill Monroe Sings Country Songs*, Coral Records, 20099; *Classic Bluegrass Instrumentals*, Rebel/Canada (Box 72, Station G, Toronto, Ontario, Canada, M4M 3E8); *The Classic Bluegrass Recordings*, County (dist. by CBS), CCS-104. **With others:** *Lester Flatt Live Bluegrass Festival*, Victor, APLI-0588; *Stars Of The Grand Ole Opry, 1926-1974*, RCA, 2-0466; *Original Bluegrass Sound With Lester Flatt & Earl Scruggs*, Rounder, Special Series 05.

# RICKY NELSON

By Jas Obrecht

NEXT TO ELVIS PRESLEY, RICKY NELSON WAS PROBably the most visible of all the early rock and roll stars. His two-minute song segments at the end of his parents' popular *The Adventures Of Ozzie And Harriet* TV show brought rock and roll into millions of homes, and somehow made it all right. After all, most parents had seen the handsome, clean-cut kid with impeccable diction grow up right on their TV screens. He proved to be a fine singer whose taste ranged from rockabilly and blues to country, and his tough sneer and sometimes gritty, raw sound attracted millions of fans. More than two decades later, Nelson still played over 200 dates a year.

The son of bandleader Ozzie Nelson and singer Harriet Hilliard, Eric Hillard Nelson was born on May 8, 1940, in Teaneck, New Jersey. He made his debut appearance on his parents' radio show at age eight, and in 1952 began portraying himself in his family's popular TV series. In 1957, at age 16, Ricky decided to record a rock and roll song to please a girlfriend who was infatuated with Elvis. Verve Records signed him and released "I'm Walkin'" backed with "A Teenager's Romance." The first TV sequence of Ricky playing acoustic guitar and singing at a party followed, and seven days later the 45 had sold over a million copies. Ricky then switched to the Imperial label, and over the next four years released a string of hits including "Stood Up," "Be-Bop Baby," "Believe What You Say," "Poor Little Fool," "Waitin' In School," "Lonesome Town," "It's Late," "Hello Mary Lou," and "Travelin' Man." Largely free of over-orchestration and studio gimmicks, his records were fresh and exciting, and several had an authentic rockabilly sound. His regular backup band—with Louisana-born James Burton on guitar—was considered to be one of the best in rock and roll. Ricky's appearances in such films as *The Wackiest Ship In The Army* and Howard Hawks' *Rio Bravo* also contributed to his popularity.

In 1963, after amassing sales of 35 million records—including 17 Top 10 hits and nine gold records—Rick, only 22, switched to Decca Records. The association produced an occasional hit. Late in the decade he recorded two country albums, *Country Fever* and *Bright Lights And Country Music.* With the Stone Canyon Band backing him, he catapulted himself back into the public eye with his 1972 hit, "Garden Party." His LP, *Playing To Win*, placed him squarely back in mainstream rock and roll. In addition to guitar, Rick also played drums, clarinet, and piano.

\* \* \* \*

*WERE YOU VERY INTERESTED IN ROCK AND ROLL before you recorded "A Teenager's Romance" to please a girlfriend?*

Yeah, very much so. I remember the first truly rock and roll record that I ever heard was Carl Perkins' "Blue Suede Shoes."

*Did you play much guitar on the* Playing To Win *album?*

I just played acoustic rhythm.

*Who is the guitarist in your current band?*

A fellow by the name of Bobby Neal. When I was with Epic I went down to Memphis to record an album, and I heard him and really liked the way he plays.

*What kind of guitars do you own?*

I have a Martin D-35. I've had it since I was 17.

*Do you play lead?*

Not really. I tried it a couple of times, and it took a little while to get it on tape [*laughs*], so I leave that up to somebody else.

*How young were you when you started playing guitar?*

Oh, gee, let me see. I think I was probably about 14.

*What other influences did you bring with you into the studio at that time?*

You couldn't help but be influenced by Elvis a little bit. At that time my main idol was probably Carl Perkins. I really idolized him and tried to sound like him. I used a stand-up slap bass at that time. Actually, electric basses came in about '57.

*Who were the studio musicians you used for the Verve sessions?*

People like Barney Kessel. They were mainly jazz players who really didn't understand rock and roll. There was a whole group of people like Howard Roberts, who were really great jazz players, but they just never quite made it as far as playing rock and roll.

*Was Joe Maphis your guitarist when you were with Imperial?*

Yeah, he was. Joe played all the leads on the first album, like

hall and thought, "Wow!" I loved the way he played.

*Did you suggest using country-style licks to him, or did he bring his knowledge with him?*

Well, he was from the South, so it was just an automatic kind of thing. It's a certain feel—now they call it rockabilly, I guess, for lack of a label. I gave him almost complete freedom, unless I heard a specific thing that I wanted to hear him play. You know, I was thinking about James, and I think he was probably the first to come up with anything like slinky strings. When we recorded "Believe What You Say," I remember him coming in the studio and going, "Hey, listen to this!" He'd put banjo strings on his guitar so he could bend them way up.

*Are you still in touch with Burton?*

Every now and then I talk to him.

*How were your first singles recorded?*

We had one studio that we recorded in. It was just one room with a chamber upstairs for echo. We'd all go down there and work out the arrangements right in the studio. There was no such thing as a producer at that time; they were A&R men. Jimmy Haskell was the go-between for Imperial Records and myself. I remember Jimmy used to hold up chord symbols because nobody could read. All of a sudden he'd bring out a big *A*, and then a *C*. So that was the extent of reading music. The recording techniques were really just straight-ahead. We'd record the drums and bass really out front on the basic track if we were going to lay vocals and things on it. We ended up being about four generations down because they used to overdub.

*Compared to today, what was the turnaround time between the session and the release of the record?*

It was a lot more healthy back then. We'd record like on a Friday night, and the record would be out in all the stores on Tuesday or Wednesday. By the end of that week it would have sold a million records if you got lucky.

*Did you pick the tunes yourself?*

Yeah, I did, which was a real luxury.

*At 16, how clear of a vision did you have of the final product?*

Very clear. I tried to buy up all the Sun Records and emulate them because I loved that sound.

*Was there a lot of pressure in being compared to Elvis?*

Oh, yeah. At that time everybody that stood up and played a guitar was compared to Elvis. And it really wasn't a pressure for me; it was something that I always felt was very flattering.

*Did you have much artistic control over your career when you were that young?*

Yeah, during the summer. Actually, the first thing I ever played was the Ohio State Fair. It's a large step from your bathroom to 20,000 people.

*Did you see* The Buddy Holly Story?

Yeah, I did.

*Was that an accurate representation of what rock and roll tours were like in the '50s?*

I just met Buddy Holly very briefly. Gene Vincent and I were really good friends. We used to jam a lot. My other friends during that time were Eddie Cochran, the Everly Brothers, and people like that. I know they used to go on those Dick Clark bus tours for like three or four months of one-nighters. I was very fortunate at that time to be able to play billings by myself, so I never really had to do that.

*Compared to today, what was the concert scene like back*

"Boppin' The Blues" and "Waitin' In School." There was a show called *Town Hall Party* that Tex Ritter, Merle Travis, and Joe Maphis were on. I got to know them because I dated Laurie Collins at that time, who was sort of a protege of Joe Maphis. I used to go down there every Saturday night when I was 15 and just sort of hang out. I got to meet all the people and hear all the stories. I really liked the way Joe played.

*Who are the best guitarists you've worked with?*

Oh boy, it's so hard to say. I think the two best are probably James Burton, who is really an innovator in guitar playing, and Bobby Neal. But it's so hard to generalize because they have really different styles.

*Was Burton well-known at the time he joined your band?*

He wasn't well-known at all, really. The first time I heard him was in the office at Imperial Records. He came from the *Louisiana Hayride*, and I was looking for a band at that time. I was 16, and so was James. I heard this guitar playing at the end of the *then at rock and roll shows?*

It was really the very beginnings of rock and roll, and people were getting their clothes torn off. It was very physical.

*The Burnettes wrote a number of your hits. How did you become involved with them?*

Well, I met Dorsey and Johnny right around the same time I knew Eddie Cochran and Gene Vincent. They had driven out from Memphis, and they pulled up in my driveway—this was after my first record. They were very persistent. They just opened their trunk and took out their guitars and started playing. I really did like the way they sang. They had a whole bunch of what are considered to be rockabilly songs right now. During that time I ended up with a handful of writers that I could more or less count on for material—Baker Knight, and Dorsey and Johnny Burnette. Subsequently I got to know them very well.

*What are your favorite cuts from the late '50s and early '60s?*

I'm not sure. It's so hard to say because they all had kind of a different flavor to them. At least I tried to make them different. I think "Lonesome Town" has a special meaning for me. It was probably one of the first records with just an acoustic guitar and the vocals.

*Have you wholeheartedly embraced advances in recording technology over the years?*

No. It's kind of a constant battle for me because all of the magical things have nothing to do with the technology. If anything, I think the technology gets in the way of overtones— you know, the generations-down tightening. Like "Hello Mary Lou" was about eight generations down. All of a sudden, we'd go to about the seventh generation and the cowbell started sounding like another kind of instrument. Those kinds of things are very difficult to duplicate.

*Do you find it more difficult to put together an album today?*

I always have to keep in mind that if the technology part of it is heard on record, it never quite makes it. So in a way it's a little more difficult for me. Every record company wants me to have a producer, which can make it easy if you have the right combination. If a producer can come in with really good material, it can kind of ease the burden and let you record. But if you get a producer who wants to change your image and this and that— you know what I mean.

*Did you enjoy producing your* Garden Party *album?*

Yeah, I really did. I wrote the song "Garden Party" in one night on one piece of paper—I didn't want to *move*. It was very strange because it was there to be written, and I could hear exactly what I wanted it to sound like on record. Then when I went into the studio and it started sounding that way, it was really exciting.

*What was the origin of that song?*

A promoter had been after me for about four years to do a rock and roll revival, and I was really opposed to it. He caught me at a weak moment because I had just formed the Stone Canyon Band, and I was writing a lot of material and playing colleges. So musically I was going in a whole other direction. I just thought, "Okay, I've never played Madison Square Garden," and started thinking of reasons why I should do it. I never quite convinced myself, really. I've never been very good at faking it like that. I really have to make a complete commitment to whatever I'm doing in order to have it be the least bit successful, and not just talk myself into it. I felt very out of place being there that night. It was a learning experience for me, a reminder to myself that you've got to do what you believe in.

*What do you view as the best period in rock and roll?*

I think right now it's wide open. And from playing all over—not just L.A. and New York, but *all* over the country—I think that people are really willing to accept all kinds of music. And for the first time, I don't think it has to necessarily fit into a specific slot, as far as *people* go. Maybe radio stations and the promotion people are going to have to fit it into a slot to get it played.

*Are there any contemporary rock performers you enjoy listening to?*

I like Pat Benatar a lot. I think she's great. There are so many bands, and they all have their own personalities. They end up having their own sound, which I think is great. It's a very healthy thing.

*Do you tour much?*

Oh yeah, really a lot—200 days a year. We've been doing a lot of high schools, and they are really rewarding because we're playing to a whole new group of people that just accept you at face value. It's a real good feeling when they like old songs like "Believe What You Say," which is a basic three-chord rock and roll song. If anything, punk rock and all that has come around a complete circle to the kind of music that I really understand and enjoy playing.

*Do you play your guitar much outside of performing?*

Yeah, I use it to play myself in and out of moods and to write. And it's weird—the best songs I've written have come from times when I wasn't necessarily thinking about writing songs or anything specific. It's just maybe a mood, and something started to happen. That's how "Garden Party" started out.

*Do you have any advice you'd give to young performers?*

I think you have to really enjoy performing a lot—that's something that has to be a prerequisite for anybody doing any kind of a job. I don't see how you can do a real good job on something that you're just going through the motions of doing. I thoroughly enjoy what I'm doing. [*Ed. Note: On New Year's Eve, 1985, Ricky Nelson, guitarist Bobby Neal, and band perished in an airplane tragedy in Texas.*]

---

## A SELECTED RICKY NELSON DISCOGRAPHY

(On United Artists): *Ricky*, LM 1004; *Legendary Masters*, LWB 9960; *Garden Party*, Decca, DL7-5391; *Four You*, Epic, 36868; *Playing To Win*, Capitol, SOO 12109. (On MCA): *All My Best*, 6163; *Decca Years*, 1517. (On Liberty): *I Need You*, LN 10304; *Legendary Masters*, LXB-9960; *Souvenirs*, LN-10205; *Teenage Idol*, LN 10253; *Rick Nelson Greatest Hits*, Rhino, RNLP 215; *Memphis Sessions*, Epic, FE 40388.

# WILLIE NELSON

**By Jim Hatlo**

WILLIE NELSON IS A MAN OF SURPRISES. "IMPROBable" is the mildest word that describes the course of his career from sideman to superstar, a career marked by so many odd twists, turns, and bumps that the story would be hard to pass off as convincing fiction. It isn't out of character, then, that as an instrumentalist he plays a type of guitar that country bandleaders aren't supposed to play, uses a technique usually reserved for another type of guitar altogether, and first chose to do so for one of the least likely reasons.

In place of the obligatory pearl-monogramed steel-string, Shotgun Willie packs a Martin short-scale N-20 *classical* guitar, one of perhaps only 277 ever built. In country circles, let alone the string music world at large, Martin classicals are about as common as Porsche limousines. And while manicured fingers are considered *de rigeur* for the playing of classical guitars, Willie uses a flatpick—which accounts for one of his instruments trademarks. In the soundboard, a ragged gash extends from near the lower quadrant of the soundhole rosette down almost to the treble end of the bridge saddle. Classical guitars traditionally do not have pickguards. Willie's instrument, after 15 years of flatpicking, provides an object lesson in why steel-string guitars usually *do.*

Even if the famous auxiliary soundhole, surrounded by pick-abraded bare wood, with skeletal brace ends and edges peeking through, never had formed on Willie's N-20, there would have been no question of the guitar's identity. Besides its battle scars, the soundboard bears the autographs of such artists as Roger Miller and Johnny Bush, along with other graffiti left—at the owner's invitation—during Willie's days as a Nashville songwriter who couldn't quite go over the top as a performer.

Why did Willie Nelson start using a classical guitar in the first place? Test your musical intuition by choosing one of the following: Willie switched to classical guitar because he wanted to *(a)*favor a weak left hand by changing to the lower tension of nylon strings; *(b)* inject an element of mariachi music into his Texas-based country stylings; *(c)* get a guitar that was strikingly different from those of his performing peers; *(d)* sound like France's Gypsy jazz guitar virtuoso, Django Reinhardt.

The correct answer is *(d).*

Any similarities between the style of Nelson and the style of Reinhardt are purely intentional. "I wanted to look for a guitar that I could use to find that tone that Django was getting," Willie says, referring to the sound of Django's unusual Selmer-Maccaferri steel-string acoustics. "The guitar that I am using now is the closest that I could find to that."

Most guitarists would figure that Willie was drawn to a nylon-string instrument because of its comparatively easygoing action. But he says that, in fact, the opposite is true.

"The action is really a lot slower than what you'd get on a regular Fender electric or something, which I used to play all the time," he explains. "I played a lot of Fenders and a lot of Gibsons—all electrics. I really didn't play the acoustic guitar onstage then, for the simple reason that the fingering was more difficult. But finally I sort of settled for the harder action to get the tone I wanted."

As a performer, Willie also settled for harder action to get the kind of results he wanted. For years he channelled royalties from a successful songwriting career into a money-losing band, so that he could play his music the way he wanted, with his "family" of loyal sidemen. He went against the Nashville grain in the early '70s, switching to a non-country label, recording in New York, and moving his base of operations to Texas. That earned him the label "outlaw," but it helped launch a new wave in country music that eventually overflowed into the rock and pop markets and carried Willie Nelson to megastar status. At present, his roll call of recording credits includes no less than eight gold albums, six platinum albums, one double-platinum album, and one triple-platinum album.

Ironically—or perhaps, characteristically—the triple-platinum album isn't country at all. It is *Stardust,* Willie's 1978 tribute to the standards (like "Stardust," "Blue Skies," "September Song," and "All Of Me") that he heard and loved as a boy in the '40s.

Born in the teeth of the Depression, April 1933, Willie grew up in Abbott, Texas, south of Fort Worth. His mother left home when he was six months old, and he was raised by his grandparents. His grandfather, a blacksmith, gave Willie his first guitar lesson at age six. Willie's grandmother, who wrote gospel songs, also played guitar. "I started out with a thumbpick," Willie recalls, "because that was what my grandparents used, so I was taught that way. But later on I began to hear players like Eldon Shamblin [of Bob Wills' Texas Playboys], and they used a straight pick. So I changed because that music was more what I wanted to play. When I was a kid I used to play the mandolin—fool with it a lot, and the banjo, and everything that had strings on it. I usually could get some sort of sound out of them. But I never really tried to get good on anything other than a guitar."

His older sister, Bobbie (now the pianist in Willie's band), was taking piano lessons, so the sheet music she brought home supplemented the songs he heard on the radio—World War II pop hits like "Coming In On A Wing And A Prayer" and "Don't Sit Under The Apple Tree (With Anyone Else But Me)." Through radio he also drank in *Grand Ole Opry* country music, western swing, and jazz. As he grew bigger, Willie earned $3 a day picking cotton with black field hands. What made the work bearable for him was the blues and work songs they sang.

At age 10 Willie made his professional debut, playing in a Bohemian polka band for $8 a night. He began working in a small group with Bobbie's husband on bass, and the local football coach on trumpet. Gradually he evolved a guitar style influenced by such players as Johnny Smith, Hank Garland, George Barnes, Barney Kessel, and Django Reinhardt. "I liked those rhythms that Django's band laid down, too," says Willie, "the stuff his brother Joseph played on rhythm guitar." Perennially eclectic, he also was drawn to the music of flamenco guitarist Carlos Montoya. "The Spanish flavor was something I always enjoyed anyway," he says, "so Montoya was one of my favorites from the beginning."

After high school he served a short stint in the Air Force during the Korean War, then spent the '50s working as a door-to-door salesman (variously selling vacuum cleaners, bibles, and encyclopedias), a plumber's helper, a used-car salesman, a janitor, a Sunday school teacher, and a disc jockey, all the while playing in bars and honky-tonks. And writing music. One of his first successful songs was "Family Bible." He sold the rights to it for $50, so he could buy groceries for his family. In 1959, he wrote his classic "Night Life," which would eventually be recorded by more than 70 different artists and sell over 30 million copies. But two years later he sold the rights to it for $150, which he used to buy a second-hand Buick. He used the Buick to move to Nashville.

Willie's work won quick recognition in Music City. Songwriter Hank Cochran heard Willie one night in Tootsie's Orchid Lounge, the bar that served as the unofficial artists' club room for the neighboring Grand Ole Opry, and signed him to a publishing contract. Singer Ray Price, who with Cochran was a part-owner in the publishing company, also was impressed. He made "Night Life" his theme song, and hired its author as a bass player.

Soon Patsy Cline had a huge hit with Nelson's "Crazy," and Faron Young had another with Willie's "Hello Walls." Liberty signed Willie to a recording contract, and he scored his first Top 10 country hit in 1962 with the single "Touch Me." He became a regular member of the *Grand Ole Opry* in 1964, and the following year he signed with RCA. But though he recorded more than a dozen albums for RCA between 1965 and 1971, Willie didn't enjoy the kind of success that other artists were having with his material.

One reason was his phrasing. Intrigued by crooner Frank Sinatra's knack for singing off, or against, the beat, Willie had adopted the technique in his own music. (That kind of phrasing often turns up in Willie's guitar solos.) But his producers saw Willie's use of rhythmical license as a liability, not an asset—and often remixed his studio tapes to get his voice back *on* the beat.

The results weren't impressive, commercially; and artistically they were frustrating for Willie. His substantial songwriting income allowed him to hold his road band together, however, and they kept the faith in live performances. "The music I played on a bandstand was better than the music I played in the studio," he once told Al Reinert of *New York Times Magazine.* "For one thing, I'd be using my own band, and we'd have a better feel for it—be more relaxed. We'd have an audience to play for, and it was just a whole lot more fun."

In 1969, in the middle of his second divorce, Willie's Nashville house burned down. His guitar was one of the few things he was able to save from the flames. While Willie's home was being rebuilt, he moved back to Texas—and stayed. He made the relocation official in 1972. Meanwhile, Willie and his

**The untraditional Willie Nelson has defined his own branch of progressive country music.**

band began hitting the Southwest tour circuit again; and with the expiration of his RCA contract, he left the Nashville studios behind as well. In 1971 he signed with Atlantic, which was venturing into the country market. It was a good move for both parties.

Given a free hand, Willie took his own band to New York to record *Shotgun Willie*. Finished in less than two days, the LP brought their "outlaw" sound out into the open. Within six months, sales of *Shotgun Willie* had surpassed the sales of all his Nashville albums combined.

From there the successes began to snowball. *Phases And Stages*, completed in 1974 as Atlantic wound down its country operations, sold 400,000 copies. Meanwhile, the Nashville songwriting fraternity saluted his earlier contributions to country music by inducting him into the Nashville Songwriters Hall Of Fame in 1973.

Willie formed his own record company, signed a distribution agreement with Columbia, and in 1975 released *Red-Headed Stranger*. From that came the single "Blue Eyes Cryin' In The Rain," which gave him his first Top 10 country hit in 13 years and won him his first Grammy Award. (It also documented a rare reversion to fingerstyle playing on the guitar solo. "I didn't use a pick on that one," Willie says. "Sometimes I use my thumb by itself, to get a softer sound. On 'Blue Eyes,' that was strictly thumb and fingers.")

*Red-Headed Stranger* was certified gold in March 1976, and before the month was out Willie shared in the plaudits as RCA's *The Outlaws*—a compilation featuring the music of Willie, Waylon Jennings, Jessi Colter, and Tompall Glaser—also earned gold record status. Honors and hit records came almost predictably thereafter. Among his laurels to date are eight Country Music Association awards, including Best Album (twice), Best Singer (twice), Best Vocal Duo (with Waylon Jennings in 1976, with Merle Haggard in 1983, and with Julio Iglesias in 1984), and Entertainer of the Year—a title conferred on him in 1979 by both the CMA and the Academy of Country Music.

Willie no longer has to worry about breaking even outside the studio. This summer, Willie Nelson & Family was number 14 in *Billboard Magazine's* list of top-grossing concert appearances (a roster on which the much-hyped Victory Tour by the Jacksons sewed up six of the top 12 spots). Willie also is listed as one of the top ten money-earners on the Las Vegas showroom circuit

(along with his old idol, Frank Sinatra).

But despite all the justifiable to-do about his gilt-edged performing status, Willie still prefers to think of himself first and foremost as a picker.

"What I always liked to do was be the guitar player," he says. "Somewhere along the way, I started being the singer. I'm not sure how that happened. I think one night the front man didn't show up, and I wound up fronting the band and doing the singing. And I don't know if that was really the best day of my life! I really do like to be just the guitar player, sometimes. It's very enjoyable when the only responsibility you have is playing the guitar."

\* \* \* \*

*WHEN YOU ARE PLAYING LEAD, WHAT'S GOING ON IN your mind? Are you thinking of the chord changes, or melodic patterns on the fretboard, or modes related to the key of the tune, or positions you like to work from?*

Not consciously. I think probably if somebody put a computer on me, they'd find I use a lot of things the same way. But consciously—I just play off the top of my head. On the songs that I do a lot, I guess I'm subconsciously aware of the chord structures and I just play whatever notes I hear that fall within those. I really don't think about all that. I guess I'm playing from somewhere else.

*Do you work out solos ahead of time? Often, when you're fronting your band, your solos will restate the melody. But in some situations—on the* Angel Eyes *album, for example—you'll take what sounds like a more spontaneous lead break.*

It's all how I feel at the moment. I really am not confined to playing anything the same way. I don't have any arrangements that I try to follow, other than the basic things that are always there in a tune—the stuff that you can't get around. Whenever anyone in the band takes choruses, they just play what they want to play.

*Back in 1976 when you were interviewed by our sister magazine,* Guitar Player, *you said that in doing solos you didn't get into a lot of minor scales, because you felt you were major-chord oriented. Now that you're playing things closer to mainstream jazz, is that still true?*

I think so. I love minor chords, and I have written some songs with minors in them. But basically, the songs that I listened to and learned in the beginning were major-chord songs.

*Is that when you developed your feeling for standards like "Stardust"? Would it be fair to say that growing up with that kind of material helped you learn how to put together well-crafted melodies?*

I think it very well could have. I was always exposed to those songs through the radio and through music that came into the house—sheet music, and so forth. I love good melodies, so I'm sure that had a lot of influence on me.

*Through albums like* Stardust *and* Angel Eyes, *you've probably influenced a lot of younger musicians yourself, giving them their first exposure to standards and jazz. Do you have any other styles of music up your sleeve—material you might record in the future?*

There are some of the older styles I still haven't done, like

Stephen Foster songs, and old Sons Of The Pioneers things—the real cowboy songs like "Leaning On The Old Top Rail" and "Empty Cot In The Bunkhouse Tonight." All of those classics are still there to do.

*Often you're functioning as a rhythm player. In your opinion, what goes into really playing rhythm as well as it can be played?*

I think you have to know the chord forms. I think guys like Paul Buskirk and Homer Haynes are two of my favorites because of their styles. [*Ed. Note: Mandolinist Paul Buskirk and guitarist Henry "Homer" Haynes (half of the team of Homer & Jethro) had strong elements of swing in their music.*] It's 4/4 rhythm and it's done with drums; but I really like the sound of the kind of rhythm section where you just have an upright bass and the rhythm guitar.

*Does a rhythm guitarist need a special sensitivity to where the lead player is going?*

Yes, I think that's an innate thing that most good rhythm guitarists know, because most rhythm guitar players are also lead guitar players, to a certain degree. So you just have a feel of when to play and when not to play, or how loud to play.

*When you're chording, do you ever use your thumb to fret notes?*

Yeah, a lot of times. I do that especially in open-chord rhythms. For instance, on a [first-position] *D* chord I'll use the thumb on the low *E* string to play an *F#*.

*You generally use Fender medium flatpicks on your nylon-string guitar, instead of fingerpicking it. How often do you change picks? Some steel-string players have told us they go through a half-dozen a night, because the picks get worn and start sounding scratchy. But it would seem that nylon strings would be easier on a flatpick.*

I guess a normal person probably would be able to make them last longer, but there's one tune we do each night—"Bloody Mary Morning"—where I'll go through a pick every time I play it.

*You can hear the difference? The pick starts to sound rough?*
No—I just break it.

*Do you play with the point of the pick, or do you turn it and use the rounded corner for a mellower sound, as some players do?*

I try to keep it on the point, but in the course of "Bloody Mary Morning" I play every side of it, I think! I use up a couple of picks a night, because "Bloody Mary Morning" will take care of one, and "Whiskey River" will eat up another; so I'll go through at least two picks, and maybe three, every show.

*You used to use ball-end La Bella nylon strings. Are you still staying with that brand?*

As far as I know, I am. The strings are automatically changed on my guitar every few days by a guy in our crew, and I'm not sure if he is still using La Bellas or not. I can't tell any difference.

*Are there certain strings you're more likely to break than others? Some players find that the G string is the first to go, for example.*

I very rarely break strings. In fact, I don't remember the last string I broke. The picks go before the strings do, because the nylon strings are more flexible.

*The nylon strings are one of the things that set your sound apart; but the way you amplify your guitar has a lot to do with that, too, doesn't it.*

I think so. It's a Baldwin amp with a Martin classical guitar—which is kind of a bastard situation. I've tried other combinations, and I don't get the same sound that I do with this one, which was really accidental.

*Didn't the pickup itself come from a Baldwin guitar that got broken?*

Yeah, I had it taken out of the Baldwin and put in this one years ago, by Shot Jackson's place in Nashville. [*Ed. Note: In the late '60s, after Baldwin acquired Gretsch and began marketing a line of guitar amplifiers, the company briefly offered a classical guitar model with a ceramic piezo-electric pickup, and a companion amplifier designed for a "natural" tone response.*] I've never changed it. I've tried to keep everything exactly the same, and the amplifier is still the same one. They don't make Baldwins any more, you know. Each time I come across a used Baldwin amp, I try to buy it so I can use the parts for replacements on this one. I've got a couple of them.

*You've had a lot of work done on your guitar to keep it in service through all your years of touring. Who handles the repairs?*

A guy named Newman in Austin, Texas. He has a guitar shop in the Opera House in Austin, and he's been fixing my guitar for years.

*Do you carry any other acoustic guitars on the road with you, or keep some at home that you just use for recording?*

I have a couple of guitars around the house, and sometimes I have one on the bus just to fool around with, but my stage guitar is my main guitar. The others are a variety of things—just whatever is available. It varies from one day to the next, really.

*How many days a year are you on the road?*

I think probably somewhere between 200 and 250. That's this year. It's been like that practically every year, and each year I say, 'Next year I'm going to slow down.' But I still like doing it. I just enjoy playing music a lot.

---

### A SELECTED WILLIE NELSON DISCOGRAPHY

**Solo albums** (on Columbia): *To Lefty From Willie*, PC-34965; *Stardust*, JC-35306; *Somewhere Over The Rainbow*, FC-36883; *Red Headed Stranger*, KC-33482; *The Sound In Your Mind*, KC-34092. (On RCA): *Willie Nelson, Live*, APLI-1487; *The Outlaws*, RCA, APLI-1321; *What Can You Do To Me Now?*, APLI-1234; *Yesterday's Wine*, ANLI-1102; *The Words Don't Fit The Picture*, LSP-4653; *Spotlight On Willie Nelson*, RCA/Camden, ACLI-0705. (On United Artists): *The Best Of Willie Nelson*, UA-LA086-G; *Country Willie*, UA-LA410-G. (On Atlantic): *Phases & Stages*, 7291; *Shotgun Willie*, 7262. **With Leon Russell:** *One For The Road*, Columbia, KC2 36064. **With Roger Miller:** *Old Friends*, Columbia, PC-38013, **With Johnny Cash/Waylon Jennings/Kris Kristofferson:** *Highwayman*, Columbia, FC 40056.

# GRAND OLE OPRY

By Robert K. Oermann

COUNTRY MUSIC'S "MOTHER CHURCH" IS THE *GRAND Ole Opry*, both a radio show (still broadcast over Nashville's station WSM) and an institution that are without parallel in American music. Today it is perhaps best known for its vocal stars, the Porter Wagoners, Conway Twittys, Loretta Lynns, and Dolly Partons of show business' rhinestone set. But the venerable Opry has always been a magnet for country instrumentalists of superior ability. Through the years this oldest of American radio shows has showcased performers who, through their very presence on the Opry, made significant instrumental contribu-

tions to popular music, and thereby helped foster the growth of new playing styles. Because of the exposure given to those great artists, for more than a half a century the Opry has profoundly affected the evolution of acoustic string music in America.

When the *Grand Ole Opry* was founded in 1925, it was designed to feature instrumentalists. The program's original guiding spirit, the "Solemn Old Judge" George D. Hay, perceived the *Grand Ole Opry* as a showcase for the pickers and stylists of the rural mid-South. This had the effect of preserving and promoting musical styles that were fading in sophisticated urban areas. Thus, one of the early Opry's most important cultural contributions was its popularization of the breakdowns, jigs, reels, and fiddle tunes that now form the backbone of country instrumentation. Hay actively solicited string-band musicians who could play the lively music of square dances; and he originally referred to the program as a radio "Saturday night barn dance." Most of the early Opry performers were local farmers and tradesmen. Hay admonished them to "keep it close to the ground" musically. He also dressed them up in hillbilly attire and gave them colorful names like Gully Jumpers, Fruit Jar Drinkers, Dixie Clodhoppers, and Possum Hunters. With musical advice and a suitable entertainment image, he turned them loose on the world with his weekly exclamation, "Take it away, boys!"

The first performer George Hay discovered was a 77-year-old fiddler named Uncle Jimmy Thompson. Uncle Jimmy's debut performance over WSM radio on November 28, 1925, is the accepted date for the birth of the *Grand Ole Opry*. Thompson was a Tennessean who had spent much of his youth in Texas. Thus, he had synthesized the tradition-based Tennessee fiddle style and the more showy Texas style by the time he began winning fiddle contests. He reportedly knew over 375 fiddle tunes and boasted that he could play for eight hours straight without repeating himself. His debut WSM number is said to have been "Tennessee Waggoner"; and his recordings ("Karo," "Billy Wilson," "Lynchburg"), were also of vintage fiddle pieces. Uncle Jimmy was the Nashville area fiddle champion of 1926, the year that the old-time fiddle craze peaked in the U.S.

Many of the best early Opry fiddlers led the hoedown bands. George Wilkerson of the Fruit Jar Drinkers, Oscar Stone of the Possum Hunters, Charlie Arlington of the Gully Jumpers, and Gale Binkley of the Dixie Clodhoppers, were all excellent square-dance fiddlers. In addition to Uncle Jimmy, there were several to demonstrate their flashy styles. These included Uncle Bunt Stephens, Henry Bandy, Sid Harkreader, and Blind Joe Mangrum.

In the '20s the fiddle was the dominant string instrument in country music. Country music did not become guitar-based until the '30s. Thus, the old-time fiddle tunes formed the Opry's musical cornerstone.

Despite this, there were several notable early Opry performers who became widely renowned on other instruments. In fact, three of the Opry's biggest stars actually were harmonica players. The first man to play country music over Nashville radio (before Hay founded the Opry) was harmonica player Dr. Humphrey Bate, the leader of the Possum Hunters. Bate recorded more than Uncle Jimmy Thompson, broadcast for a longer period of time, and went on tour before any other Opry act hit the road. His string band's music was arguably better than

Thompson's. Bate traded off leads with his fiddlers, playing in a clean, clear precise style that made him extremely popular. Nevertheless, elderly Uncle Jimmy's showmanship and Hay's promotion of Thompson as the Opry's founding act have overshadowed Bate's considerable contribution.

Dr. Humphrey Bate influenced Herman Crook, who began playing Nashville house parties with his brother and wife before moving to radio in 1926. Herman transposed many classic fiddle tunes for the harmonica and developed a startling, rapid style that remains quite impressive. Today, at the age of 84, Herman Crook still stands up to the WSM microphone each week to play behind the high-stepping clog dancers on the program.

The third harmonica player on the show was "The Harmonica Wizard," Deford Bailey. Bailey was unquestionably one of the most musically innovative performers that ever appeared on the program. He was a crippled black man who played a synthesis of white hillbilly music and blues/jazz. His repertoire ranged from railroad songs to fiddle melodies to lazy blues. He could mesmerize an audience with harmonica and nothing more. It was Bailey's performance style, in fact, that named the radio show.

The barn dance followed a classical music program one Saturday night in 1927, and Deford was scheduled to open with his "Pan American Blues," a number that imitated the rush of a locomotive. Coincidentally, the classical program ended with a symphonic piece depicting a train. George D. Hay ad-libbed, "For the past hour we have been listening to music taken largely from Grand Opera; but from now on, we will present the *Grand Ole Opry!*" Deford Bailey wailed into his harmonica solo, and the barn dance had a name forever more.

Bailey once called Uncle Dave Macon, "the best white banjo player I ever heard." Deford and Uncle Dave were the *Grand Ole Opry*'s first real "stars"; and in his own way Macon was the musical match of the black hillbilly. Uncle Dave was a master of the clawhammer, or frailing, old-time banjo style. He utilized his techniques on a wide variety of material, including vaudeville numbers, folk songs, gospel melodies, and dance tunes. He was a wide-open stylist who banged and flailed wildly on his instrument, more concerned with showmanship than musicianship; but even today he is revered and imitated by students of old-time banjo.

In 1928 Macon brought the Opry its first great guitarist, Sam McGee, a blacksmith whom Uncle Dave discovered playing "Missouri Waltz" on a little Martin guitar in Franklin, Tennessee. Uncle Dave became McGee's mentor and employer, and introduced the world to one of the most creative guitarists in the history of country music. The technical virtuosity he displayed on his many recordings is still impressive today. Influenced equally by ragtime, blues, sedate parlor music, and dance tunes, McGee brought verve and panache to old-time guitar playing. His brother/partner Kirk McGee is known principally as a singer, but he is no slouch as a guitar picker, either. Kirk prefers the more serious, stately, sentimental numbers to his late brother's light-hearted romps; and he can still be heard performing these on the modern Opry.

Early Opry shows also featured the hammered dulcimer. This lovely instrument was played by Kitty Cora Cline, but after she left the program its intricate, delicate, bell-like tones were not heard on the *Grand Ole Opry* for some 50 years. Grandpa Jones' daughter Alissa brought the hammered dulcimer back, in

The Ryman Auditorium, the original home of the *Grand Ole Opry*.

the '80s.

Obed "Dad" Pickard, known as the One-Man Orchestra, supposedly could play any instrument in the orchestra except the clarinet; and on late-'20s Opry shows he performed with fiddle, mandolin, guitar, Jew's harp, and banjo. If recorded evidence is any guide, however, Pickard was more of a novelty act than he was a musical prodigy. On the other hand, his Pickard Family, as vocal popularizers of authentic folk songs, had few peers.

In the '30s the *Grand Ole Opry* acquired the services of one of the greatest old-time fiddlers of the South, Fiddlin' Arthur Smith. Only the late Clayton McMichen of Georgia came close to him in this art form. Smith came to the Opry in 1930 to work with Sam McGee and Uncle Dave Macon, but his superb technique was already developed by then. His style, with its extraordinary drive and speed, anticipated bluegrass fiddling. His combination of a long bow technqiue with masterful noting and a breakneck pace made him the most influential fiddler of his era.

When Arthur Smith recorded for the first time in 1935, his accompanists were Alton and Rabon Delmore. The Delmore Brothers had joined the *Grand Ole Opry* in 1932. They were unusual among brother-duet acts of the '30s for several reasons. Their songs had a heavy blues influence, whereas most similar teams drew inspiration from gospel or mountain music. They were also considerably more adept as instrumentalists than were many of their contemporaries; and their rippling twin-guitar runs gave them a sound like no other.

Alton, the duet's composer, developed the Delmore Brothers' sound from his eccentric tenor guitar playing. He had developed the style by playing his flat-top like a banjo; and he taught it to Rabon. He also believed in using the guitar as a melody instrument and practiced by playing songs on it as though it were a piano or violin. This, too, was unusual, for the guitar was almost always used as a rhythm instrument in country music of that time. Maybelle Carter and Riley Puckett also were bringing the guitar out of the rhythm shadows and into the lead instrument spotlight during this period.

The great Roy Acuff arrived at the *Grand Ole Opry* in 1938. His contributions to country music history are as a singer, songwriter, and businessman. As an instrumentalist he is something of a lightweight; but the ranks of his Smoky Mountain Boys band have been filled with superb musicians. The current edition, for instance, includes the brilliant dobro stylist Pete "Bashful Brother Oswald" Kirby, the dynamic harmonica virtuoso Ohio Wheeler, the gifted flat-top picker Charlie Collins, and the masterfully fluid fiddler Howdy Forrester. No lover of acoustic music could fail to give this combination its due as one of the purest delights of any Opry Saturday night.

The same can be said of Bill Monroe's Blue Grass Boys, through which have passed some of the finest acoustic musicians in the world. Monroe came to the Opry in October 1939, and set about building the group that would come to define and name a new musical genre. David "Stringbean" Akeman, later a solo Opry star, was an early old-style banjo player in the Blue Grass Boys. Monroe's fiddlers have included Carl Story, Jimmy Shumate, Howdy Forrester, Chubby Wise, Bobby Hicks, Richard Greene, Buddy Spicher, Vassar Clements, Byron Berline, Tommy Jackson, Benny Williams, and Kenny Baker. His guitarists have included Clyde Moody, Mac Wiseman, Jimmy

Martin, Carl Butler, Lester Flatt, Peter Rowan, Del McCoury, Jackie Phelps, Bob Fowler, and Roland White. All of these men were masters of their instruments and contributed mightily to the development of what Monroe calls "my music." Nevertheless, historians point to the hiring of Earl Scruggs into the band in 1945 as the true beginning of bluegrass music.

Scruggs' innovative three-finger style revolutionized banjo playing. Until him, Opry banjo pickers like Uncle Dave Macon, Grandpa Jones, and Stringbean, had worked within the old clawhammer or drop-thumb styles. Earl's rapid three-finger rolls rained notes on the audience in a clean, precise, yet complex shower of sound. This, more than any other factor, defined the emerging bluegrass style.

Earl Scruggs and Lester Flatt left Monroe in the late '40s and founded their own group. Flatt's singing, songwriting, and distinctive guitar runs, coupled with Scruggs-style banjo, made Flatt And Scruggs the most popular bluegrass band in history. They appeared regularly on the *Grand Ole Opry* from 1955 to 1969.

Monroe replaced Scruggs with Don Reno, who developed his own three-finger style independently of Earl. The equally-gifted Sonny Osborne succeeded Reno. In the '60s Blue Grass Boy Bill Keith lifted banjo picking to new heights with his chromatic style, which allowed players to flow up and down the scales with the fluidity of a fiddler. Vic Jordan, Curtis McPeake, Joe Drumright, Don Stover, and Butch Robins have been just a few of Monroe's other outstanding banjo men over the years.

Bill Monroe was by no means the Opry's only early mandolin master. Lonzo & Oscar, who joined the Opry in 1942, are generally thought of as a comedy act; but in serious musical moments they could more than hold their own. Rollin "Oscar" Sullivan looks goofy, yet he is a dynamic snappy mandolinist when the occasion demands. In recent years, he has displayed this talent more and more on Opry shows.

Jesse McReynolds, perhaps the most respected country mandolin player of all, joined the Opry in 1964. As half of Jim And Jesse, he has employed such top-of-the-line band members as banjo pickers Bobby Thompson, Vic Jordan, and Allen Shelton, fiddlers Vassar Clements and Blaine Sprouse. The Osborne Brothers also joined the show in 1964. Bobby's mandolin prowess, Sonny's banjo playing, and the pair's use of electric instruments resulted in the coining of the term "newgrass" to identify their bluegrass hybrid style.

Electric instruments, like bluegrass, first came to the Opry in the '40s. Paul Howard, who joined the cast in 1942, believes his band was the first to use electric guitar on the hallowed stage; but Sam McGee always claimed he predated this. Pee Wee King, who most definitely brought the accordion to center stage on the show, had an electric guitar in his band when he rejoined the Opry in 1941; and Ernest Tubb brought one from the Texas honky-tonks when he joined in 1942.

Tubb's Texas Troubadours have included several fine pickers, notably pioneer country electric guitarists Jimmie Short and Billy Byrd, and steel guitar legends Jerry Byrd and Buddy Emmons. Emmons, who with Shot Jackson virtually invented the modern pedal steel guitar, was also a member of Ray Price's Cherokee Cowboys band and of Jimmy Dickens' band, both of which were Opry acts of considerable stature. His astounding jazz-based stylings have graced a number of excellent solo albums in the past decade, and his creativity has influenced acoustic musicians as well as electric instrumentalists.

Johnny And Jack became an Opry act in 1947, left to join the *Louisiana Hayride* in Shreveport, Louisiana, then came back to the Opry in 1952. Besides bringing the future Queen of Country Music, Kitty Wells, with them, these two contributed the innovations of rumba and Latin rhythms in their playing.

Hank Snow also developed the country rumba style. Chiefly known as a singing stylist, Snow is also a brilliant flat-top guitarist. On the occasions when he treats the Opry audience to instrumental solos he demonstrates great taste and finesse.

Mother Maybelle Carter and the Carter Sisters joined the *Grand Ole Opry* in 1950. The Mother of Country Music was at the peak of her powers as an instrumentalist at this time. In the early '30s Maybelle's guitar style of picking melody on the bass strings while brushing time on the treble ones lifted the instrument out of its role as a rhythm-keeper. Her playing, coupled with Gene Autry's Sears catalog marketing of the guitar, were probably the most important factors in bringing it to the forefront of American popular music. Even today, beginning guitarists pick out Carter Family melodies in Mother Maybelle's style. Maybelle Carter was never a flashy instrumental soloist, but her technique of lightly sketching in melodies was deceptively simple. Her clean, concise, crisp playing was consistently excellent. In later years, when she felt her guitar style had slipped, she switched to autoharp and transformed it as well. Not content to strum chords on the instrument, she began picking out dainty, intricate melodies on the complex, multi-stringed autoharp.

Maybelle brought daughter Helen along. At first, Helen was that rare creature, the country accordion player; but in time her mother passed the guitar gauntlet to her. An even more significant contribution of the Carter sisters' act, however, was its additional guitar accompanist, Chet Atkins.

Atkins had been in Nashville once before, but it was as a part of Maybelle Carter's show that he arrived to stay. Mr. Guitar was soon performing solo spots on the *Grand Ole Opry*; and from there he moved into Nashville studio work. His versatility, quick-study talent, and faultless execution are legendary. Now the most recorded instrumentalist in history, this virtuoso tackles jazz, classical, flamenco, and country techniques with equal ease.

Chet, 1982's Instrumentalist of the Year in the annual Country Music Association awards, has recorded with several Opry guitarists. He and Hank Snow have teamed up on acoustic duets; and he also has played with Don Gibson, who joined the show in 1958. Gibson's considerable songwriting talents have tended to overshadow his great gifts as an Atkins-influenced guitarist.

Billy Grammer joined the Opry in 1959. He remains a weekly *Grand Ole Opry* performer today. Billy is, of course, the originator of the Grammer Guitar. An electric guitar stylist, Grammer initially innovated the use of pickups for amplification. He has recently switched to flat-top picking of sentimental melodies and folk songs. He plays with intriguing variations in volume and sustains, and superbly brings out the nuances of melody.

Not all was innovation and instrumental experimentation in the '50s. The bands of Hank Williams, Webb Pierce, Faron Young, Marty Robbins, Stonewall Jackson, Carl Smith, Ray Price, and Porter Wagoner contained dozens of outstanding instru-

mentalists who were firmly rooted in country tradition. Porter's exuberant fiddler Mac Magaha and Stonewall's one-time harmonica player Charlie McCoy are just two examples.

Eddy Arnold brought steel guitar pioneer Roy Wiggins to Nashville in 1944, and kept him on the Opry into the '50s. He remains on the show today, backing acts like Ernie Ashworth.

Wilma Lee and Stoney Cooper brought their fusion of mountain music and bluegrass to the Opry in 1957. Their Clinch Mountain Clan has included dobro stylists Buck Graves and Bill Carver, and bluegrass banjo wizards Vic Jordan and Butch Robins. In addition, Wilma Lee is an adept clawhammer banjo picker; and Stoney was, of course a master fiddler.

Another longtime Opry "show" or "trick" fiddler was Curly Fox. He still occasionally makes spectacular guest appearances. When Fox and his late wife Texas Ruby were more regular Opry members in the '50s, a frequent Saturday night guest was Floyd Cramer, the famous "slip-note" piano innovator.

The Everly Brothers were once *Grand Ole Opry* members who brought rockabilly guitar-playing to the show. So did Johnny Cash, who brought both Luther and Carl Perkins with him when he played Opry engagements.

Doug Kershaw, when he was a *Grand Ole Opry* member, demonstrated the manic, sawing Cajun fiddle style that has made him renowned. Jimmy C. Newman has maintained the Cajun tradition on the *Grand Ole Opry*. His Cajun Country band, featuring concertina, electric guitar, and fiddle leads is one of the most exciting groups to be seen on the current shows.

Women came into their own in country music during the '60s and '70s. Of the Opry's many female stars, the most interesting instrumentalists are Dolly Parton and Barbara Mandrell. Although Parton seldom demonstrates it, she is an extremely capable country guitarist and banjoist. Mandrell actually began her career as an instrumental performer. As a teenager she was a professional steel guitar demonstrator/instructor; and she still features this aspect of her talents in her live shows. She also adroitly plays banjo, sax, and drums.

In recent years the *Grand Ole Opry* has held up its instrumental tradition admirably. In fact, the show's 1982 cast additions are two of the finest instrumental units on today's scene. The nouveau-western group Riders In The Sky features the fluid guitar rhythms of Doug Green, as well as the superb country-jazz lead fiddling of Woody Paul. Ricky Skaggs, winner of the Country Music Association's 1982 Best Male Vocalist and Horizon awards, has a band that is arguably the tightest country group on the road today. Ricky's multi-instrumental abilities on mandolin, fiddle, banjo, and guitar are awesome. Under his leadership, his band is fired and inspired. British rocker Ray Flacke [electric guitar], ex-Poco member George Grantham [drums], R&B trained Jesse Chambers [bass], Bill Monroe veteran Bobby Hicks [fiddle], gospel-influenced Mickey Merritt [piano], commercial country journeymen Bruce Bouton [steel guitar], and bluegrass utility man Lou Reid [guitar, fiddle, banjo, bass] make sweet music indeed when they take flight with Skaggs.

Both Skaggs' group and the Opry's house band were nominated for Instrumental Group of the Year honors by the Country Music Association in 1982. Those groups, and the other gifted instrumentalists who step up to the WSM microphones each week are upholding the glorius Opry tradition of great picking that began back in 1925.

# TEX RITTER

**By Doug Green**

WOODWARD MAURICE RITTER WAS BORN TO A prominent east Texas family near Murvaul, in Panola County, on January 12, 1905. He was not a cowboy, as such, but he grew up with a love of and a respect for cowboy lore and music. Although he majored in pre-law at the University of Texas in Austin, he spent much of his time absorbing the learning of cowboy folk-song scholars J. Frank Dobie and John A. Lomax.

Ritter went to law school for a year at Northwestern University in Illinois before the call of the entertainment business became too strong. He headed for New York in the late '20s. By 1930, he was appearing in the role of Cord Elam while doubling as understudy to the lead in the successful Broadway production of *Green Grow The Lilacs.* It was the first of five Broadway shows in which he was to appear during the early '30s.

Aside from his work on Broadway, Woodward Ritter—soon to acquire the nickname Tex—was a busy man. He obtained work on two separate radio shows, co-hosting the WHN *Barn Dance,* New York's answer to the *Grand Ole Opry;* and singing and acting in *Cowboy Tom's Round-up.* In addition, he made his first records while in New York, recording for Uncle Art Satherley at ARC (the American Record Company). His first recording—never released—was "The Cowboy's Christmas Ball," cut on October 31, 1932; his most popular in his brief stay with ARC was "Rye Whiskey."

In 1935 Tex moved to Decca Records, then in its infancy. There he recorded a number of authentic cowboy songs, including "Get Along Little Dogies" and "Sam Hall," and later recorded songs from his films for the label. His years with Decca were frustrating, however, because although his sales were steady no hit records emerged.

With the sudden, unexpected, and overwhelming cinema success of Gene Autry as a singing cowboy, most studios and producers rushed out to look for singing cowboys of their own. Edward Finney, working out a deal with Grand National, settled on Tex Ritter as a prospect. "I wanted to make a series that would be really western, with a personality who sang a good song," Finney said later. "I listened to some of the records he (Ritter) had made for Decca and they were exactly what I had in mind."

Finney could not have made a better choice. While many studios attempted to foist operatic and pop singers on the public as singing cowboys, Ritter, though not truly a cowboy, was a Texan with a great love of genuine cowboy songs and lore. His rough-hewn voice suggested authority and authenticity unmatched among singing cowboys, making him an extraordinarily effective, believable singer. The believability accounted for much of his success on film and on record. Though their voices were different, Ritter and Autry had what other singing cowboys lacked; a laid-back unpretentious quality in their styles and tones that matched cowboy music and the cowboy image. No pop singer could duplicate it.

Tex Ritter's first film for Grand National was *Song Of The Gringo,* released November 22, 1936. It was quickly followed by *Headin' For The Rio Grande,* released December 20. Tex made 12 films for Grand National before moving over to Monogram in 1938, where he made 20 more. Two of these Monogram films were especially interesting: *Take Me Back To Oklahoma* (1940) featured the first film appearances of Bob Wills and his Texas Playboys; *The Pioneers* (1941) marked the film debut of Red Foley.

Tex and Wild Bill Elliot began co-starring in a series of eight films for Columbia midway through 1941. Tex then co-starred with Johnny Mack Brown in a similar series for Universal during 1942 and 1943. In 1944 he starred in two final films for Universal before beginning a series—of which he was ultimately not proud—for the low-budget PRC outfit. His PRC pictures ended with *Flaming Bullets,* his 60th film, late in 1945. Although Tex appeared in several more films through the years, a couple of them country music spectaculars of the '60s, *Flaming Bullets* closed out his career as a singing cowboy. In fact, it marked the beginning of the end of the singing cowboy film, for after World War II that genre became a dying entertainment form.

Of all the singing cowboys, Tex, Gene Autry, and Jimmy Wakely were the lucky ones: They were real country singers who had more than their screen presence to rely on. All were able to continue profitable and successful recording careers while their contemporaries just died on the vine.

Ritter's recording career hit a remarkable hot streak shortly after he signed with the newly formed Capitol label in 1942. The first song he recorded for Capitol proved to be his first real hit

America. In addition, he and longtime friend and business partner Johnny Bond co-hosted the popular Los Angeles television program *Town Hall Party* from 1953 to 1960. The show proved to be the launching ground for a number of entertainers, including Freddie Hart, and the then 11-year-old Barbara Mandrell, and it featured such musical heavyweights as Merle Travis in addition to its genial co-hosts.

Doubtless the highlight of Ritter's career in the '50s was the success of "High Noon," which he recorded in 1952. It became immensely popular the following year as the theme of the film of the same name, ultimately winning an Academy Award.

A lifelong student of western history and a deep lover of traditional music, Tex was instrumental in planning and organizing the Country Music Foundation and the Country Music Hall of Fame in the early '60s. A tireless supporter and booster of country music, Tex was eager to establish a place where its history would be carefully preserved. He was also largely responsible for inducing the renowned Missouri muralist Thomas Hart Benton to undertake painting "The Sources of Country Music," and was instrumental in getting that art project funded. It is to Ritter's memory that the painting, now a major exhibit at the Country Music Hall of Fame, is dedicated.

Tex was himself elected to the Country Music Hall of Fame in 1964. The following year he left Hollywood, feeling perhaps that the country music scene there was paling. He moved to Nashville, where he became a member of the *Grand Ole Opry* and began hosting a late-night radio program over WSM. Acting on a lifelong dream he even made a bid for political office, running for the U.S. Senate in 1970.

No dilettante as an instrumentalist, Tex owned a small collection of extremely fine guitars and had used several of them in his films. In later years he favored a Fender flat-top for performing, doubtless feeling more secure with it on the road in that it was far more replaceable than his Gibson SJ-200, his Martin OOO-45, or even the Martin D-28 he used for a time in the '50s.

If he was in poor health late in his life he didn't show it. He continued a rigorous touring schedule though well into his '60s and he maintained his keen interest in country music and its history. He died of a sudden heart attack on January 3, 1974, in Nashville.

Tex Ritter was unquestionably one of the most popular singers and actors in the history of country music, but he was much more: He was genuinely, passionately interested in the lore of country music and in its protection and preservation, and through his untiring efforts much of that historical preservation was accomplished. He was a kind and thoughtful man who spoke for the dignity of country music, both in Hollywood and on tour, through four decades of that music's growth. He was what every entertainer would hope to be; unaffected at his peak, gracious in his decline, and concerned with his music's origins and excellence throughout. There will never be another quite like him.

record, "Jingle Jangle Jingle," and the first song of his next session was a bigger hit yet: "There's A New Moon Over My Shoulder," recorded late in 1943 and tremendously popular in 1944. "I'm Wasting My Tears On You" was another big 1944 record. Hit records came thick and fast in 1945, with "You Two Timed Me One Time Too Often," "Rye Whiskey," "Green Grow The Lilacs," and "Boll Weevil."

The hits did not come in quite such a rush after that, but they came steadily, with Capitol recordings such as "Deck of Cards" (1948), "High Noon" (1952), "The Wayward Wind" (1956), and "I Dreamed Of A Hillbilly Heaven" (1961).

After the singing cowboy era began to fade, Ritter's film career was dwindling as his recording career was on the upsurge, Tex became one of the most traveled entertainers in

---

**A SELECTED TEX RITTER DISCOGRAPHY**

**Solo albums:** (on Capitol): *American Legend*, SKC-11241; *Hillbilly Heaven*, SN-16201. (On Gusto): *Country Gospel*, 0069; *Riding Hard*, 0082.

# HARGUS "PIG" ROBBINS

By Doug B. Green

ON OCTOBER 11TH, 1976, AN ATTRACTIVE OPRYLAND attendant led a tall, husky, blind pianist to center stage at the *Grand Ole Opry* house, where, before a national televison audience, he was presented with the country Music Association Award for top country instrumentalist of the year, topping such luminaries as Chet Atkins, Charlie McCoy, Johnny Gimble, and Roy Clark.

For Hargus "Pig" Robbins, this award represented the culmination of years of dedication and hard work. Although not widely known to the general public, this young man who plunked his first notes out while in grade school at the Tennessee School for the Blind is one of the most respected—and most widely heard—session musicians in Nashville's thriving studio scene. His playing can be heard on scores of popular country music albums, including Tom T. Hall's *Faster Horses*, George Jones' *Alone Again*, Johnny Rodriguez' *Reflecting*, and Charley Pride's *From Me To You*, which contains what Robbins feels is his most representative piano work in the song, "Wonder Could I Live There Any More."

Robbins was born near the tiny community of Spring City in the Tennessee Appalachians, to a family whose only interest in music lay in singing hymns and humming tunes around the house. Beginning in the first grade, he attended the Tennessee School for the Blind in Nashville, an institution noted for its music programs. There, at the age of seven, Hargus began taking piano lessons.

Robbins is quick to admit that he was a difficult student after a couple of years. "I was kind of hard-headed," he remembers. "I got to thinking I knew more than the teacher." Part of the problem might have been the regimen. "Classical! That was their whole bit," Robbins explains. "They frown upon tunes or boogie-woogie or rock and roll or whatever. But if you've got some ability, you're not just going to stick with the classical stuff. I started figuring out anything I could hear on the radio. The early stuff, I guess, was hillbilly, because that's what I'd heard all my life, and then I kind of got into dixieland, and then rock and roll came along."

Although influenced by such varied piano stylists as Ramsey Lewis and Floyd Cramer, Robbins didn't restrict himself to

piano. From the fourth grade on, he played trumpet in the brass band; then, with the advent of rock and roll, he bought a saxophone in the late '50s and taught himself to play it. "I worked a couple of gigs with it," Robbins says with a laugh, "but I never did become a Boots Randolph! But it was fun, and in a lot of places we would play, the piano wasn't in good enough shape to really compete with the loud guitars and drums anyway."

The piano was still his main love, however, and it was with this instrument that Robbins began doing session work in the growing Nashville studio scene of the late '50s. "I tried to write some songs with this family that wrote songs," he recalls, "and of course I played when we made the demo. We'd take the tape around without much luck, but people would comment, 'Who's playing the piano?' Of course, I told them it was me, so they called me to do some demos for the publishing companies."

The transition from demo player to full-fledged studio musician was quick, due partly to reasons other than talent. "Floyd Cramer had come out with 'Last Date' and then kind of retired from the recording scene after that," Robbins explains, "and when he quit, I was really just about the only one around who could play in that pedal style that was so popular, and that didn't hurt me any. Then, too, the business was really growing, and that kind of made room for another band, because one or two bands had it more or less sewed up before. It was an exciting time for me. I couldn't wait to get up out of bed in the morning to get at it."

Robbins didn't just duplicate Cramer's "bent note" or "pedal sound," so called because it was based on the phrasing of the then-new pedal steel guitar. He also developed his own distinct style at the keyboard by featuring the melody in the left hand played against chords in the right. Robbins calls this his "Maybelle Carter" technique, because it echoes the famous guitar style Carter pioneered in the '20s by playing the melody on the bass strings and strumming the treble for rhythm.

"What I like on records is a lot of full rhythm," Robbins notes. "To me, that means a lot of octaves in the right hand. It just fills up a record and gives it a lot of midrange. Now, on the pedals, I just use a very light sustain, if any, and occasionally the

**Hargus "Pig" Robbins' ability to play in the popular "pedal style" made him much in demand in the Nashville studio scene.**

soft pedal if the producer wants it super soft and muted, but I do this very sparingly. I think a lot of piano players make the mistake of using too much sustain, because to me it all runs together and becomes messy sounding. It just doesn't sound good on record."

Having owned an Aeolian Winter, two Everetts, and a Wurlitzer electric piano, Robbins currently plays a Baldwin grand at home. "It's about four years old, and has just been restrung," he says. "It looks like hell, but it sounds great." In the Nashville studios, however, Robbins plays a wide selection of pianos. "There's quite a lot of difference in the pianos around town," he observes. "I like the Columbia B studio the best. They've got a Steinway Model B, a 7'1" grand, the action's not too heavy and it's not too light, and the sound is just fantastic! I don't usually like a Baldwin; they're just too stiff and too heavy. I know this contradicts everything I've said, because I own a Baldwin, but this particular Baldwin is the closest thing I've found to that Steinway over at Columbia. I don't know if it's just that it's old and has gotten loosened up over the years or what.

"It's the same with the Rhodes electric piano," he continues. "I love the sound, but the action is just so darn stiff. The Wurlitzer electric has a light action, but the Rhodes is the one they usually have in the studios."

In recent years, Robbins has been playing electric keyboards more frequently. In addition to electric piano, he has used a Hohner Clavinet on a number of sessions, and played both a Yamaha synthesizer and electric piano on George Jones' "Her Name Is . . ." and Conway Twitty's "Games That Daddies Play." "I think the acoustic piano will always be around," Robbins says, "but the synthesizers and the Clavinet and the electric piano have definitely found a growing place. I think the phase shifter on the electric piano sounds beautiful! Then there's the organ, of course, which is like the harpsichord to me, in that you find one in every studio but you don't use it but eight or ten times a year. Most of the organ work I do is for gospel recordings, but somebody may want one on a country record next week."

Robbins has no particular preferences in amplifiers. "Most of the electric pianos, like the Wurlitzer, have their own amp built in," he points out. "I just usually plug the Rhodes into the studio amp, whatever it is, or take it direct into the board. The amp doesn't really play that much of a role in the studio. To cut out the noise of the amp, they usually take as many instruments direct as they can."

Robbins' conversation about the piano is laced with references to producers, sessions, and records. He is totally a creature of the recording studios, and is in his element in them. He rarely plays in public—"Just twice a year, at the Fan Fair in the spring and the Disc Jockey convention in the fall"—and is happiest and most at ease as a session player. "If you're in a session and hit a clinker, you can always go and take it back," he notes, "but if you're out there in the middle of the stage, well, if you hit one, hell, it's gone!"

Although Robbins recorded feature albums for Mercury in 1963, Time in 1964, Decca in the mid-'60s, and Chart in 1968 and 1969, none of these records is currently distributed. However, Elektra will soon release a new Hargus Robbins LP, tentatively titled *Instrumentalist Of The Year*. Five of the cuts were composed by Robbins, who claims, "I wanted to find some different material, and to do a lot of original stuff. I wouldn't have done the album unless I felt I could have come up with something different."

What sort of practicing does Robbins do at home? "Oh, I have to limber up every Monday morning at least," he says with a chuckle, "and I do sit down and look for licks or combinations of notes, or different sounds I might be able to use on a record, but I doubt that I could play a tune all the way through, because I'm not at all into that part of piano playing. We're basically trained as studio musicians to complement a song. That's all we're trained for, and at the end of a session, we probably couldn't tell you what the first song was. We're into it and out of it and on to the next session."

More than ever before, the piano has become part of the sound of modern country music, as pianist/singers like Charlie Rich, Ronnie Milsap, and Jerry Lee Lewis are changing the all-guitar look and sound of that style. But the CMA Instrumentalist Of The Year doesn't consider this a sign of a musical revolution in the making at Nashville.

"On records," he observes, "some producers dig keyboards and some don't. On some records, they'll lean to steel or guitar or voices, and on some to keyboards. It all depends on their likes and dislikes. Of course, if you can come up with a good lick, they'll put it on there. If you could come up with a different sound, you might be able to put out an interesting album of your own, and if you're lucky, you'll come up with a tune that people dig."

---

**A SELECTED HARGUS "PIG" ROBBINS DISCOGRAPHY**

**With Tom T. Hall:** *Faster Horses*, Mercury, SRM-1-1076. **With George Jones:** *Alone Again*, Epic, KE 34290. **With Johnny Rodriguez:** *Reflecting*, Mercury, SRM-1-1110. **With Charlie Pride:** *From Me To You*, RCA, SLP-4468.

---

# ROOTS OF ROCKABILLY

**By Dan Forte**

*Oh, well, I woke up this mornin',*
*and I looked out the door.*
*I can tell that old milkcow*
*by the way she lows . . .*

"**H**OLD IT, FELLAS! THAT DON'T *MOVE* ME. LET'S GET real, real gone for a change."

"Real, real gone for a change" is one of the great understatements in rock and roll history. After interrupting the bluesy intro to Sleepy John Estes' "Milkcow Blues" at a December 1954 session at Memphis' Sun Studio, Elvis Presley—along with guitarist Scotty Moore and bassist Bill Black—got real gone indeed and demonstrated vividly the changes that they were about to exert on pop music.

Elvis' mixture of country roots, black blues, boogie-woogie, youthful energy, and unabashed sexuality was dubbed rockabilly, "cat music," and Elvis was "The Hillbilly Cat." The supercharged, guitar-dominated rockabilly of Elvis, Eddie Cochran, Gene Vincent And The Blue Caps, Buddy Holly, and their contemporaries was a cornerstone of early rock and roll, along with the pumping pianos of Little Richard and Jerry Lee Lewis, the close-harmony doo-wop of urban vocal groups, the highly original guitar work of Chuck Berry, and several other sub-styles that reflected varying proportions of the music's

**Rockabilly's most widely heard lead guitarist, Scotty Moore, (left), contributed blistering solos and country-flavored fills to Elvis' (right) early hits.**

**Bill Haley was the first boss of rock, both as a singer and guitar player.**

ingredients.

Just what is rockabilly—a sound, a style, an era? It's all of these. For the most part, rockabilly started as music performed by Southern whites, aimed at their own peer group, young whites. Most of its musicians had a solid foundation in country and western and the *Grand Ole Opry*, but were exposed to rural black music as well. No one embodied this seeming dichotomy more than Elvis Presley.

Bill Haley And The Comets may have scored the first national rock hit with "Rock Around The Clock," but they lacked the fire, the reckless abandon that permeated Elvis' early sessions for Sun Records. The playing was there but not the feel, the underlying mood. Although Haley's beginnings were in country music, the Comets (previously named the Saddlemen, complete with steel guitar) were more a white version of Louis Jordan's jump band, the Tympani Five—in fact, both recorded for Decca and were produced by Milt Gabler. (Although there has been some debate as to who played the phenomenal guitar break on "Rock Around The Clock," Gabler recalls that it was Danny Cedrove, not the group's subsequent lead player, Fran Beecher. This is substantiated by the fact that Cedrove played virtually the exact same solo on Haley's "Rock The Joint," recorded in 1952 for the Essex label.)

Haley's brand of country was closer to western swing, and his black influences (such as Jordan) were more sophisticated—as much jazz as blues. In contrast, Elvis' inspirations were both rural—white bluegrass and country blues—as evidenced by his very first single, which coupled Arthur "Big Boy" Crudup's blues. "That's All Right," with Bill Monroe's "Blue Moon Of Kentucky." Both, of course, were hepped up to boogie-woogie pace. Bill Haley may have given teens of the '50s a hit song they could dance to, but Elvis gave them an identity, a

model. He was more than just a singer; he was sideburns and pink and black shirt-jacks. He was a kid, just like them. He was also undeniably Southern. Blues harpist Charlie Musselwhite (who, while still in high school in Memphis, would occasionally come along when Elvis would rent movie theaters, skating rinks, or the fairground for private parties) emphasizes, "The Yankees had put us down for so long, I just can't express how *important* it was when Elvis made it. He was immediately recognizable as being Southern; the minute he opened his mouth, we knew he was just like us."

Elvis also did much for the guitar's identity. As Jerry Hopkins, author of *Elvis* [Simon & Schuster], points out: "Elvis made it all right for men to play guitar. Of course, there were male guitar players before Elvis, but it wasn't really considered a masculine thing to do." Elvis not only made it all right to play guitar, he made it necessary. But, while those who followed in his footsteps (including Gene Vincent and Ricky Nelson) used the guitar mainly as a prop, Elvis' acoustic was an integral part, perhaps the most important element, of his early recording. As Scotty Moore remembered in a *Guitar Player* interview: "His playing did add to the group, because he more or less tied things together from the rhythm standpoint. For the most part, I think you could say that once we'd get a rhythm pattern going that felt good with the way Elvis wanted to sing it, we'd work everything else in around that. The rhythm was the primary thing. Any lead work was really secondary at that point."

If Elvis' acoustic rhythm helped give rock its backbone, Moore's electric embellishments contributed to fleshing out the rest of the music, in the process inspiring dozens of future guitar heroes. (Keith Richards reportedly never leaves on a Stones tour without a sound system for his hotel room and a tape of Presley's *The Sun Sessions*.) Like most guitarists of the early '50s, Scotty was influenced by the most popular instrumentalists of the day: Chet Atkins, Merle Travis, and Les Paul. The eclectic Moore also lists jazz innovator Tal Farlow, blues great B.B. King, and "everybody I heard" as influences.

Moore grew up in Humbolt, Tennessee, about 80 miles from Memphis, listening to the guitar music his father and three older brothers played. "They played some country," he recounts, "and what's considered bluegrass now, along with some other things, mainly for their own enjoyment," Scotty joined the family ensemble when he was eight, with a Kalamazoo acoustic, and didn't get his first electric until being stationed in Japan while in the Navy.

In his search for a white artist with a black sound and feel, Sun Records' Sam Phillips teamed Elvis with Moore and bassist Bill Black, having heard their group, the Starlight Wranglers. "We played primarily country," Scotty says of the group, "but from playing honky-tonks and what have you, you had to play everything, even though you did it with basically a country band. We just called it honky-tonk music."

With the limited instrumentation of Elvis' trio, Moore was given the freedom to do anything and everything on his all-gold Gibson ES-295 hollowbody electric. "This was the first opportunity, without my really knowing it, that I had to really mix it all up," he explains. "I mean, it wasn't a planned thing. But I loved blues and I loved country, and I played *some* fingerstyle a la Chet and Merle. And with the few instruments we had, you just did everything you could to make it sound bigger, you know."

*The Sun Sessions,* recorded in 1954 and '55, still constitutes one of the greatest albums in rock history. Listening to Moore's double-string bends on "Baby, Let's Play House," it's easy to see why that song inspired Jimmy Page to take up guitar. Scotty's fills and leads on "Just Because," "Trying To Get To You," and "I Don't Care If The Sun Don't Shine" stand as mini-masterpieces, rendered even more impressive by the fact that they were completely improvised. "It was *all* improvisation," he laughs.

Ironically, once Elvis' Sun contract was sold to RCA, Scotty found himself playing lead backed by his idol, Chet Atkins, who produced and played rhythm on the first few RCA sessions, including "Heartbreak Hotel." The lead work heard on Elvis' recordings of "A Fool Such As I," "Little Sister," and "Big Hunk O' Love" is by none other than Hank Garland, undoubtedly the most radical of the Nashville studio pickers back then. Garland also recorded with Jerry Lee Lewis, Charlie Rich, and several one-shot rockabilly bands.

When Elvis moved from Sun to RCA, Sam Phillips concentrated on rockabilly guitarist/vocalist Carl Perkins, who scored twice with his composition "Blue Suede Shoes." His own version of the song hit #1 on the national charts in 1956, prior to Presley's success with "Heartbreak Hotel." Elvis' subsequent recording of "Blue Suede Shoes" also became a smash hit. One can only speculate as to how popular Perkins might have become had he not sustained a fractured and broken shoulder in an automobile accident just as his career seemed to be taking off. But Perkins was no Elvis; he was more hillbilly, as his first efforts for Sun, such as "Movie Magg" and "Turn Around," illustrate.

But Carl Perkins could do two things that Elvis Presley couldn't: He could write catchy, original songs, and he could play hot lead guitar. Both talents inspired the likes of Ricky Nelson, who recorded Carl's "Boppin' The Blues" and "Your True Love," and the Beatles, with George Harrison playing numerous Perkins-inflected solos, particularly on "Matchbox," "Honey Don't," and "Everybody's Trying To Be My Baby"—all written by Perkins.

Carl Perkins was born in 1932 in Ridgely, Tennessee, and grew up in dire poverty, the son of a sharecropper who suffered from tuberculosis. He got his first guitar at age five and, like Elvis, had his musical roots in both blues and hillbilly music. In a 1975 *Guitar Player* interview, he told Dennis Hensley about a black farmer named John Westbrook, his first guitar mentor. "I'd go over to his front porch at night," he said, "after I'd worked ten hours a day in the fields. We'd burn some straw grass stalks to smoke the mosquitoes away and just sit and pick for hours . . . . John played black blues on the guitar, and I liked his sound; he did a lot of string pushing and choking. I'd imitate his licks and runs. During that time, I always listened to the *Grand Ole Opry* show on radio, and I memorized the songs of Ernest Tubb and Bill Monroe. When I'd sing the country favorites, I'd lace them with some of old John Westbrooks's blues guitar licks, and that's

**Carl Perkins may have been influenced by Atkins and Travis, but he created a truly original style of his own.**

how my personal style developed."

Perkins went through numerous guitars in his early years, so it's difficult to say which songs were recorded with which models. The booklet accompanying Charly Records' three-record boxed set, *Carl Perkins—The Sun Years,* includes a 1954 photo of the Perkins Brothers Band featuring Carl on what appears to be a 3/4-size electric. The sheet music to "Blue Suede Shoes" shows him holding a '52/'53 type gold-top Les Paul with a trapeze tailpiece. Other photos picture him with Fender Telecasters and Stratocasters, and he later helped popularize the Gibson ES-5 Switchmaster three-pickup hollowbody before switching to Epiphone's version of the same concept.

The simple but effective guitar style that Perkins honed shared many of the same qualities that Chuck Berry displayed—the simplicity, the rhythmic drive, and the two-note bends. The sound was trebly and decidedly electric. But Carl also displayed a melodic sense on the ballads and more country-flavored numbers. He may have been influenced by Atkins, Travis, or other guitarists of the period, but he turned it into something truly original.

Chuck Berry's influence, of course, pervaded *all* rock and roll guitarists who followed, to some degree. Too much in his own vein to be categorized as rockabilly, Chuck came damn close on occasion. The fact that he recorded for Chicago's Chess label is a matter of race more than musical style; musically, he had a lot more in common with Elvis than with Muddy Waters, Little Walter, and his other labelmates. His first hit single, "Maybellene," with its raucous but well-crafted multi-string lead, is as close to country as it is to anything resembling blues. When Fred Stuckey interviewed Berry for a 1971 *Guitar Player* interview, he asked him if he was playing rock and roll before 1955. "In a sense," the guitarist answered. "It wasn't named then. It was boogie-woogie. It was even called jazz once—jive, you know. I heard a lot of country music stuff and copied a lot. I guess I couldn't have said I was playing country, but I was stabbing at it."

With the presence of Sun Studios, Memphis was Rockabilly Headquarters, although not all of the city's hepcats recorded for Sun. One exception was Memphis Golden Gloves boxing champion Johnny Burnette. Billed as the Rock 'N Roll Trio, Johnny (on lead vocals and rhythm guitar), brother Dorsey Burnette (on upright bass), and Paul Burlison (lead guitar) forged a primal-scream style of rockabilly that bordered on the maniacal. After Sam Phillips passed on their demo tapes, the group went to New York, where it won top honors on *Ted Mack's Amateur Hour* TV show three weeks in succession, landing a record deal with Decca in the process.

Whatever Burlison lacked in technique and finesse, he more than made up for in guts and energy. As guitarist Jimmie Vaughn of the Fabulous Thunderbirds states, "To me, he made the whole thing up—the rock and roll wildman. I still haven't heard anybody play wilder than him, as far as rock and roll or rockabilly." Yet another vivid example of a player synthesizing black and white influences, Burlison played guitar with his own country band over radio station KWEM in West Memphis, Arkansas, and in the slot that followed his show he backed blues shouter Chester "Howlin' Wolf" Burnett, because Wolf's regular guitarist, Willie Johnson, was working in the fields during the day. "We had to go to a studio *behind* the studio my band played in," Paul details, "and Chester couldn't even call our names out. See, blacks and whites just didn't play together, not back in '51."

Burlison's style on Telecaster was unorthodox, to say the least. For example, on "Train Kept A-Rollin'" (which inspired cover versions by the Yardbirds featuring Jeff Beck, and Aerosmith), Burlison plays octaves throughout the song, fretting the first and sixth *E* strings with the index and thumb of his left hand while plucking with the index and thumb of his right hand. This unusual technique is continued up and down the neck for his solo break, which like all of Burlison's leads was totally improvised. Add to this the fact that the 1956 recording is one of the first to employ intentional guitar distortion—fuzztone, if you will. "We were playing in Cleveland, Ohio," Paul explained in a 1978 *Guitar Player* interview, "and just before the show the leather strap on my blonde Fender amp broke, and the amp fell to the floor. When I plugged the guitar in, it had a real fuzzy sound. I looked in the back of the amp and one of the tubes was barely sticking in the prongs; it was acting as a rheostat. The guitar sounded pretty good, and I left the tube the way it was. Whenever I wanted to get that sound, I'd just reach back and loosen the tube. You could tell when you were getting it—it sounded real funky." Burlison also used the loose-tube effect on the Trio's version of "Honey Hush."

Finding themselves without an "Elvis" of their own, Capitol Records held an audition/contest that a Virginian named Gene Vincent won handily with his group, the Blue Caps. Gene's earliest successes—including "Be-Bop-A-Lulu," "Woman Love," and "Race With The Devil"—set his hyperventilating vocals against the phenomenal, complex guitar work of Cliff Gallup. But Gallup returned to Virginia after a brief taste of life on the road, and in January of 1957 Vincent hired a South Carolina country guitarist named Johnny Meeks after hearing him play once in a bar. "In between Cliff Gallup and me," Johnny clarifies, "there was a guitar player named Russell Willaford, who played a Telecaster. He was only with the Blue Caps about a week—two weeks max—but he got to be in the movie *The Girl Can't Help It.* When I joined the group, it was Gene, Paul Peek on rhythm, Bobby Jones on bass, and Dickie Harrell, the only original Blue Cap left, on drums."

On Meeks' first session with Vincent, the group recorded "Lotta Lovin'," "Wear My Ring," "Dance To The Bop," and "I've Got It." "I was playing a Stratocaster when Gene hired me," Johnny recalls. "But he was a Gretsch man, so he bought me some sunburst Gretsch. Later we got an endorsement from Leo Fender, so we all got white Fenders, and I got a white Strat with my name on it."

Though he was playing pure country before joining wildman Vincent, Meeks lists Chet Atkins, Chuck Berry ("for that driving sound"), B.B. King, and "all the blues players" as influences. When he joined the Blue Caps, Johnny admits, "Cliff Gallup was a helluva lot better player than me—much more advanced. A very precise player. But I had that teenage, driving sound that Gene liked. I tried learning the solos note-for-note off Gene's records, but he told me not to. He wanted me to play *my* stuff. Only on 'Be-Bop-A-Lula' did I stay pretty close to the record." Johnny's piercing single-note style can be heard prominently on "Teenage Partner" and Vincent's arrangement of "Summertime" (both from Vincent's *Record Date* LP, reissued by EMI in Europe). Vincent also recorded one of Meeks' compositions, "Say Momma," which Johnny recently recorded with rockabilly revivalists the Hypnotics on Rhino Records' *LA Rockabilly* anthology.

If Cliff Gallup was rockabilly's most advanced guitar player, James Burton would have to be the genre's most versatile. Born in Shreveport, Louisiana, in 1940, Burton got his first guitar at age 13 and became staff guitarist on the *Louisiana Hayride* radio show less than two years later. The distinctive lead guitar on Dale Hawkins' rockabilly hit "Susie Q" was none other than James at age 15. That was the first in an unparalleled string of hit records for which Burton has supplied guitar parts. The roster of artists that James worked with during his illustrious studio career is as varied as it is lengthy, including Frank Sinatra, the Byrds, the Osmonds, Johnny Mathis, the Supremes, and Waylon Jennings. He has also toured extensively with Emmylou Harris, led Elvis Presley's group from the King's 1969 concert comeback until his death in 1977, and has played with John Denver since Elvis' death.

But for rockabilly fans, the association Burton is remembered for most is his tenure as lead guitarist with Ricky Nelson, which was beamed to households all over America on the *Ozzie And Harriet* TV show. Though he was often passed off as just another mass-marketed teen idol, Ricky Nelson made some first-rate rockabilly records. he idolized Carl Perkins, picked excellent material (including several tunes written by Johnny and Dorsey Burnette), and surrounded himself with a top-notch band that included Burton on guitar and Joe Osbourn on bass. Prior to hooking up with Burton, Nelson employed bluegrass-turned-electric veteran Joe Maphis on his early hits, including "Boppin' The Blues," "Bebop Baby," "Stood Up," and "Waitin' In School." Surprisingly, the aggressive sliding-and-choking leads played by Maphis sound raunchier than the sure-handed cleanness and glassy tone displayed by the young Burton, who almost always had complete freedom on Nelson's recordings.

With some early training on steel guitar, James employs a rather strange picking technique combining a flatpick held between his thumb and forefinger, and a metal fingerpick on his middle finger. Coupled with Burton's eccentric taste, this accounts for one of the most identifiable guitar sounds in popular music, not to mention some monster solos. For starters, dig "It's Late," "Hello, Mary Lou," "Shirley Lee," and "Believe What You Say" (all on the double-set, *Ricky Nelson*). James' solo on Nelson's version of "Milcow Blues" was so memorable he used it as the basis of his break on Merle Haggard's "Workin' Man Blues" several years later.

The James Burton style has inspired a legion of country and rock pickers, including *Guitar Player* Readers Poll country winner Albert Lee, James' successor in Emmylou Harris' Hot Band, who not coincidentally favors Telecasters, J.B.'s trademark. And, although his basic guitar style bears little resemblance to Burton's, the Kinks' Dave Davies enthused, "Oh, James Burton was my idol!" in a 1977 *Guitar Player* interview, "There were no really good guitarists in pop music or rock," he went on. "James Burton was bridging the gap between country music, if you will, and commercialism. When we were on the *Shindig* TV show in '65, I was over the moon, because James Burton was in the Shindogs [the show's house band, with guitarist Delaney Bramlett, drummer Chuck Blackwell, bassist Glenn D Hardin, and vocalist Joey Cooper]. I've still got his records at home— those great solos on 'Hello Mary Lou' and the other Ricky Nelson

Scotty Moore, pictured here playing a Gibson L-5, inspired dozens of future guitar heroes who heard his electric embellishments to Elvis' sound.

records." James Burton is one of the few examples of a teenage rocker turned studio veteran, of an individual stylist whose services have been in demand for 25 years.

Though each was best known for his singing and song-writing, Eddie Cochran and Buddy Holly were also accomplished lead guitarists. Both had their roots in country music— Holly first recording with Bob Montgomery as Buddy & Bob,

The Rock 'N Roll Trio, with Paul Burlison (seated) with primal-scream Telecaster.

and Eddie singing duets with Hank Cochran (no relation)—but, like all rockabilly artists, they loved rhythm and blues. And, of course, both died young and at the peak of their careers—Holly in the 1959 plane crash that also took the lives of Ritchie Valens and the Big Bopper, and Cochran in a 1960 car crash that Gene Vincent barely survived. Ironically, Cochran's hit "Three Stars" was dedicated to Holly, Valens, and the Big Bopper.

Lubbock, Texas' Buddy Holly was possibly the most eclectic of the '50s rockabilly artists. During his all-too-brief recording career, he performed rockabilly rave-ups, ballads, straight R&B, and catchy pop tunes. His clear Stratocaster sound was the focal point of most of his early efforts, and the stripped-down instrumentation of his group, the Crickets, helps explain his driving, rhythmic style. Whereas Elvis' original trio consisted of bass, lead, and rhythm guitar, the Crickets comprised bassist Joe Mauldin, drummer Jerry Allison, and Buddy as the solo guitar player. Thus Holly played lead *and* rhythm, often simultaneously as on "Peggy Sue" and "Not Fade Away," which was inspired by one of his biggest influences, Bo Diddley. Buddy was also adept at single-string leads, but always played heavily on the beat. Listen, for example, to his guitar breaks on "That'll Be The Day," "I'm Looking For Someone To Love," and "Rock Me My Baby," which sound as though they were worked out well in advance.

Oklahoma-born Eddie Cochran was a much more facile player than Holly, obviously influenced by more sophisticated players such as Chet Atkins and Merle Travis. Eddie could play gritty blues, as on "Hallelujah, I Love Her So" or "My Way," or Atkins-tinged pull-offs as on "Twenty Flight Rock." The Atkins influence is also prevalent on "Sittin' In The Balcony" with its slap-back echo. Like Holly, Cochran seldom strayed far from the thunderous, all-essential beat.

Of course, for every rockabilly guitarist who made a lasting impression, there were dozens who were never heard from again. There were also several notable players who for one reason or another never got the recognition their playing should have commanded. Roland Janes' simple but effective reverb-laden Chuck Berry licks were present on most of Jerry Lee Lewis' Sun recordings, such as "Breathless," "Little Queenie," and "Whole Lotta Shakin' Going On," but always in the shadow of the Killer's boogie-woogie piano.

Two adolescent flashes who, surprisingly, fell from the limelight after rockabilly's demise were Joe Bennett of the Sparkletones and Larry Collins of the Collins Kids. At 16, Bennett was the oldest member of the Sparkletones when they recorded for ABC paramount in 1957 (at age 12, rhythm guitarist Howard "Sparky" Childress was the youngest member). Bennett's fiery, mature playing was but one impressive element in the group's recordings, such as their hit "Black Slacks," which was somewhat of an anthem to the rockabilly image; "With a cat chain down to my knees/I ain't nothin' but a real cool breeze."

The Collins Kids, Larry and older sister Lorrie, recorded for CBS in the '50s when Larry was only 13. The pair mixed country and rockabilly, with Larry picking dazzling, rapid-fire leads on a custom-made doubleneck Mosrite, modeled after Joe Maphis', with a short neck tuned an octave above standard pitch. Collins, in fact, recorded a furiously paced duet with Maphis entitled "Hurricane," which must be head to be believed; this has been reissued on Epic's *Introducing Larry And Lorrie. . . The Collins Kids.*

**Brian Setzer rocks out on a Gibson ES-295.**

A number of factors contributed to rockabilly's demise around the turn of the decade: Elvis' induction into the Army and his move from raw rockabilly to movie soundtrack production numbers and other mainstream material, Jerry Lee Lewis' marriage to his 13-year-old cousin and subsequent blacklisting, and the deaths of Buddy Holly and Eddie Cochran. Also, music business executives who had written off rock and roll as a fad had a change of heart when they realized that there was money to be made from the teenage market. The era of the clean-cut Teen Idol was ushered in, with pop music churned out assembly-line style by songwriters such as Carole King, Neil Sedaka, and Barry Mann. Ironically, rockabilly was dealt its final, seemingly fatal blow when the Beatles took the world by storm, often recycling rockabilly tunes and licks. Give a listen to George Harrison's solo on "Can't Buy Me Love," to give but one example—a mixture of Chet Atkins and Carl Perkins guitar figures.

Throughout the '60s and early '70s, rockabilly was little more than nostalgia. Many of the genre's artists returned to the southern roadhouses they got their start in. Some, like Jerry Lee Lewis, turned to country music, and a few—notably Gene Vincent—enjoyed some success in Europe. Rockabilly had virtually no effect on sales or airplay, with the exception of a couple of rockabilly-flavored tunes by Queen and Led Zeppelin, two bands who otherwise exhibited no rockabilly roots. Major labels would have nothing to do with the "greasy kid's stuff," so up-and-coming younger bands and a few obscure old-timers (such as Charlie Feathers and Johnny Caroll) recorded for tiny independent labels such as Rockin' Ronny Weisner's living room operation. Rollin' Rock, which released the Blasters' debut album, *American Music.* At the same time, England's Charly label became America's rockabilly caretaker, releasing lavish reissues of Sun material by Carl Perkins, Roy Orbison,

Jerry Lew Lewis, and others.

In the late '70s, rockabilly made an unlikely comeback on the shoulders of the punk/new wave movements, with which it shared a back-to-basics approach and a do-it-yourself attitude. Veterans such as upright bassist/vocalist Ray Campi, who'd been plunking away for years, found themselves playing punk clubs on bills with groups like San Francisco's Dead Kennedys. With the help of the eclectic Welsh producer/guitarist Dave Edmunds, the East Coast-based Stray Cats took England by storm and within a couple of years were topping the American charts with authentic Gene Vincent- and Eddie Cochran-derived originals penned by lead guitarist Brian Setzer.

The Stray Cats, of course, weren't the only neo-rockabilly group, just the most successful. There are doubtless more bands and guitarists playing cat music in 1983 than there were in 1958. Robert Gordon's stellar unit brought Link Wray out of obscurity and now features the consummate talents of Danny Gatton. The Blasters' Alvin brothers, Phil and Dave, have added rich new material to rockabilly's repertoire. And hot on the heels of his tours with Emmylou Harris and Eric Clapton, Albert Lee released a recent self-titled LP that should keep country and rock players sweating for a good while to come.

Rockabilly has also seeped into other styles with some very interesting results. Guitarist Billy Zoom, of the innovative Los Angeles new wave band X, sees his role in the group as re-cycling at extremely high volume and speed the rockabilly licks he played in his pre-X days (he once backed Gene Vincent and also recorded several sides for Rollin' Rock). X's version of Jerry Lee Lewis' "Breathless," in the soundtrack of the movie by the same name, is a good example of this. One of the most interesting new bands to come along is Los Lobos, featuring David Hildalgo on guitar and accordion and Cesar Rosas on guitar and bajo sexto. Their impressive Slash debut album entitled *And A Time To Dance,* produced by T-Bone Burnette and Blasters saxman Steve Berlin, mixes rockabilly with Ritchie Valens Tex-Mex and norteño music.

Perhaps the most encouraging sign of the rockabilly revival is the long-awaited recognition it's brought to some of rock's unsung pioneers. Carl Perkins now tours backed by his two sons, ironically *opening* shows for Robert Gordon or the Blasters. He also made a cameo appearance on Paul McCartney's *Tug Of War* album. After eight years as the leader of Elvis Presley's band (during which time, he proudly states, "I never missed a show"). James Burton is still the most in-demand country picker in the L.A. studios. Scotty Moore works on the other side of the glass these days as an engineer in Nashville, but recently broke out his guitar for an RCA project entitled *I Was The One* which placed remastered recordings of Elvis' original vocals alongside re-recorded instrumental tracks played note-for-note by the original musicians.

But the most significant development of the rockabilly movement has been its acceptance by the media. Rockabilly is marketable. The success of the Blasters prompted Warner Brothers to add the entire Slash label to their distribution line. Fashion designers have discovered that pink and black go well together. Lounge crooner John Davidson greased his hair back for a recent *Tonight Show* wherein he sang the Stray Cats' "Rock This Town." Following his computer-age album *Trans,* Neil Young has released a rockabilly LP entitled *Everybody's Rocking.* In the works is a major feature film, tentatively titled *Rockabilly;* Johnny Meeks is the music consultant. And premiering on NBC's fall season is *Boone,* a show about a pre-Elvis teenager who's shy in class but rocks out when he gets onstage with his rockabilly band.

What next? Can a rockabilly game show be too far off? Stay tuned.

---

## A SELECTED DISCOGRAPHY OF ROCKABILLY GUITAR

**Eddie Cochran** (on Liberty): *Eddie Cochran,* LST 7172; *Cherished Memories,* 1109; *Memorial Album,* 1127; *Singing To My Baby,* 1158; *My Way,* 1205; *Never To Be Forgotten,* LRP 3220; *Great Hits,* LN-10204; *Summertime Blues,* Sunset, 5123; *Legendary Masters,* United Artists, LWB-9959; *The Eddie Cochran Singles Album* (an English import), United Artists, UCSP 20. **Bill Haley:** "Rock Around The Clock" on *Golden Hits,* MCA, 2-4010, and "Rock The Joint" on *Rock With Billy Haley,* Essex, ESLP 202. **Elvis Presley:** "That's All Right," "Blue Moon Of Kentucky," "Baby, Let's Play House," "Just Because," "Trying To Get To You," and "I Don't Care If The Sun Don't Shine" on *The Sun Sessions,* RCA, APM1-1675. "Heartbreak Hotel" and "A Fool Such As I" on *Legendary Performer,* RCA, CPL1-0341; "Little Sister" and "Big Hunk O' Love" on *Golden Records,* RCA, AQL1-1701. Rerecorded Sun cuts issued as *I Was The One,* RCA, AHL1-4678. **Carl Perkins:** "Blue Suede Shoes," "Movie Magg," and "Turn Around" on *Blue Suede Shoes,* Sun, 112; *Original Sun Greatest Hits,* Rhino, RNCD. **Chuck Berry:** "Maybelline" on *Chuck Berry's Golden Decade,* Chess, 2CH-1514. **The Rock 'N Roll Trio:** "Train Kept A-Rollin'" and "Honey Hush" on *Johnny Burnette And The Rock 'N Roll Trio,* Solid Smoke [Box 22372, San Francisco, CA 94122], SS-8001.

**Cliff Gallup** (with Gene Vincent): *Bop That Just Won't Stop,* Capitol, N-16290; *Gene Vincent's Greatest Hits,* Capitol, N-16208. **Johnny Meeks** (with Gene Vincent): *A Gene Vincent Record Date,* Capitol, T 1059. **Dale Hawkins:** "Suzie Q" available as a 45. **Ricky Nelson:** All cuts with James Burton or Joe Maphis are on *Ricky Nelson,* Liberty. LXB-9960. **Buddy Holly:** "That'll Be The Day," "Peggy Sue," and "Not Fade Away" on *20 Golden Greats,* MCA, 3040.

**The Sparkletones:** *Black Slacks,* MCA, 1553. **Jerry Lee Lewis:** All Roland Janes cuts are on *Original Golden Hits—Vol. 1.* Sun, 102. **The Collins Kids:** *Introducing Larry And Lorrie. . . The Collins Kids,* Epic, PE 38457. **X:** "Breathless" on *More Fun In The New World,* Elektra, 60283. **Los Lobos:** *. . . And A Time To Dance,* Slash, 23963-1. **Neil Young:** *Everybody's Rockin',* Geffen, GHS-4013.

# EARL SCRUGGS

By Jim Hatlo

IN THE PAST, THE DETAILS OF EARL'S DEPARTURE FROM Flatt And Scruggs were a closed subject. Today, however, he discusses them freely, offering insights here that have never appeared in print. But though those comments have historic significance, they are overshadowed by the significance of his latest endeavor. The most historic chapter in Earl's career may remain to be written, as Earl Scruggs and Rodney Dillard step side by side into the '80s.

\* \* \* \*

*WHEN YOU FIRST BEGAN PLAYING WITH BILL MONROE, how did you know what kind of technique to use, or what kind of runs to play?*

I just played my own style. I had two tunes down pretty well then: "Sally Goodin" and "Dear Old Dixie." "Sally Goodin" I thought he could relate to, and "Dear Old Dixie" — I didn't know how to try that on him. But I did those two tunes deliberately because they were so different. At that time "Dear Old Dixie" wasn't being played at all, but I thought I'd give him both tunes.

*How did you know that your music would fit, and that he would want you to stay?*

Oh, I knew in my mind that it would work. I thought it was right because of his catalog of songs and the material he had. We got down to the Opry and we played all the way through. His closing show was at 10:00. The last bus out of Nashville was at 10:00, or 10:05, or something like that. Bill still hadn't said anything about whether he wanted me to go to work with him or not. So I just picked up my banjo and said, "That's it, I've got to catch this bus." He looked at me and said, "We'll leave at 10:00 Monday," just like that. I said, "I can't." At the time I had a touch of the flu; and for another thing, my clothes were in Knoxville. So I told him, "I've got to go to Carolina for a few days," and he said "Well, be back next Saturday," and that's how I began working with him. He never did say, "You can have the job."

*At the time when you joined Bill Monroe, who else was in the Blue Grass Boys?*

He had his brother Birch playing bass, Sally Forrester [wife of fiddler Howdy Forrester] playing accordion, Jim Andrews playing tenor banjo and doing comedy, Lester on the guitar, Jim Shumate with the fiddle, and him with the mandolin. That was the band.

*You said that when you came into Monroe's band there was an accordion and a tenor banjo. How do you feel today when you hear all the talk about changing the instruments in a bluegrass band?*

The banjo, in itself, was a *real* change. The Solemn Ol' Judge [George Dewey Hay, the *Grand Ole Opry* emcee from 1927 to 1951], when he used to put me on the stage, he'd say, "Here's Bill and Earl with his fancy 5-string banjo." He never referred to it as just "his banjo"; he'd always add the word "fancy." The banjo was almost as much a part of making the band sound different as putting an electric instrument into the band.

*How about the dobro? When did you introduce it into the Foggy Mountain Boys?*

Josh Graves came on in — I think it was 1955. We actually hired Josh to play bass. We needed a bass player and we needed a comedian. Josh was working with Mac Wiseman over at WRVA in Richmond, Virginia. So he came over and was playing bass, and we thought it [the dobro] was so good that we'd try a few tunes with him. The audiences just loved it. As soon as everything sort of settled, we hired a bass player — Jake Tullock —and put Josh on dobro full-time. There wasn't any bounce-back from anyone that I recall, saying, "This is not the way it should be."

*Why do you think today's audiences have more difficulty accepting a change, such as adding a drummer to a bluegrass band?*

To me, I think they should at least give it a listening chance. Now, there are a lot of bad drummers that should be criticized, just as well as pickers. But I think a good, tasteful drummer is a great asset to the group. Before we even had the acoustic upright bass, a bluegrass band was just the guitar, the fiddle, the mandolin, and the banjo. Even the doghouse [upright] bass was quite a bit of a "no-no" as far as a lot of people were concerned. But it turned out that it was a great asset, with a lot of bottom that

**Even though Lester Flatt (left) and Earl Scruggs were closer to each other than to their own brothers, their partnership came to an unhappy end in 1969 when each wished to do different things in music.**

helped to fill in the sound. If drums are played tastefully, it sure sounds better than a bunch of musicians stomping their feet on the floor to get a beat.

*Do the drums provide a different kind of rhythm than the bass?*

Yes, they do. They give the bass more of a chance to do what the bass is supposed to do. When Jake used to play bass with us, he had the fourth string running down real loose and he would slap it against the fingerboard, and that was nothing except a substitute for the drum. I think if drumming is done tastefully, it's an asset; and I believe that it will be accepted by everybody, in time. I must tell you that I even looked down my nose at the drums — before I began to play with them.

*Could you tell us more about your relationship with Lester Flatt?*

Lester and I were almost like brothers. In fact, we used to talk once in a while about how he and I were closer than we were with our own brothers. During the years, we had eaten every meal together, ridden in cars thousands of miles together, and our thinking and discussions were pretty much the same way about music and everything. It just was a good, real close relationship. The reason for the breakup came, I guess, mainly because I wanted to try something different. Actually, before the breakup, we had signed a contract with Columbia Records — it was an attractive contract —and in the deal we had to start taking some advice from the record people as far as what they thought was commercial, as opposed to some of the stuff we were cutting. Our stuff just was not selling. *Now* those tunes are selling. If they had been selling *then* as well as they are selling now, the record people would have been happy. But it didn't work that way. Another situation was that [Earl's sons] Randy and Gary were coming along musically. Some of their music,

and some of their buddies who dropped in, sounded so good that I just wanted to try something else. It wasn't a bad feeling toward each other [between him and Lester] as much as it was that I felt I was depriving myself of some things. By that, I mean that I *love* bluegrass music, and I still like to play it; but I do like to mix in some other music for my own personal satisfaction, because if I don't, I can get a little bogged down and a little depressed. You can just get a little tired of playing the same thing over and over.

*Do you ever get tired of playing "Foggy Mountain Break-down," or "Earl's Breakdown"?*

I do, until I see the reaction coming back from the audience. When I go into the tune, I am out to entertain. If I start a show, and the audience is the least bit relaxed, I'll leave the tune off for a while. Once I see their expression and that they're enjoying it, that turns me on to it again.

*We talk so much about bluegrass music. How would you define it?*

Well, I was just thinking about an article I read the other day. You know Bill [Monroe] has the credit for being the "Father of Bluegrass." That article said that the banjo was the only indispensable instrument in bluegrass music. Now, I don't want to take credit for it, but I do think you've got to have the style of banjo in there. Then to make it complete, you need the fiddle, mandolin, guitar, and bass. The dobro is a real asset because it gives you a wider range of material you can do, since it can fill in so many empty spots.

*Does bluegrass have to be strictly acoustic?*

[*Pause*] No. To make it back in the '40s and '50s and '60s, it would've had to have been acoustic. If you get a balance with the drums, and whatever the song is calling for — if it's calling for sustaining notes — I don't see any reason why some electrical instruments couldn't be added. Anything to make the song sound a little better, is my way of looking at it.

*Was there one period in which you felt most prolific with your instrumentals?*

I got into trying to write tunes when I worked with Bill. We used to do a lot of rehearsing. By that I mean, Bill had a four-seat, stretched-out 1941 Chevrolet limousine, and he and I would sit in the back seat while traveling and go over some of the old songs Bill knew but didn't use in his show, like "Molly And Tenbrooks," and "Little Joe," and some of those songs. We'd ride a lot of nights after a show, going to another gig, and sit back there and pick. He was writing some new songs, Lester was writing some new songs, and I was helping. I never wrote any [instrumentals or lyrics] that I got credit for while I was with Bill. After Lester and I organized the Foggy Mountain Boys in 1948, I started putting some ideas that I had all along into tunes. The first one was "Foggy Mountain Breakdown." As far as my writing is concerned, sometimes I might write a couple in three or four months and then it might be two or three years before another one would come around that I felt strong enough about to record.

*During what time span were the greater portion of your instrumentals created?*

"Foggy Mountain Breakdown" was in 1948 and "Earl's Breakdown" came in '51. I think it was less than a year after that, that "Flint Hill Special" came. That's when I put the other tuner on the banjo and used two tuners. [*Ed. Note: Earl first began using one "Scruggs tuner" on the* D *string, and later added a*

*second tuner for the G string.]* I just don't remember what years it was that I did tunes like "Ground Speed," or "Shuckin' The Corn," or "Randy Lynn Rag," or those types of tunes.

*Do you feel that same creative process is continuing now?*

Yes, I think it is. I've got a couple of tunes started that I think are going to materialize into something pretty good. If any one of them doesn't, I'm going to scrap it. There are too many good tunes already written to add some bad ones.

*Now that the music style will be changing slightly, will you continue to use a pickup on the banjo during your shows?*

Yes, I think so. There are a couple of reasons for it: I can get better balance. I really hate to see a group on the stage, and not be able to hear some of the pickers. Not that I want to be heard all the time, but I want to be able to blend in with the group. About the only way I know to do it is to continue using a pickup.

*The design styles of bluegrass instruments have gotten to be quite a status-symbol thing. Have you had a preference for the design style of your banjos, such as inlay patterns, wood finish, or plating?*

No, I never have. In fact, Louise [Earl's wife] has told me a lot of times that I have the worst-looking banjo of anybody in the business. Really, the sound is what I'm looking for. I keep my banjo up as far as frets and other adjustments are concerned, but if the varnish gets looking worn, that doesn't upset me that much. I've recently had my banjo re-done, but it wasn't just for beautification; it was just because it really needed it, and I had the time off to go and have it done. Years ago, when I sent the banjo back to the [Gibson] factory, they put those inlays in there [*pointing to a painting showing his banjo with a "bowtie" inlay pattern*]. A little later, that began to bug me a bit and I thought it needed a change. I hadn't thought that much about it until somebody told me they could replace the original inlay. I do like for it to look as original as possible.

*Several people have said, "If Earl Scruggs had played a Paramount banjo, it would have been the bluegrass banjo, and the Gibson banjo would have been unpopular." How did you get into the Gibson banjos?*

My first banjo was a mail-order banjo. I thought it came from Sears Roebuck, but my brother said it came from Montgomery Ward. But it looked like a Kay banjo. It didn't have any name on it — it was just a cheap banjo. When I was growing up, I was only exposed to a couple of good banjos, and they just happened to be Gibsons. That turned me on to looking for one, and I ran across mine in a pawn shop. That's how I got into it. I've never played a Paramount. I do think that most of the people who were using Paramounts were tenor banjo players, especially in the Carolinas. The Gibson was too hollow-sounding for a straight pick, and needed a mute or something.

*When you were performing with the Earl Scruggs Revue, there was a lot of distance onstage between performers. In your bluegrass band, you worked a lot closer together. Which do you prefer?*

I would rather work close. Lester and I used to work with one mike. It seemed that working into one mike would give you that living-room type of playing together. I get a better feel for the music working close than I do just getting a feedback from the monitor — you know, just hearing the parts from the monitor and not from someone standing next to you.

*Does using a pickup mean that you won't have to work close to other musicians in the future?*

No, I think we will be working shoulder to shoulder, but we just won't have to swarm into one mike for the instrumentals. I think it also looks a little more uniform and gives a better appearance.

*What do you see as the music for the new band?*

It's going to be pretty much a mixture of many things. A lot of the old Flatt And Scruggs stuff, as well as some of the Dillards stuff. We have two or three shows worked out, but we have to try it on the audiences first to see what has to be added or changed. So, it's kind of hard to answer that question. I didn't know until a few weeks ago that Rodney plays the dobro. I also talked to Josh Graves about working some with me on dobro, and I've toyed with that idea.

*Is it certain that Josh will join you?*

Josh says he will, but he's got some bookings himself that may keep him from joining us for a while. It will bring back old memories. I am sure that we can work off each other, and that will make it exciting.

*Will the new band's music be a mixture of Earl Scruggs' experiences?*

Yes, it will be a mixture. If it has to have a title, I guess it will just be American music. But I will be doing many of my best tunes that I did before, with Lester. We've been rehearsing them, and they really sounded good.

**A SELECTED EARL SCRUGGS DISCOGRAPHY**

**With The Earl Scruggs Revue** (on Columbia): *Country Chart Busters, Vols. 1 & 2*, C-32618, C-327720; *Family Portrait*, PC-34336; *Earl Scruggs Revue*, KC-32426; *Today And Forever*, JC-36084. **With Lester Flatt:** *Flatt And Scruggs With The Foggy Mountain Boys*, Mercury/Phonogram, MG-020542 (re-released as Pickwick JS-6093). (On Columbia): *Flatt & Scruggs At Carnegie Hall*, CS-8845; *Flatt & Scruggs Greatest Hits*, CS-9370; *Story Of Bonnie And Clyde*, CS-8751; *World Of Flatt & Scruggs*, CG-31964. (On Rounder): *The Golden Era*, Special Series 05; *Don't Get Above Your Raisin'*, Special Series 08. *The Original Sound*, Mercury, MG 20773. **With Bill Monroe:** *Original Bluegrass Sound*, Rounder, Special Series 06. **Singles:** *Blue Moon Of Kentucky*, 1-11176; *Drive To The Country*, 3-10992; *Give Me A Sign*, 1-11176; *I Could Sure Use The Feeling*, 3-10992; *Play Me No Sad Songs*, 1-11106. (On Mercury/Phonogram): *Back To The Cross*, 7063; *Cora Is Gone*, 7059; *Pain In The Heart*, 7061; *Take Me In Your Loveboat*, 7067; *Till The Dew Drops Fall Upon*, 7068. **Out of print:** *Foggy Mountain Banjo*, Columbia, CL-1364; *Folk Songs Of Our Land*, Columbia, CL-1830; *Hear The Whistles Blow;* Columbia, CL-2686; *Flatt & Scruggs Foggy Mountain Chimes*, Harmony Club (Box 925, Hollywood, CA 90068), HS-11401; *Flatt & Scruggs With The Foggy Mountain Boys*, Columbia, HL-7250; *Nashville Airplane*, Columbia, CS 9741.

# ELDON SHAMBLIN

By Richard Lieberson

**I**N THE SOUTHWEST OF THE 1930'S, BOB WILLS AND Milton Brown began to bring jazz and pop influences to the old-time fiddle band music, creating a hybrid that came to be known as western swing. The great Bob Wills band can boast many outstanding musicians, including steel guitarist Leon ("Take It Away Leon") McAuliffe, fiddlers Jesse Ashlock, Louis Tierney, Johnny Gimble, and Keith Coleman, pianist Al Stricklin, singer Tommy Duncan, mandolinist Tiny Moore, and guitarist Eldon Shamblin. Eldon is not as well known as some of the other pillars of the Wills band because Bob rarely called his name out on the records, as he did to announce solos by the other musicians.

Eldon, a native of Weatherford, Oklahoma, who started playing at 17, developed his unique style of rhythm guitar while working with the Texas Playboys in the late '30s. He began to introduce substitute and passing chords into the standard progressions, arranging his voicings so as to maintain a moving bass line. His method of linking inversions together, coupled with a strong rhythmic sense, was one of the most important elements in the Wills rhythm section. Shamblin was to the Wills band what guitarist Freddie Greene was, and is, to Count Basie's band.

Eldon did a good deal of arranging for the band, and collaborated with Leon McAuliffe on the beautiful steel guitar/ standard guitar duets heard on "Bob Wills Special," "Twin Guitar Special," and other numbers. While primarily known as a rhythm guitarist, Eldon is an adept and creative lead man.

Eldon's style is heard to good advantage on *Bob Wills And His Texas Playboys: For The Last Time*, recorded in December of 1973 with an all-star cast of Wills alumni. The guitar here stands out more than on the original recordings of the '30s and '40s. Further examples of his work can be found on *The Bob Wills Anthology*, which contains many of the great original recordings, and Merle Haggard's *Tribute To The Best Damn Fiddle Player In The World*, a tribute to Wills, featuring Haggard's fine band, The Strangers, in addition to some Wills veterans.

Eldon impresses as a warm and articulate man with broad musical tastes. Currently working with Speedy West and His Swing Band, he occasionally performs with Merle Haggard, as well as Marjene Fox. Eldon makes his home in Tulsa, Okalahoma.

\*   \*   \*   \*

*W*HAT WERE YOU DOING BEFORE JOINING THE WILLS *band? Had you already started playing professionally?*

I started out in Oklahoma City, playing the beer joints for tips. Rough, you know, but musicians, if they love it, they'll just stay with it, as long as they can eat. I had a 30-minute radio program by myself, playing guitar and singing. My pay for that show was 55 cents worth of meals a day. And that was one of the better jobs in Oklahoma City in those days. I came to Tulsa in '35 with the Alabama Boys—that's Cotton Thompson, the Tierney brothers (Louis and Mancell), and Harley Huggins. Most of them later went with the Wills band. I met them in a club in Oklahoma City and had them up on my radio show. About eight months later they called me, and I came to Tulsa as a vocalist on KVOO. I never did like to sing, so I stayed there a couple of years, and decided I better learn to play a little bit. After the Alabama Boys, I got a job as staff guitarist on KTUL—that was a CBS station. Around radio stations at the time, you had a lot of staff musicians. I played with girl singers, groups, everything. I played with one group, we had one of those big harps, a piano, a clarinet, guitar, and bass. We were playing swing classics, strange as it may seem. Bob heard me on this radio show and called me. I went on the Wills band in 1937.

*Who was playing guitar before you joined?*

Guy by the name of Herman Arnspiger. He was with the original Light Crust Doughboys, him and Bob and Milton Brown. He played strictly what I call country, old-fashioned type of guitar. But he was fine, for his style.

*Did you start picking up the guitar on your own?*

Right. Like a lot of musicians, never took any music, had any lessons. If you had anybody to take lessons from, you didn't have the money. By case of necessity, you learned to play and hoped you learned the right thing, so you could survive on it.

*Who did you listen to when you were starting?*

Eddie Lang was the only guitar man I had heard on record. Here in Tulsa, there weren't any guitar players. As I got into the business, Django Reinhardt was my favorite. And Charlie Christian, over there in Oklahoma City. I never listened to country or western music. I said, "I'm not going to listen to that, because I'm playing that, I'm gonna listen to something I feel is further advanced. So I always listened to Benny Goodman, the big bands, Basie. I know, back when I was a kid, if a guy could

**Texas Playboy Eldon Shamblin (center) in session with Leon McAuliff (left) and Smokey Dacus (right).**

play, it didn't make any difference if he was black, white, yellow, green, or what—you just sat down and played. I think that's always been one of the controlling factors in the music industry. If people like your playing, don't make no difference if your hair's long, short, or you don't have any, or anything else.

*Did you ever get to see Charlie Christian play?*

You didn't really have a chance to hear anybody. All the years I was on the Wills band, we worked six nights a week, and sometimes seven. We had a religious show one day, I was in the vocal quartet. Sundays, I bet I played hundreds of funerals. We had a 12:30 broadcast every day. We played in town two nights a week, and the rest of the time we travelled—grind, grind, grind.

*How did you develop that style of rhythm with the moving bass line?*

We were recording "Take Me Back To Tulsa," about 1940. Wills came over to me—the only time in all the years that Mr. Wills ever told me how or what to play—and said, "Now Eldon, I want you to put a lot of runs in this thing." From that time on I assumed that's what he wanted, so I developed the style by case of necessity, I guess. Another reason was, bass fiddle never meant much to Bob. He would say, "This old boy sings pretty good, so we can make a bass man out of him." He had some good bass men, but that was after World War II. I developed the style because we never had any good bass men—kind of compensates for it, see? The bass patterns I use are based on what I call "practical theory." In other words, make it fit and make it sound good; that's the name of the game.

*If you were playing one of those passing diminished chords, the other rhythm wouldn't be playing it, would they?*

Not necessarily. Lots of times I've thought about this conflicting with the bass, but it don't seem to, because you got a melodic thing going. It's just like a bunch of wind instruments playing against each other. As long as you get moving in the right direction, where it fits, it don't seem to conflict.

*Did you play much lead with Wills?*

I played a little bit, but not really. Wills depended on guitar for rhythm, even though he had drums, bass, piano, and everything. You could miss one lick, and he'd get mad.

*Unlike a lot of guys with Wills in the old days, you seem to know your musical theory pretty well.*

Oh yeah, you have to; how can you play without it? In the old days, Wills just had a bunch of guys, you see, and a lot of them didn't try to advance themselves music-wise. Consequently, the band grew out from under them. The later guys like

Johnny Gimble, Tiny Moore; they're not just ear men. They're good theory people in additon. They can arrange or do anything they want to. I used to buy these full band arrangements and study each part, because it was so mystifying to me. I analyzed each part, to tie it all together. That's the way I studied harmony. I done this at an early age, when I first got on the Wills band.

*How did you work out the twin stuff between you and Leon?*

We'd both work on the lead part, and I done the harmony. The first one we did was "Bob Wills Special." We'd never heard anything like that, you see. Right at that time we'd just got some amplifiers. It was quite a chore, when you're not used to it, phrasing and all that stuff. We were just kids then, had to be '38 or '39. Man! After the war practically everything was done in two or three parts—"Bubbles In My Beer," "Faded Love,"—all those things I done.

*Did you ever do any arranging?*

Yeah, I done a lot of arranging. My first little thing was "Big Beaver." I also did the horns of "San Antonio Rose." We had an arranger; he since died. He was a sax man, Granville King. We had a lot of Glenn Miller stuff, you know: five saxes, five brass, two trombones, three trumpets, plus the strings. It was a real nice thing.

*Did Wills know any theory or do any arranging?*

No. But Wills was a guy with lots of ideas. He had that uncanny ability of knowing what the people want and pursuing it. I feel Haggard's the same way. Every time I work with Haggard, I think of how much he's like the old man in so many ways. He's got a dynamic personality with a hard crust. There's no doubt who's running the band. Wills was very domineering, but a fine guy. You knew you had to get on the ball. He didn't have to say that, he'd just look at you. Had them black eyes that went right through you. The guy has to be admired because he was a humanitarian. Never saw him turn anybody down in his life. If he felt like they needed anything, he'd give it to them. And this speaks pretty well for a guy, in this age we're living in. Money didn't mean much to Bob. And his word was his bond. There's very few of them type people left. A lot of promoters took advantage of him, as the world changed. He was a real hard-working showman. He never failed to amaze me. Each night was a challenge because you never knew what he was going to do. We didn't have any cut-and-dry things, no routines. He liked to play it off-the-cuff. You didn't know when you was going to get a chorus. And that kept the band alive, too. He just [Eldon imitates Wills pointing with fiddle bow]. Of course when we had the big band you had some of your stuff arranged, because we was reading everything. It's hard to play them off-the-cuff.

*Wills stuff sometimes had extra beats and irregular meter. Was it tricky to play?*

You bet. But you know what? You develop. I got to where I played with him so long he could skip beats, and I wouldn't even notice. I'd skip with him. Take a tune like "Sitting On Top Of The World." Bob sang that song out of meter, and he never sang it the same way twice. But it didn't really matter. As long as you were watching, what difference did it make? Then, in later years, I went to work on Leon's band, and I never could play that song. Well, this proved a point to me. It don't really matter if you play one way, whether it's in meter or note; you get used to playing it, and then someboy plays it like its supposed to be played, and you can't play it. Now this used to bug a lot of musicians when Wills'd skip a two-beat deal. Like horn men for example. They're not used to it. Of course after they would finally get used to it then it would be all right.

*I spoke to a guy who said the beat of the band was uneven, tough to dance to.*

I can explain that for you, I think. Wills said, "Okay, people out there are dancing. If you get their blood to boiling, and you stay at the same tempo, they're gonna think you're dragging." He liked that tempo to increase. He didn't want it to be like "Tiger Rag," but he wanted a gradual increase in that tempo. Isn't that a weird thing? But that was his theory.

*What kind of guitar were you using with Wills?*

We didn't have any electric guitars at first. We had a man right here in Tulsa, Bob Ridley, built an amplifier, and I used a little crystal mike on my Gibson Super-400. I had to cut a notch in my bridge to slide that little crystal mike under. This was the most horrible thing that you've ever heard in your life. This would nearly make a man go commit suicide. One night you'd play it, your *E* string would be hotter than a pistol, and you couldn't hear your *B* or *G*. The next night maybe your *B* was hot, and the others wouldn't sound. Then they come out with an electric guitar like Leon used for steels. It was a standard Rickenbacker, but the body was about like a ukelele. It had a little teeny body but a regular guitar neck. I played it in a broadcast one day, and the old man like to flipped. He said, "I like the sound of that thing, but there ain't nobody in this world going to know you're playing a guitar." So he wouldn't let me play it. We had a fine guitar man in Dallas. This guy would eat that thing up alive! But when he played, he crossed his legs and stuck his feet out. He played so easy you couldn't hardly see his hand moving. He lasted two weeks and then the old man fired him. Wills said, "I know he's a fine guitar man, but if you got 500 people out there, they hear this, and they can't figure where's it's coming from." He felt like if a guy didn't look like he was doing something, he just wasn't doing something, no difference how good he's playing.

*When you did twin stuff with Leon were you playing an acoustic with a crystal mike?*

No, I think about that point Gibson came out with an amplified guitar. I had a Gibson guitar and a Gibson amplifier. I don't remember what model it was, but it was one of the first ones to come out. It wasn't very good, really.

*Tell me about the Stratocaster you're using now.*

This was give to me by Mr. Fender in 1954. It was a demonstrator. It's been banged and beat, and the frets is wore, but I've had no problems with it whatsoever. It's been a good one.

*What kind of strings do you use?*

Nothing special. Medium strings. I tried light rock and roll strings, and after one night they're through. The way it is, I have to change them about once a week. I tried flatwound, but they're not good for the type of things I do.

*Did you stay with Wills straight from the time you joined?*

Outside of about a year. A lot of the guys quit and enlisted when World War II came along, but I decided to weather the storm. I just stayed till they drug me in the army. I came out and Leon started his band, and I went to work with him. But I was only with Leon about nine or ten months, and then Wills called me and made me an offer, so I decided to go back. I finally left him in '56 and went down to Big Springs, Texas, and played with a guy by the name of Hoyle Nix; he was on this last album. Nix idolized the Wills music—sounds like him, copies him. I came back to Tulsa in 1960, because I had a family and two daughters lived here. I was getting pretty far into the piano tuning business and electronic organ service work. I didn't really want to get back on the road in the music business. I taught at the Guitar House here for five years, and after that I had my business built up to where I had all kinds of business. I play the Miss Oklahoma Pagent every year; I play a lot of things like that. I just kind of enjoy it once in a while; I wouldn't want a steady diet of it. Once in a while it's kind of a kick. If somebody calls me for a job, and I think, "Could be I'll enjoy this," I'll do it. If I don't think I'll enjoy it, I won't do it; the money don't matter that much. And I won't play western jobs, if it's not a top-notch guy. I prefer to play the cocktail things and pop trios. Country clubs, private clubs, no public deals at all. I don't play in public, I just don't like it. I prefer pop trios, where people don't pay no attention to you and you don't beat your brains out.

*Have you played any rock dates?*

No. I like rock and roll, and I wish I could play it, but I don't like it well enough to learn it. You try to do the things you believe in, you do a better job. When we played Wolftrap Farm and Chicago University, I was noticing how the young people were responding to our western type of music. You talked to people and they know all about you, from way back, and this mystified me. They had your life history! I said, "Man, what kind of deal's this?" I couldn't figure out what was happening. Us guys back here, we figure it's deader than a doornail. But this last album we made, Tommy Allsup told me we were going to get a gold record on that thing. I was really amazed. The thing I've discovered about people that like western music, they love it. They'll go to any extent to hear it. The clientele on the Wills band was always that way. They'd drive 500 miles just to get to hear it. When we was touring this part of the country years ago we used to have families that would take a two week's vacation, and all they would do is be at every dance we played, every night. And that's the way they'd spend their vacation. This is a little weird to me. The masses didn't go, but the ones that liked it, loved it. You may not have many, but if they know about it, goddamn, they'll be there.

---

**A SELECTED ELDON SHAMBLIN DISCOGRAPHY**

**Solo album:** *Guitar Genius*, Delta, 1007. **With Tiny Moore & Jethro Burns:** *Back To Back*, Kaleidoscope, F-9. **With Bob Wills:** *Bob Wills And His Texas Playboys*, United Artists, UA-LA 216-J-2; *The Bob Wills Anthology*, Columbia, KG 32146. **With Merle Haggard:** *Tribute To The Best Damn Fiddle Player In The World*, Capitol, ST-628. **With others:** *S' Wonderful*, Flying Fish, FF-035.

# RICKY SKAGGS

**By Jim Hatlo**

WHAT DID THE FUTURE HOLD FOR RICKY SKAGGS, sideman *par excellence* with Emmylou Harris' Hot Band and with the Whites? "I'd like something for myself," he replied. "It's time to get my own career started."

That was in 1980, just after Ricky had finished a sizzling show with Harris at northern California's first (and last) Stanford Country And Bluegrass Festival. He was speaking with a certain acoustic music magazine just into its second year of publication. Many of the magazine's readers had already heard of Ricky Skaggs. The rest of America, by and large, had not.

It was a safe bet that the talented 26-year-old multi-instrumentalist's future would be bright. But no one suspected how quickly it would dawn, or how dazzling it would be. Within a few years, he would be a phenomenon.

Yes indeed, Ricky Skaggs started his own career and got something for himself. He got a new image, trading his post-Beatles locks for a blow-dry coiffure worthy of a country front man. He got his own band. And in 1982 he got awards like Best New Artist and Best New Male Vocalist from the Academy of Country Music, and Best Male Vocalist from the Country Music Association. He copped the Ralph Stanley Dove Award from the Gospel Music Association. In 1983 he and his band got the Touring Band Of The Year award from the Academy, and the Instrumental Group Of The Year award from the CMA. They won them again in 1984, and got their third straight Bluegrass Act Of The Year award from *Music City News*. Ricky shared in a Grammy award for Best Country Instrumental (after playing "Fireball" in a reunion with the New South, on the live LP *Bluegrass: The Greatest Show On Earth*). *Cashbox* magazine gave him another Male Vocalist Of The Year award. (Along the way, his gifts as a multi-instrumentalist also earned him repeat honors in the annual *Frets* Readers Poll.)

It wasn't the hairdo. Ricky Skaggs' impact on the record-buying public made the industry sit up and take notice. No one could call a string of eight #1 country singles a fluke. The eighth, "Uncle Pen," marked the first time since the *Billboard* charts began in 1949 that a bluegrass tune by a solo artist had achieved the #1 slot.

Ricky's albums didn't do too poorly, either, *Waiting For The Sun To Shine, Highways And Heartaches,* and *Don't Cheat In Our Hometown* all went gold in the U.S. and Canada (the first two are now platinum, north of the border), and his latest, *Country Boy,* is headed in the same direction.

The waves he has made have rocked boats in waters well past the headlands of country music. *Esquire* magazine, which spent two years studying over 5,000 nominees for its first-ever *Esquire* Register Edition, published in December 1984 to honor "a new breed of American hero," included Ricky Skaggs on its roster. He was thereby certified as being among "The Best Of The New Generation: Men And Women Under Forty Who Are Changing America," along with people like actresses Meryl Streep and Sissy Spacek, rock innovator David Byrne, basketball whiz Julius Erving, Nashville Network star David Holt, Olympic diver Greg Louganis, Apple computer wunderkind Stephen Wozniak, trumpeter Wynton Marsalis, Windham Hill Records founder Will Ackerman, and filmmaker Stephen Spielberg.

Ricky earned his place among *Esquire*'s 272 movers and shakers by playing "music that proudly asserts its pure country roots," the magazine said, even though "contemporary Nashville logic dictates crossover pop slickness."

"He has made it in the country music business on his own terms," *Esquire* wrote. "His three successful Epic albums have encouraged other artists to put the country back into country music."

Skaggs' amazing success has brought hope to lots of other traditional country and bluegrass musicians, those still wandering in the relative wilderness of country fair bookings and small independent record labels. If Ricky Skaggs, formerly of Ralph Stanley's Clinch Mountain Boys, formerly of the Country Gentlemen, formerly of J.D. Crowe And The New South, formerly of Boone Creek—if *he* can reach the Promised Land, then they have a fighting chance to get there, too. Ricky is giving them all the help he can. Through his influence, the 1983 Academy of Country Music awards telecast included a special video clip—narrated by Ricky—introducing a national audience to the joys of bluegrass festivals.

Ironically, the new messiah of traditional music is still fighting a minor rear-guard action against bluegrass pharisees

114

**Ricky Skaggs on acoustic/electric guitar.**

who condemn him for not being "pure" enough. His chief offense: going outside the faith by intermarrying traditional tunes with electric instruments and uptown hot licks.

"I've never said that we play bluegrass music," Ricky responds. "We play bluegrass-*influenced* music. We've been winning Bluegrass Act Of The Year every year at the *Music City News* awards, and it's real hard for me to go up and accept that, because we're not a bluegrass act. I know what bluegrass is; I've played it all my life. But for people outside it, I'm probably the most bluegrass thing they've ever heard on country radio. I use the fiddles and mandolins and a lot of instruments that are real vital to bluegrass, and because of my voice being high, and the harmonies we use, I think they tag me with the bluegrass label. But I know the difference.

"We play bluegrass festivals now and then, maybe one or two a year. I'm a little apprehensive about going to a festival because I would never want to disappoint anybody or let them down; but the people always love it. No one has ever given us a hard time at a bluegrass festival."

What about the legitimacy of electric instruments—pedal steel and electric guitar, for instance?

"Bill Monroe would never have used them," Ricky says, "but that's no reason not to use them. I wasn't afraid to go with instruments like that in my band because I can mix them in there with the acoustic music in a way that they're just instruments like everything else. If you can do it in a way that enhances the music, then I don't think there is anything wrong with it."

Unlike such country artists as Jerry Reed and Glen Campbell, hot pickers who let their instrumental skills fade into the background once they achieved star status, Ricky is playing as much instrumental music as ever. "I still play the fiddle and I still play the mandolin," he says. "I'm playing guitar, too—and

I'm playing a lot of electric guitar now."

Purists who turned Ricky's picture to the wall when he added electric instruments may now be plastering it over altogether, but the change has actually helped balance the band's sound. Ricky's diversification into electric picking came after his first lead guitarist, Ray Flacke, wearied of the road and left the band in 1984 to pursue a studio and teaching career.

"I'd had a Telecaster-type 'bender' guitar [a custom solid-body with a built-in, spring-loaded device for raising the pitch of the second string] for a couple of years," Ricky says, "but I hadn't had much reason to use it, with Ray in the group. When he left I auditioned a couple of guitar players, but they really weren't what I was looking for. My wife, Sharon [White], talked me into playing lead guitar myself. She's always had a lot of faith in me. 'I've heard you play,' she said, 'and I know you can.' I kept telling her I wasn't ready to do it, but she wouldn't let up until I agreed to give it a try. I'm really glad she wouldn't take no for an answer."

With Ricky's hand on the volume knob, the band's sound level has come down from its former high-water mark. "When Ray was with us," he says, "it used to be kind of like a domino effect. We would try to get the stage quieter, but then if Ray turned up, Bruce (Bouton, on pedal steel) would turn up, and then the fiddles would turn up, because everybody was trying to get back to being able to hear themselves again. But now the stage volume has dropped considerably. I've been playing my mandolin and fiddle all acoustic—just through the microphones—because we're not nearly as loud as we used to be."

Ricky is proud of his instrumental accomplishments, even though he doesn't sneeze at the awards he has won as a vocalist. In discussing favorite cuts from his albums, he likes to dwell on the instrumental breaks. "I was real happy with the way my fiddle solo in 'You've Got A Lover' [a #1 single from *Highways And Heartaches*] came out," he says. "On *Country Boy,* I'm playing plenty of acoustic solos. Most of the album is real acoustic. I'm playing a lot of guitar on the title cut."

That is an understatement. In covering "*Country Boy,*" Skaggs was stepping onto turf that had already been fenced and posted by Albert Lee, the lightning-fingered Englishman who preceded Skaggs in Emmylou Harris' band. Lee made "Country Boy" his signature tune way back in 1971, in England, and drew raves in the U.S. for a later version on his 1979 solo album *Hiding* (A&M, SP-4750). The idea of Ricky Skaggs tackling "Country Boy" was something tantamount to Heisman Trophy winner Doug Flutie taking aim at Joe Namath's career record for Super Bowl yardage.

Skaggs was not intimidated. He appropriated Lee's killer licks, added a few variations of his own, and blazed through the tune with a ferocity that withered any doubts as to whether he was too much the jack-of-all-trades to be a big-league lead guitarist. He also turned his cross-picking chops loose on the guitar solo for "I'm Ready To Go," the gospel rouser that closes the album, and threaded a sensitive backup part through "Two Highways." Elsewhere he traded electric riffs with Bruce Bouton on "Baby, I'm In Love With You," crafted a shuffling multi-fiddle break for his cover of Peter Rowan's "Rendezvous," and added an understated mandolin track to "Patiently Waiting."

But it is perhaps "Wheel Hoss," the Bill Monroe instrumental at the end of side one, that gives Ricky the most pleasure. Not because of his creditable flat-picked guitar lead, but because

Monroe accepted Skaggs' invitation to play mandolin on the cut. The guest appearance gave Ricky a chance to pay tribute to the patriarch of bluegrass—and in effect, it conferred Monroe's blessing upon Skaggs' second-generation updating of the music.

"He did it as an overdub," says Ricky, "and it was the wildest thing in the world to look out in the studio and see Bill Monroe with headphones on. Really, technology had prevailed there! The neat thing was how his mandolin fit in with the piano and the pedal steel, and he *loved* it. He had such a great time doing it. He was so gracious and such a gentleman in the studio. He never once balked and said, 'Well, I'm not going to play with that because it's an electrical instrument, and that's not bluegrass.'

"When people complain because my music isn't bluegrass, I understand. But you know, in order for Bill Monroe to come in and do something like he did on 'Wheel Hoss,' he has to have respect for the kind of music that I'm doing right now.

"When I came to Nashville, there were three people that I really wanted to impress with my music. One was Bill Monroe, because he is the father of bluegrass. Then there was Ralph Stanley, because he was my first boss, and I felt I learned an awful lot from him and his kind of music. And then there was Roy Acuff, because he had seen so many of the young innovators come to the *Grand Ole Opry*, like Hank Williams and Elvis Presley.

"I think that I do have respect from those three people; and if they are happy with what I do, then anybody else can either take it or leave it. I feel that those men are real good judges of traditional country music. I mean, it's all country music as far as I'm concerned."

It's fair to say that Skaggs walked the length and breadth of country music before forging his own style. He first apprenticed at the very heart of traditionally oriented bluegrass. With Stanley's band, playing mandolin and fiddle as a 16-year-old prodigy, he was a few degrees back from the cutting edge—closer to the old mountain music that fed Monroe's imagination. If there is such a thing as an "authentic bluegrass band experience," Skaggs got one with Stanley.

"Being around with Ralph, and Curly Ray Cline, and Jack Cook, and the other guys in the band, who were 30 or 40 years older than I was—that was real neat for me," Ricky recalls. "It was something new. I learned some things that I *didn't* want to do on the road. I learned what it was like to travel with six or seven people in a station wagon, along with a bass fiddle. It keeps me humble to know that's where I came from; and if I had to go back to something like that, I would, because I love the music so much. But it really makes me appreciate what I've got now."

It was after he joined Emmylou Harris in 1978 that Ricky got a taste of those trappings of stardom—tour buses, backstage catered buffets, roadies, and other creature comforts. He could have kicked back and just enjoyed the ride. Instead, he stayed alert to the logistics of transporting and staging music entertainment on that scale. Besides being at the other end of the spectrum from the Clinch Mountain Boys technically, the Hot Band also was operating on an altogether different front musically, at the borders of rock and roll. Ricky listened, observed, met people, and began refining the ideas that were to find expression in his own successful acoustic/electrical sound.

"It was a real good education for me," he says, "going with Emmylou and taking what knowledge I had of bluegrass, and learning what I could about electric-type instruments like steel guitar, electric guitar, drums, piano, that kind of thing. I had never worked with those before. I learned as much about electronics and equipment and monitors and stuff as I possibly could. I was always snooping around and seeing what kind of amps they were using, what kind of monitors, what kind of consoles; whether a monitor cabinet was Gauss or JBL or Electro-Voice. I learned how different things sound—how certain amps or certain speakers would sound different, for instance. JBL's have a little softer bottom, maybe, than Electro-Voice.

"Having had my own group, Boone Creek (1976-78), was a good place to start. It was good to know about the problems of running a band; to see what it's like in reality out there. After I had been with Emmy two and a half years, I had cut *Sweet Temptation* (1979), and *Don't Cheat In Our Hometown*—even though that didn't come out before '83 because Sugar Hill kept it in the can until they made a deal on it with Epic. I really felt like I was to the point where I could do something on my own."

While Ricky's tour of duty in the Hot Band was the catalyst that crystallized his solo act, moving in country-rock circles also provided an education of a different sort. "Once I got into rockabilly-like music or rock and roll country, or whatever you want to call it, I got to seeing some real heavy drugs," he recalls, "and it really freaked me out, because a boy like me from eastern Kentucky had never run into those things. Drugs weren't really a big thing in bluegrass—well, sleeping pills were, or diet pills, that kind of thing. Anything to speed them up a little bit. But nothing heavier. And I was scared to death of it. I had a relative who was a real good musician, but he was an alcoholic. He just lived in the bottle, and I saw such a talent go to waste. I vowed I would never let anything like that happen to me—some kind of chemical dependency.

"When I talk about impressing Roy Acuff, that's one of the things I mean. He's seen so many young people come and go, getting involved in drugs and alcohol, or marital problems, or whatever would cause their careers to fall apart. I'm a born-again Christian, and that's probably the main thing that has kept me and my family together, and kept my career going, and kept my head on straight."

(Skaggs' beliefs have a marked influence on his programming, with gospel tunes like "Children Go" [*Don't Cheat In Our Hometown*], "I'm Ready To Go" [*Country Boy*], and "River Of Jordan [*Family & Friends*] being fixtures on his albums. "I don't come on as a real strong preacher or something like that," he says, "I was preached to that way when I was a kid, and I kind of rebelled against it, so I would never want to push that on anybody. But my religious convictions kind of keep me with one goal in life, and that's to try to be a better person every day if I can, and to let people know that there is always one door open for them, even when they think that all the doors have been closed.")

Ricky put together his award-winning band by building a core of veterans from established country acts. For example, drummer George Grantham spent 11 years with Poco; pianist Gary Smith worked over five years with Barbara Mandrell; backup singer Richard Dennison formerly sang harmony with Dolly Parton; fiddler Bobby Hicks' credits include stints with

Bill Monroe, Judy Lynn, and Porter Wagoner. As a band-leader, Ricky also looked for versatility: Steel player Bruce Bouton doubles on guitar and dobro. Multi-instrumentalist Lou Reid switches between guitar, fiddle, and banjo. Hicks occasionally moves over to the banjo.

Against that instrumental backdrop, Ricky shifts between guitar, mandolin, and fiddle, interspersed with his electric guitar and his "Mandocaster," a 5-string solidbody electric mandolin.

"I've got a 1949 Martin D-28 that I use when we're touring," he says. "I've had a Takamine pickup put inside it, and to me that's the ultimate acoustic guitar sound for the road. The pickup goes in the saddle and there's a preamp inside the guitar—which makes it kind of heavy, and you have to cut a hole in the guitar, but it's all according to what you're willing to give up for that good sound. The guitar sounds so acoustic it's scary; we've even used the pickup in the studio, instead of miking the guitar, and it sounded real good. Then I have 'Red' [a 1959 D-28 that formerly belonged to Ricky's father].

"I used Red some on the road, but I haven't used him in the studio in quite a while, now. He's going to need some work, because he's a little sick these days. So is 'Floyd.'" ("Floyd" is a custom 5-string fiddle that was built for Ricky by Arthur Conner of Floyd County, Virginia.)

"One thing I've let happen," says Ricky, "that I never used to let happen when I was playing bluegrass music all the time, is that I've let my instruments run down a little bit. I really shouldn't have done that, but I just don't have the time to look after them on the road."

Ricky has made yet another concession to success. He has given up his old practice of converting GHS nickel-wrap guitar strings into strings for his 1924 Gibson F-5 mandolin. He used to pop the ball-ends out of the strings, creating loop ends that could be attached to the mandolin's tailpiece. "I haven't found the need to do that anymore," he says. "It was great for recording though, because with the slicker mona-steel (instead of the typical bronze wrap) you didn't get so much noise from string slides." Ricky uses GHS strings on the rest of his fretted instruments, and uses a Thomastik 5-string set for his fiddle.

If Ricky has less time for the mechanics of performing, that's in part because he is devoting more energy to the strategies of showbiz. "I wanted to break the ice gently," he says of his entrance into the main country music arena. "I wanted to try to milk-feed the audience a little bit before I started trying to put some solid food—real traditional country music and blue-grass—out to them.

"I think if I had put mandolin and banjo and dobro on all my cuts for *Waiting For The Sun To Shine,* that would have been a mistake. Presentation is so important to people, and lots of times you only have one chance. You want to make sure that chance is the best shot you have. *Waiting For The Sun To Shine* was plenty country, but it was a little different. It had a little less bluegrass, and it went over easier than just jumping in abruptly and saying, 'Hey, listen to this! I'm bluegrass!'

"In the past, I think the banjo has kind of been pushed down peoples' throats. That's why I tried to come in a little more from the back door, instead of coming directly in the front door with the full bluegrass sound. So I've only had banjo on two of my singles: 'Highway 40 Blues' (played by Bela Fleck) and 'Uncle Pen' (played by Lou Reid).

"Of course, back when the album *Waiting For The Sun To Shine* came out, we didn't know what was going to happen, we had no idea that we would end up having two #1 singles from that record!"

From that benchmark, in just a few years Ricky has established the kind of track record that buys a large degree of freedom in the world of recording. Success breeds success: Witness the heavy promotional commitment CBS made to the current Ricky Skaggs tour of the Northeast. When the golden eggs are coming in, you step up the grain to the goose. But the concert fees and the promotional bucks are doing more than bankrolling a performer, as far as Ricky is concerned: They are also underwriting a vision, an idea with implications that go beyond the boundaries of Ricky Skaggs' own career.

"There is definitely a new trend in country music," he says. "I mean, it's real obvious with our eight #1 records, gold albums, and so on—things that I never dreamed would be possible for me, because I just felt there was such a limited market out there for bluegrass music. But it turned out that's really not so.

"Bluegrass is a form of country music, and it always has been. If we try to make it out like something as different as rock and roll, then we're just fooling ourselves. It started out as a kind of country music, and then Bill Monroe heard a hot banjo picker named Earl Scruggs and threw that in there, because he wanted to innovate. He wanted to be the one out there doing something different.

"What I wanted to do was to get away from playing just totally acoustic bluegrass music so I could try to mix two styles together, and do something different. I kind of see myself here in the '80s as doing what Monroe did in the '40s, as far as trying to work with something traditional—trying to keep it the same, yet change it and update it. I want to give it a new breath of life."

---

### A SELECTED RICKY SKAGGS DISCOGRAPHY

**Solo albums** (on CBS/Epic): *Favorite Country Songs,* FE-39409; *Live In London,* FE 40103; *Love's Gonna Get Ya!,* 40309; *Country Boy,* FE 49410; *Don't Cheat In Our Hometown,* FE 38954; *Highways & Heartaches,* FE 37996; *Waiting For The Sun To Shine,* FE37193. **With others:** *Sweet Temptation,* Sugar Hill (Box 4040, Duke Station, Durham, NC 27706), SH-3701; *Family & Friends,* Rounder (One Camp St., Cambridge, MA 02140), 0151. **With the Whites:** *Old Familiar Feeling,* Warner Bros., 23872-1; *More Pretty Girls Than One,* Sugar Hill, SH-3710. **With Tony Rice:** *Skaggs & Rice,* Sugar Hill, SH-3711. **With Boone Creek:** *Boone Creek,* Rounder, 0081; *One-Way Track,* Sugar Hill, SH-3701. **With Bill Monroe:** *Bill Monroe & Friends,* MCA, 5435. **With Emmylou Harris:** *Pieces Of The Sky,* Reprise, 2284; *Blue Kentucky Girl,* Warner Bros., 3318; *Roses In The Snow,* Warner Bros., 3422. **With J. D. Crowe:** *Bluegrass: The Greatest Show On Earth,* Sugar Hill, SH-2201; *The New South,* Rounder, 0044.

---

# HANK SNOW

By Dennis E. Hensley

"**I** DON'T REALLY PROFESS TO BE A GREAT GUITARIST," claims veteran country artist Hank Snow, "but since the people seem to enjoy my style of picking, I've kept at it for the past 40 years."

Canadian-born Hank Snow—better known to his fans as The Singing Ranger—came to Nashville during the early years of radio. Along with Ernest Tubb, Minnie Pearl, and other country music pioneers, Hank Snow helped establish the *Grand Ole Opry* as a world-renowned institution. Over the years his albums have been consistently strong sellers, and his singles, such as the multi-million selling "I've Been Everywhere," have remained constant chartbusters.

Hank's big break came over a quarter of a century ago, when he recorded "I'm Movin' On" and saw it rise to #1 on both pop and country charts. Since then he has made worldwide tours, has appeared on scores of television shows, has gained fame as a songwriter, and has also made numerous recordings as a solo guitarist.

Hank Snow's unique style of acoustic guitar playing has been as much part of his act as his singing. In the '50's Hank released several instrumental recordings, and in 1964 he and Chet Atkins combined talents on an instrumental album release, *Reminiscing.*

\* \* \* \*

*H*OW DID YOU LEARN TO PLAY GUITAR? DID YOU EVER take any lessons?

I took formal music lessons for over a year from an excellent instructor. Although I can play by ear, I also know theory and note reading. During one period of my life I worked as a guitar teacher for three consecutive years to supplement my income. I always enjoyed chording and working out fancy rhythm patterns, but my greatest joy and challenge came in working out lead parts. I developed a unique style of playing which blended the flatpicking of mountain music, the string pushing of bluegrass, and the chord harmonies of straight country music.

*Has any one guitarist had an influence on your style of picking?*

Thinking back, I would have to say that Carl Farr was one of my real favorites. Carl was the guitar player with the original Sons Of The Pioneers. I tried to copy the runs and ad-libs that Carl did on their recordings and in their stage act. He was a super talent. Trying to imitate Carl's technique is what made it

119

necessary for me to practice the guitar so much. He was especially good on fill-in riffs, something I've developed and used on my own vocals through the years.

*When you first began recording you released singles which were vocals, and singles which were guitar instrumentals. Was that unusual in those days?*

Yes, it was. It still is today. In the late '40s and early '50s Merle Travis recorded both instrumentals and vocals, but he and I have been about the only two to do so, at least over a long period of time. Chet Atkins used to sing a little, but he didn't do it professionally, simply for show or crowd amusement.

*Have you always done your own lead work on recordings?*

I've always been my own lead guitarist, even if it meant we had to overdub my vocal part later in order to get good voice and instrument separation.

*Do you do your own instrumental arrangements for your records?*

Chet Atkins and I have worked together on my recordings for many years. I come into the studio with my arrangements, whether vocal or instrumental, all in mind, but Chet usually has some revisions or alterations to suggest. Chet's the finest session producer in Nashville and the greatest country guitarist who ever lived, so naturally I heed his advice and appreciate his guidance. Besides, [laughs] I have to have somebody to blame it on if the record proves to be a dud.

*I understand you're building a home studio?*

Yes, and it's almost all finished now. My objective is to be able to do my instrumental lead work and my vocals at home, and then turn my tapes over to RCA and have a back-up group dubbed in.

*Do you play any instruments other than guitar?*

Not really, I enjoy working on steel guitar sometimes and I've been known to sit down to a piano, but nothing professional.

*How many guitars do you own?*

I've got a whole collection. I do stage performances and recordings with various Martin guitars, but as a hobby I buy guitars of all brands and designs and keep them at home.

*What kind of strings do you use?*

I currently am using an experimental set of new strings which Martin is developing. They've asked me to test them out for a year, and thus far they have been excellent strings. Under normal circumstances, however, I use Mapes medium gauge strings for acoustic guitar. Mapes has always supplied strings for the Martin Company, and I've always played a Martin flat-top.

*What kind of a pick do you use?*

A medium, both in size and thickness.

*Do you ever use pickups on your Martin flat-tops?*

Never, never, never! On sessions I play my guitar in front of a microphone and onstage I do the same thing. Pickups clamp steel onto the wood of the guitar, which alters the guitar's original pure sound.

*Do you do anything before a performance to limber your hands? Any special exercises?*

No, nothing special. I spent every day of my life with a guitar in my hand, so all I need to do is pick one up, check the tuning, run over a few chords, and I'm ready.

*Is it true that you are cutting down on personal appearances?*

That's true. I only tour these days from the 20th of April through the 20th of October. I take the winter months off. I go to Florida and Texas for a vacation, and I spend a lot of time at home in Nashville. I spent three decades on the road, and at this stage of the game I'm not too keen on battling those rough winter roads anymore. Of course, traveling, like picking, is in my blood, so I may end up like Roy Acuff, who has retired six times yet is still going strong.

*What do you do to avoid stage boredom?*

Well, 26 years ago I had a super-smash hit single called "I'm Movin' On," so everywhere I perform I *have* to sing that number. Everything else I can modify, however. I've recorded so many albums and collected so many songs, I've really got a large catalog of tunes to offer folks. To keep from getting stagnant, I sing different songs, and I pick different instrumentals from one performance to the next.

*You're a founding father of country music. What are your views on the modern Nashville sound?*

I'm extremely disappointed in it. I don't like it. How can they cut jazz and rock in a Nashville studio and call it country? Just because it was recorded in Nashville, that doesn't make it country. Look, I'm not against any singer or picker earning a gold record, I'm just against the way country music has been drastically altered. It's lost its solidness, its gut-level appeal. True country fans want the true country sound. Look at Willie Nelson's hit release of "Blue Eyes Crying In The Rain"—that was recorded with only four or five instruments, most of which were non-amplified. It was simple, and solid, and very country, and folks bought it like crazy. That's the kind of picking and singing I've always tried to do.

*Why, on your instrumental records, are there only four to six pieces behind you?*

Again, my main concern is to conserve the true country sound. As such, all I need is a bass, rhythm guitar, some drums, perhaps a piano, and occasionally a fiddle. Another reason for this is so that when I perform instrumentally onstage with my road band, the audience hears the same sound they've heard on my records.

*What artist has had the greatest over-all influence on your music?*

Without a doubt it was the late Jimmie Rodgers, The Singing Brakeman. His guitar licks were very basic, but they worked well in his style of music. His songs told real stories of life and mankind. In my early records I tried to copy Jimmie's singing by imitating his diction and phrasings. I soon got away from that, but in the back of my mind I'm always conscious of the impression Jimmie's music made on my life.

---

**A SELECTED HANK SNOW DISCOGRAPHY**

**Solo albums:** *Just Keep A Movin'*, Detour, 33-004; *Collector's Series*, RCA, AHL1-5497; *Golden Greats*, RCA (Australia), SP 181. **With Chet Atkins:** *Reminiscing*, RCA, LAP-5952; *Collector's Duets*, Victor, CPL1-7059.

# SONS OF THE PIONEERS

By Doug Green

THERE WERE NO COUNTRY MUSIC AWARDS BACK IN the '30s and '40s. It's too bad, because the Sons Of The Pioneers would have walked away with the Vocal Group of the Year award just as regularly as the Statler Brothers have in recent years. The Sons Of the Pioneers were creators of their own unique, personal style and type of country music, just as Bob Wills and Bill Monroe were, although the Sons Of The Pioneers have received less critical attention. Still, their contributions in style and the creation of great songs have been extremely influential, and have provided us with one of the most fascinating and exciting forms of country music, western harmony singing.

The group's long and complex history began in October 1933, when Len Slye—later known to the world as Roy Rogers—

The Sons Of The Pioneers (left to right) Hugh Farr, Bob Nolan, Pat Brady, Karl Farr, Lloyd Perryman, and Tim Spencer, rebanded after WWII and produced many hit songs, including "Cool Water."

**Above: The Sons Of The Pioneers (left to right) Pat Brady, Hugh Farr, Karl Farr, Bob Nolan, Tim Spencer, and Lloyd Perryman, c. 1946.**
**Below: The Sons Of The Pioneers (left to right) Karl Farr, Hugh Farr, Tim Spencer, Leonard Sly (Roy Rogers), Bob Nolan, and Gus Mack, c. 1935.**

coerced two fellow southern California musicians, Tim Spencer and Bob Nolan, to get back into the music business they'd quit during the Depression. The three singers formed a group they called the Pioneer Trio.

Nolan, born April 1, 1908, in New Brunswick, Canada; Spencer, born July 13, 1908, in Webb City, Missouri; and Slye, born November 5, 1911, in Duck Run, Ohio, had all migrated to the Hollywood area in the late '20s and early '30s in search of musical careers. They'd played with several bands, sometimes together and sometimes apart, but under Slye's prodding they ultimately joined forces for a venture of their own.

The three had much to offer. Nolan was a promising song-writer—he ranks among country music's greatest—who had already composed two of his classics, "Way Out There" and "Tumbling Tumbleweeds." He had a unique voice as a soloist and was a fine harmony singer. Spencer had begun to develop his talents as a songwriter, sang a strong tenor, and could solo. Slye was the guitarist, lead singer, fancy yodeler, and believe it or not, the trio's comedian.

The group was greatly strengthened in early 1934 with the addition of Hugh Farr. Farr was a fine Texas fiddler from a musical family; shortly thereafter his brother, Karl, joined the Pioneers as lead guitarist. In deference to the Farr brothers' part-Indian ancestry, and because they were too young to pass themselves off as pioneers (and mostly because it sounded a lot catchier), the group changed its name to the Sons Of The Pioneers.

The next several years were active ones for the Sons Of The Pioneers. They started appearing on radio, began a long series of musical support roles in Charles Starrett films for Columbia, and began recording for the then-new Decca label. This was also their most creative period of songwriting, one that saw them write and record such western classics (while virtually defining

the style) as "I Still Do," "Happy Roving Cowboy," "Blue Prairie," "One More Ride," "Love Song Of The Waterfall," and "Song Of The Bandit." They also began a long series of transcriptions for national distribution that probably boosted their reputation more than the records did.

Members came and went. In 1936, the group added a magnificent tenor voice when it hired 19-year-old Lloyd Perryman to replace Tim Spencer (though Spencer rejoined within the year). Slye left to begin a career in films, and with his departure the band hired Pat Brady as a comedian. Brady was also a full-time bass player, relieving Nolan of that responsibility.

Slye had previously auditioned for Universal Pictures, when Universal was looking for a singing cowboy, but he had been rejected because he looked too young. Slye got his break when Gene Autry went on strike at Republic Pictures. Autry was pressuring Republic for a salary commensurate with his box office popularity, and in response Republic began seeking a new singing cowboy to force Autry to come to terms. Slye was chosen from among hundreds of applicants. He took the name Dick Weston when he left the Sons Of The Pioneers, then changed it to the now-familiar Roy Rogers.

Though Slye was with the band only four years, he was really the sparkplug among the founders. He remained loyal to the Sons Of The Pioneers, hiring them for his Republic films beginning in 1941, and he still appears frequently with the current Pioneers.

World War II was hard on the band, as it was on most musical groups. Brady and Perryman were drafted and were replaced for the duration by bass player/comedian Shug Fisher (perhaps best known for his TV role as Shorty Kellums) and lyrical tenor Ken Carson.

When the wartime shellac shortage ended, the Sons Of The Pioneers were back in the studio, this time for RCA Victor. The sessions produced more of their greatest songs, including "Timber Trail," "Cowboy Camp Meeting," "Everlasting Hills Of Oklahoma," and probably their biggest hit, "Cool Water."

Lloyd Perryman and Pat Brady returned after the war. Although the group remained extremely busy, there were some important changes in the making.

An era ended in 1949 when Tim Spencer retired. Years on the road and a turn to religion had wearied him of a life of touring. He founded Manna Music, a successful gospel publishing company, and ran it for many years. Spencer suffered a serious stroke in 1970, and eventually died on April 26, 1974. However, he lived long enough to see one of his finest songs, "Room Full Of Roses," revived by Mickey Gilley to become a #1 record.

It was no surprise that Bob Nolan left within three months of Spencer's departure. He, too, was weary of the road, and was embittered by dishonesty within the music business. He recorded a bit on his own, and continued to record with the Pioneers until 1957, but he grew increasingly withdrawn and began secluding himself at a California mountain retreat for several months of each year. He still spends much of his time there restlessly writing songs, though few indeed have been heard in recent years.

Spencer's replacement was a former singing-cowboy film star who had been dropped by Columbia in 1947 when Gene Autry joined the studio. It may be hard to believe that *Gunsmoke*'s grizzled Festus was once a singing cowboy, but in fact Ken Curtis was one of the best, and he lent his smooth voice to many of the Pioneers' recordings.

Nolan's unusual guttural baritone might have seemed, on the surface, impossible to replace, but Tommy Doss' voice was virtually identical, and Doss was to remain a mainstay with the band from 1949 to 1963. Lloyd Perryman took over the band leadership after the departure of Spencer and Nolan. He kept the sound and style and the band itself intact through both fat and lean years.

Ken Curtis left in 1953. He was replaced by Dale Warren, the current bandleader. The rock and roll years took their toll on western harmony music, as they did on all country music. Hugh Farr became disgruntled and left in 1958. Karl Farr died of a heart attack onstage in 1961, at the age of 52. Somehow the band stayed together, and Karl Farr was succeeded by Roy Lanham, the group's present guitarist.

Lloyd Perryman, his tenor voice deepening over the years, was not only a great singer; he was also a determined man, and he kept the band going despite the problems it encountered. Just as things seemed to take an upswing—the Sons Of The Pioneers made several national television appearances, cut a fine new album for Granite Records, and began making college appearances—Perryman suffered a heart attack. He died, following open-heart surgery, on May 31, 1977, after 41 years in the saddle, 28 of them as trail boss.

Dale Warren took over the reins. He still holds them, singing lead and playing electric bass. Warren's brother-in-law, Billy Leibert, an excellent and long-respected musician, now plays accordion. Lanham plays inspired electric guitar, and Rome Johnson has been added to fill Perryman's large boots as rhythm guitarist and baritone singer. In 1974 Rusty Richards took over the tenor singing chores from Luther Nallie. Besides bringing to the group an impressive songwriting talent, Richards has provided some first-rate feature yodeling, a sound missing from the band for a number of years.

This is the group that currently carries on the Sons Of The Pioneers' long and honored tradition, and continues to build upon it. The band's resurgence continues: It recently appeared on *Dinah* and *The Merv Griffin Show*, as well as guesting several times on *Hee Haw*. The Sons Of The Pioneers were among the five finalists in nominations for the Country Music Hall of Fame last year, and doubtless will become members before too long.

They are still on the road, still bringing great western harmony singing to audiences around the country, and keeping alive a magnificent tradition in country music.

---

## A SELECTED SONS OF THE PIONEERS DISCOGRAPHY

*Tumbleweed Trails*, MCA, 730; *The Sons Of The Pioneers*, Bear, 15071; *Sons Of The Pioneers*, Columbia, FC 37439; *Way Out West*, Country Music Foundation; *The Best Of The Sons Of The Pioneers*, RCA, LSP 3476; *The Sons Of The Pioneers*, JEMF, 102.

# MERLE TRAVIS

By Mark Humphrey

"LIVING LEGEND" IS A TERM TOO OFTEN LAVISHED ON
surviving artistic also-rans, but it *does* apply to some individuals;
and nowhere is it more apt than beside the name of Merle Travis.
Merle's expressive, craggy face bespeaks the many roads traveled
in a lifetime that has taken him on a musical odyssey from the

coal country of Kentucky's Muhlenberg County to Hollywood
and beyond.

Merle Robert Travis was born November 29, 1917, at Rose-
wood, Kentucky. His father, "Uncle Rob" Travis, relaxed from the
strenuous grind of coal mining by picking a 5-string banjo, and

eight-year-old Merle was thus inspired to try his hand at the instrument. When big brother Taylor abandoned the home place, and his hand-made guitar, for a factory job in Evansville, Indiana, Merle—at age 12—was ready to take up the instrument on which he would leave his own indelible print: "Travis picking."

Merle soon found himself in the midst of a healthy finger-picking tradition, competing with the older boys of this area—Pip Stevens, Cundiff Durham, Orval Raymar, "Plucker" English, and Cola Addison. But the best of the lot were two young miners named Mose Rager and Ike Everly. Merle has always generously credited those two men with inspiring Travis picking, and to this day plays tunes he learned from them. Everly was to die a victim of black lung disease, but not before leaving the world another musical legacy—his sons, Don and Phil (the Everly Brothers). The genial Mose Rager still plays his music at home in Drakesboro, Kentucky.

The performance bug struck Merle early, and he made as many amateur show appearances as he could. A still teenaged Travis made his radio debut at a "live" broadcast from one of the infamous dance marathons in 1936, and he soon found himself working with such colorfully named bands as the Tennessee Tom Cats and the Knox County Knockabouts. "Knockabout" was an accurate description of a musician's life in those days, but Merle was unperturbed. "That was the days of the Depression,"

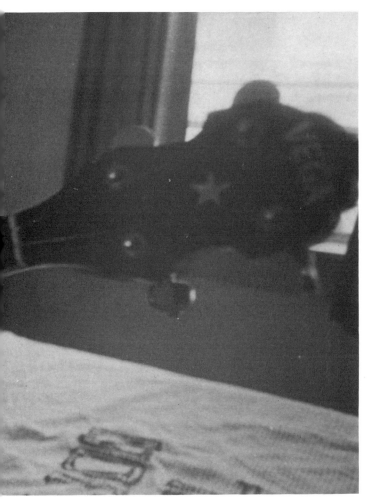

he recalls, "but people—young people like me—didn't get depressed."

Merle moved up in the world when he joined Clayton McMichen's Georgia Wildcats. McMichen was one of the most influential country fiddlers of the era, and Travis gained valuable experience in his brief stint as a Georgia Wildcat. Having done service as a Tom Cat, a Knockabout, and a Wildcat, Merle's next incarnation was as a Drifting Pioneer, one of a group with which he spent close to seven years on Cincinatti radio station WLW. "We played what today would absolutely be called bluegrass music," Merle recalls. But no bluegrass band since has looked quite like that one. Done up in buckskins and coonskin caps, the Drifting Pioneers resembled a convention of Davy Crockett fanatics.

While at WLW, Merle met Grandpa Jones and Alton and Rabon Delmore, already an established recording team as the Delmore Brothers. The Delmores, Jones, and Travis pooled their talents for a daily program of sacred songs, and dubbed themselves the Brown's Ferry Four. Today Merle laughs at the irony of a gospel group taking its name from the Delmores' bawdy "Brown's Ferry Blues." What was to become a major country and blues label, King Records, was started on the sly when Jones and Travis, then under exclusive contract with WLW, recorded as the Sheppard Brothers (the name came from a caricature Jones habitually drew). On his own for the first time, Merle assumed the name Bob McCarthy on record and waxed "When Mussolini Laid His Pistol Down." Listening to the wartime lament today, it becomes evident that Travis picking was already thoroughly developed by the time of that 1944 session.

World War II brought Merle's recording career to a halt. Following a stint in the Marines, he headed for the West Coast, where he helped another record label get started. He wrote Capitol Records' first million-seller for Tex Williams ("Smoke, Smoke, Smoke That Cigarette"), and served as session man and songwriter for all Capitol's major country acts.

Hollywood was to commercial country music in the '40s what Nashville is to it today, and Travis was very much in the thick of things. Traversing the San Fernando Valley on his motorcycle, Merle was in great demand for dances, and he played regularly with Ray Whitley's Rhythm Wranglers, a western swing band. When asked about who he worked with in the West Coast scene, Merle laughs and says, "It would be easier to ask who I *didn't* work with." Among the cast of thousands who figured in Merle's picking were Gene Autry, Johnny Bond, and Tex Ritter.

When he wasn't playing music, Merle frequently could be seen galloping down the hill after the bad guys in some of the "singing shoot-em-ups" of the day. (Merle's hilarious recollections of his Hollywood cowboy adventures are captured in volume XV, numbers 54 and 55, of the *JEMF Quarterly,* John Edwards Memorial Foundation, The Folklore and Mythology Center, University of California, Los Angeles, CA 90024.)

It was during this extremely productive postwar period that Travis designed his own solidbody electric guitar, the prototype for many other designs. It was also at Travis' behest that inventor Paul Bigsby came up with the famous Bigsby vibrato bars. A little later, Merle made a memorable appearance singing "Re-enlistment Blues" in the now classic film *From Here To Eternity.*

The '50s belonged to rock and roll, but the urban folkies of the early '60s discovered Travis-picking and, quite naturally,

Travis. As an elder statesman of country music, Merle held court at Carnegie Hall in 1962, and he appeared at the Smithsonian Institution's Festival of American Folklife in 1969. The Woodstock Generation found its country roots via the Nitty Gritty Dirt Band's album *Will The Circle Be Unbroken?*, and Merle was there, along with a host of other country and bluegrass luminaries, for the epochal 1973 recording. In 1977, Merle was inducted into the Country Music Hall of Fame. He would seem to have garnered more than enough laurels for any man to rest on. Instead, Merle has initiated a second (or is it a third?) recording career on CMH Records, receiving rave reviews from such unlikely quarters as *Rolling Stone,* which called him "one of America's greatest living guitarists" and "one of the most underated songwriters, too."

It is hard to think of any other guitarist who has exerted so much influence on so many different fields of music. Chet Atkins, "Mr. Guitar" to country music fans, said of Travis: "I can truthfully say that Merle has been the continuing influence in everything I've tried to do. I'd probably be looking at the rear end of a mule if it weren't for Merle." The young Doc Watson listened eagerly to Merle's radio broadcasts with the Brown's Ferry Four, and passed along what he absorbed to a new generation of folk, bluegrass, and country pickers. "Doc's Guitar" was inspired by Travis' "Blue Smoke" and each time he plays "Deep River Blues," Watson acknowledges the influence of those '40s radio shows by putting the Travis guitar style together with a Delmore Brothers song. Both Atkins and Watson named children for their favorite guitarist.

The folk revival of the late '40s (remember Burl Ives, Josh White, and the Weavers?) was given a renewed vitality by Merle's *Folk Songs Of The Hills* album, a pleasant contrast to the ersatz folk fabrications of that era. Nearly a decade later, rock and roll felt a Travis influence. Guitarist Scotty Moore's immediate source of inspiration may have been Chet Atkins, but it was a driving version of Travis picking the propelled the instrumental breaks on the early Elvis Presley hits. Neither country music, nor folk music, nor rock and roll would be quite what they are today had it not been for the influence of a very humble, tremendously talented man from rural Kentucky.

\*  \*  \*  \*

*W*HERE YOU GREW UP, THE WOODS WERE THICK WITH *banjo pickers and fingerpicking guitarists, and Bill Monroe was raised 19 miles away. Were there many fiddlers around?*

Yeah, I got hooked on fiddling. I used to try to play a fiddle, too. There was an old man named Uncle Merit Addison who lived up on the road—we lived 'way down in the woods—in Ebenezer, Kentucky. That's where I was raised. And Uncle Merit played the fiddle. I'd heard him play a couple of times. Maybe I was ten years old. He was an old man. I'd go up there and say, "Uncle Merit, play me one on the fiddle." And he'd start to twisting his wrist and say, "My ol' wrist ain't as nimble as it used to be, son." But I'd bug him so much he'd say. "Okay, crawl under the bed and get me the fiddle." And I'd crawl under the bed and get this old box that looked like a coffin. And he'd unhook the latch, take the fiddle out, tune it a little bit, and spit on the keys—and then he'd fiddle! So I liked that fiddle—putting the rosin on the bow, and the fiddle smelled so good when he

opened the case. I thought, "When I grow up, I'll be a fiddler just like Uncle Merit."

*What was your first guitar like, the one your brother Taylor built?*

I forget now exactly what kind of wood he made that of. But it was a flat-top guitar. He was always handy at anything like that. So he decided he'd build a guitar, and he did. Then Taylor moved to Indiana. He got a job at a factory up there, and that beat coal mining. He wrote a letter back, and at the end of the letter he said, "Give Merle the guitar." Then I took an interest in it.

*You've always credited Ike Everly and Mose Roger with inspiring "Travis picking." If we could go back in time and hear Roger and Everly, in what way would they remind us of Merle Travis?*

Oh, they probably played better than I do. You wouldn't have to go back in time, all you'd have to do is go to Drakesboro, Kentucky, to hear Mose.

*What sort of records did you hear when you were growing up?*

The first records I remember hearing were Edison cylinders. Then we traded the Edison machine for a Westrola phonograph. Victor made the Victrola and Westinghouse made Westrola. My uncle had a whole bunch of records—Carson Robison, Vernon Dalhart, and all that. We had a guitar solo by Nick Lucas. One side was called "Picking The Guitar" and the other side was called "Teasing The Frets" [now reissued on Yazoo, *Pioneers Of The Jazz Guitar*]. Me and my younger brother, John, we'd play it over and over again. And boy, we'd say, "Can't that feller play! Wow!" We also had one by Chris Bouchillon. He was a comedian and he'd talk, and man, if he hadn't been talking people would've said what a great guitar player he was. He'd play fingerpicking style behind his talking stuff, like "Born In Hard Luck," and it was fine, good picking. We didn't know there was a name called country music or a name called popular music. It was all just music if we knew it and played it. We probably played some of it wrong and some of it right.

*Did you make a record of a guitar solo called "Everly Rag"?*

I recorded it one time for radio transcriptions. They had such things as fillers, and I had gone in to do some transcriptions [for radio spots]. Some of them only lasted 15 seconds. A fellow named Joe Allison went to Capitol records and said, "You should release all those transcriptions on an album by Travis," and they did. They made up names to the tunes—one was called "Louisville Clog" and one was called "Pigmeat Stomp."

*That was the album* Walkin' The Strings. *That's kind of a rarity, isn't it?*

Well, it should be [*laughs*]! I didn't know this thing was released and I was somewhere playing a show, and somebody came in, saying, "Play 'Pigmeat Stomp.'" And I said, "You've got me there, I don't believe I've ever heard it." He said, "Well, you should, you recorded it." I said, "Well, you're thinking of someone else. I'm sure I never recorded 'Pigmeat Stomp.'" He said, "You sure did!" And I said, "Well, now buddy, I'd like to see a record of it." He said, "I've got it out in the car [*laughs*]."

*Was this an album of acoustic or electric guitar instrumentals?*

That's the funny thing. The boys down at Capitol Records always seemed to get all screwed up in what they tried to do with me. Not one single tune on the *Walkin' The Strings* album had an electric guitar note in it. And on the cover was me sitting there

**Travis Picking, a style developed by and named after Merle, is identified by alternating fingerpicking melodies and muted bass notes (picked on the lower strings by the thumb).**

just as big as life with an electric guitar. Now then, one time I got a bunch of good musicians there in Hollywood, and I went down to recut some of the old stuff that I'd done in the '40s. This was in the '60s. The title of the album was *Travis*. I didn't pick one note of acoustic guitar, and on the jacket they put a picture of me with an acoustic flat-top roundhole guitar, leaning up against a rock. I declare, I believe that if I'd made an album with me playing the clarinet, they'd have had me on the cover with a dulcimer.

*Most people think you pick with just the thumb and first finger, but sometimes you use two fingers.*

Sometimes I use three, like in "Caravan." Years ago, I used just thumb and index finger. In that style, you can get a choke

sound like this [*damps the strings of his guitar with the palm of his right hand*], or you can play with open strings.

*How did you develop that choking effect?*

Mose Rager played like that.

*You've been using a fingerpick some on your index finger while demonstrating these techniques. Is that something you've started using recently?*

Before this contract with CMH Records I was to do an album in Nashville with dobro player Shot Jackson. I was there, and my index fingernail broke off to the quick. Without that, I can't play anything at all. Not that I pick with the fingernail, but I use it as a brace. So Shot Jackson said, "Why don't you try a steel pick?" I put

127

**Merle Travis (left), with Doc Watson. Doc named his son Merle after his favorite guitarist.**

it on and said, "Good Lord, I couldn't play with one of these things to save my life." He said, "If you practiced you probably could. Then you wouldn't have to worry about your fingernails." So we called and cancelled the session, because I couldn't play without the fingernail. But Shot said, "Take that pick anyhow." I've been messing with it, and you get real good sound out of it.

*In your left-hand style, you play with your thumb a lot, and according to Tommy Flint's book* The Merle Travis Guitar Style *[Mel Bay Publications, Pacific, MO 63069], you don't play barre chords.*

Oh sure, I play barre chords. But mostly I don't. Mostly I just grab a guitar neck like a hoe handle. [*Travis has calluses on his left thumb.*]

*You played some nice harmonics on your recording of "On A Bicycle Built For Two" on the Capitol album* The Merle Travis Guitar. *What's the trick to harmonics?*

Well, you pick with the thumb and damp with the first finger 12 frets up from the note you're fretting.

*Did you ever play in alternate tunings?*

Yes, I've played some in open G (*D-G-D-G-B-D*). That's a good tuning for blues. When I was a kid, I used to pick some in that tuning, fretting with a bottle. That's no big deal. Everybody's done that. Then there's one where you tune the fifth string [*A*] up to *B*. That one is very good for playing rich, orchestral jazz-type chords.

*Didn't you record something where you put a high* E *string on for the third string, and tuned that up an octave above normal pitch for the third-string G?*

Right. It was like the top *E* string fretted at the third fret. I recorded with that string setup on "Beer Barrel Polka" and "Black Diamond Blues."

*What string gauges do you use?*

You'll find me awfully dumb when you ask me what gauge these guitar strings are. I have no more idea than the man in the moon what gauge any of these strings are. I just go in and say, "Give me a set of Gibson electric and a set of Martin acoustic," and I put 'em on and forget about it. When I open up the package and look at those numbers, I have no idea what they all mean.

*Did you ever use flatwound strings?*

Yeah, but I never had much luck with them because they died too quick. After about one day they'd just go "thump, thump." Maybe they've improved.

*Do you change your strings very often?*

Not very often. If I'm recording a guitar solo, I like to have strings that are fairly new because you get a better ring from them.

*What kind of thumbpicks are you using?*

Some little old thin thumbpicks that are hard to find, but if I can find them I use them. I have no idea who makes them.

*Tell us about your hybrid acoustic guitar.*

It's a D-28 Martin with a Bigsby neck.

*How old is the Martin body?*

I probably bought it in 1939. I had Paul Bigsby put that neck on just after he made that first solidbody electric guitar [1947]. I liked the neck so well, the size and everything, that I had him put one on the Martin. Now the neck on this Gibson Super 400 is exactly the size of the Bigsby neck. That's not a regular Gibson neck. It's smaller and thinner.

*You've been playing the body of your acoustic guitar for about 40 years and the neck for about 30. Have you had to modify it at all in recent years?*

I put a new bridge on it not long ago.

*How did you develop some of your famous solos—"Walkin' The Strings," "Cannonball Rag," and "Blue Smoke," for instance?*

"Walking The Strings" and "Cannonball Rag" are actually dolled-up versions of a couple of little old tunes that Ike and Mose used to play. "Blue Smoke," now there's one where you use three fingers. "Cannonball Rag" is a round-robin tune. There's a million tunes like that.

*What do you mean by a "round-robin"?*

A round-robin chord progression, like "Salty Dog." [*To illustrate, Merle plays a C-A7-D7-G-C chord progression.*] That's a round-robin.

*Do you have any favorites among your instrumentals?*

No, I don't. I like to play slow pieces better than fast pieces. I like to put a rhythm and bass track on tape and sit and play with them, because every time you'll play it different. I do that as a pastime.

*What about practice? Through the years you've been so busy working that you probably haven't had to worry about it, but I guess that at some point you did some woodshedding.*

I don't think I ever said, "I think I'll sit down and practice." because if I wasn't in the mood there wouldn't be a bit of use in practicing. Now, since I've been talking to you I've been sitting here picking on the guitar, because I'm a fidgety person. I'm like Johnny Cash, I'm not a person that can sit down and sit still and stare. If you weren't here, I'd be out cutting grass, or inside helping Dorothy can beans. I'm always busy. So I always have a guitar sitting around, and when I'm doing nothing else, I play. When I'm sitting watching TV, I play every commercial and everything with them. Without even knowing it, I do it. I just feel better with a guitar in my hands. That's about all the practice I do.

*When did you first hear Chet Atkins?*

The first time I heard him really turn loose was in about 1945. Chet had written me a letter or two, and I had met him in Nashville. He told me he listened to me on the radio from Cincinnati. He said "I try to play the guitar like you." I'd been out of the Marine Corps a short while, and I was going back to Cincinnati to visit friends. It was a cold morning; we did our radio shows early in the morning, before daylight in the wintertime. Well, Chet Atkins was on the radio at the time in WLW in Cincinnati. And I was listening to the radio, and the announcer said, "Now we'll have a guitar solo from Chet Atkins." He started playing, and I pulled the car over. It was snowing like crazy, but I just sat there and listened to him and I thought, "Wow!"

*The impact of your influence seems to fall pretty evenly between acoustic and electric pickers. Like Atkins and Jerry Reed, you're often seen in acoustic or amplified sets. Do you have any comments on the acoustic-versus-electric controversy?*

I admire people who stick by their principles. I've heard people say, "I would *never* play an electric instrument. I play an acoustic guitar, period." But then when they go to perform, they will gripe their heads off unless the hall as a $100,000.00 public address system in order that listeners can hear the guitar amplified through that system. Why not have one like this [*indicating his trademark Gibson Super 400*] with the pickups on it and the amplifier sitting down by you so you can adjust it yourself? It's exactly the same thing. If you make a record, the man in the control room turns the controls up to make the guitarist's instrument sound big and pretty and loud. That's exactly why the pickups are put on here. This is it. The acoustic guitar purists all mean well, but they haven't stopped to think, "Now wait—this is a guitar with the microphone under the strings instead of out in front of it."

*So you don't change your style at all playing acoustic or electric guitar?*

No.

*What was your first electric guitar?*

It was a Gibson L-10 with a DeArmond pickup. The first time I used it on radio was on a program called *Plantation Party*, a network show. That would've been in 1939 or 1940.

*Do you have any words of advice for young musicians trying to start in the business?*

I think I'd just say keep pickin', and if you have it, somebody's going to discover it. You're not going to wind up working down at the corner shoe store if you have the talent of a Les Paul or a Chet Atkins.

*In your song "Three Times Seven," you sing. "I just won't tame, I'm gonna be the same 'til I'm three times twenty-one." You'll be a year past three times 21 on November 29. Would you care to make any comments summing up your career thus far?*

I'm just about there [*laughs*]! That's true, I said, "I just won't tame, I'm gonna be the same 'til I'm three times twenty-one." I also wrote something in a magazine article one time. I said that when I'm 90 years old and some young fellow is playing the Galaxy Theater on the planet Mars. I hope I'm the old guy sitting back there watching the door and listening to the show. That's how much I love the business. [*Ed. Note: Merle died of cardiopulmonary arrest on October 20, 1983.*]

---

**A SELECTED MERLE TRAVIS DISCOGRAPHY**

**Solo albums:** *Rough, Rowdy, And Blue*, CMH (Box 39439, Los Angeles, CA 90039), 6262; *Country Hits Of The '40s*, Capitol, 650; *Light Singin' & Heavy Pickin'*, CMH, 6245; *The Best Of Merle Travis*, Capitol, SM-2662; *The Merle Travis Guitar*, Capitol, SM-650; *The Merle Travis Story*, CMH, 9018. **With others:** *Country Giants/Merle Travis & Joe Maphis*, CMH, 9017; *The Atkins-Travis Traveling Show*, RCA, AHL 1-0479; *Will The Circle Be Unbroken?*, United Artists, 9801; *Walnut Valley Spring Thing*, Takoma (Box 5369, Santa Monica, CA 90405), 1054.

# Doc Watson

**By Jon Sievert**

PROBABLY THE MOST INFLUENTIAL AND COMMERCI-
ally enduring instrumentalist to emerge from the '60s folk
experience was a blind singer/guitarist from Deep Gap, North
Carolina: Arthel "Doc" Watson. Doc was not only a compelling
vocalist with a rich baritone and a vast repertoire of Blue Ridge
Mountain music, but a true virtuoso of the flatpicked acoustic
guitar.

The effect Doc had on guitarists was immediate. Until he
showed what could be done, the vast majority of budding folk
guitarists were content to assume the traditional role of vocal
accompaniment and rhythmic backup. When Doc turned up,
flatpicking the lead to fiddle tunes at blazing speed, the fallout
was immediate. Gifted young guitarists Clarence White of the
Kentucky Colonels and John Herald of the Greenbriar Boys
were among the most important of those immediately affected.
Doc's genius established once and for all the validity of the
flatpicked acoustic guitar as a lead instrument.

Arthel Watson's story begins on March 3, 1923. One of nine
children of Annie and General Dixon Watson, he contracted an
eye disease as an infant that left him blind before he was two
years old. Hymns he heard sitting on his mother's lap in church,
and the old-time ballads she sang around the house, formed
some of his first memories of music. His father was also a singer,
and something of a banjo picker, and led the family every night
in Bible reading and hymn singing.

Doc got his first musical instrument, a harmonica, at an early
age, and thereafter received a new one each Christmas. Before
long he had strung a single steel wire to the woodshed's sliding
door and tuned it to his harmonica so he could provide his own
bass accompaniment while he played.

When Doc was seven the musical world began to open up
for him. His father bought a table model Victrola from an uncle,
and included in the purchase were a stack of recordings by such
groups as Gid Tanner and the Skillet Lickers, the Carolin Tar
Heels, and the Carter Family. The collection soon grew to
include recordings by Jimmie Rodgers, Riley Puckett, and
Mississippi John Hurt.

Because of his blindness and his family's poverty, Doc did
not start school until he was ten. His parents sent him to North

Carolina's School for the Blind, in Raleigh. When he came home
the following summer his father offered to build him a banjo.
Doc accepted and took to the new instrument immediately,
learning to frail several tunes.

A couple of years later, when he was 12, Doc heard a
classmate playing a guitar. Soon he had learned a few chords
himself, and after he returned home he made a deal with his
father and got his first guitar, a $12.00 Stella. Not long afterward
he teamed with his brother, Linny, to learn many of the region's
old-time mountain tunes and many of the new songs he was
hearing on the *Grand Ole Opry* and the clear-channel bootleg
Mexican radio stations. Doc's early performances were mostly
limited to front-porch playing with relatives and neighbors until
the pressure of making payments on his first Martin convinced
him to try singing in the streets.

Doc acquired his nickname when he was 18. He and a friend
were getting ready to play for a remote radio broadcast at a
furniture store, and the announcer decided the "Arthel" was too
cumbersome to use of the air. "Call him 'Doc,'" a lady in the
crowd suggested. The name stuck (Doc says there is no truth to
the story that it derives from the Dr. Watson of Sherlock Holmes
lore).

In 1947 Doc met and married Rosa Lee Carlton, daughter of
a fine old-time mountain fiddler named Gaither Carlton.
Gaither was a walking repository of old tunes indigenous to his
isolated mountain home and he passed along many that remain
part of Doc's repertoire today.

Despite his blossoming talent, Doc still was not earning any
money from his skills. After his marriage he took to tuning
pianos to help feed his family. It wasn't until 1953, when he was
30, that he became a successful working musician. That was the
year he met Jack Williams, a piano player from Tennessee who
was fronting a country and western swing band. Williams was
impressed by Doc's talent and invited him to play lead guitar in
the band. Shortly thereafter Doc traded in his D-28 for a 1953 Les
Paul Standard and became an electric guitarist. (Even today Doc
carries those '50s tunes with him, and he delights in occasionally astounding audiences with a hot encore rendition of "Blue
Suede Shoes" or "Tutti Frutti.")

Because the band did not have a fiddle player, Williams called on Doc to provide the lead part on fiddle tunes for square dancing. Thus, ironically, it was on the electric guitar that Doc developed and honed the style for which he was to become so famous on the acoustic guitar.

The association with Williams lasted nearly eight years. The band toured eastern Tennessee and western North Carolina, playing VFW halls and square dances. During that period Doc continued to pick and sing old-time music with his family. He also played with a neighbor, Clarence "Tom" Ashley, who had been an original member of the Carolina Tar Heels.

In 1960, as the folk boom was just beginning, Ashley was sought out by two young musicologists named Ralph Rinzler and Eugene Earle. Anxious to record Ashley, Rinzler and Earle happened to get Doc Watson on banjo and guitar in the bargain. The results of that meeting are still available on a pair of albums, *Old-Time Music At Clarence Ashley's* [Folkways].

Rinzler was excited by the sessions, especially by Doc's unique talent. He immediately began making plans to get Ashley and Doc to New York to perform their old-time mountain music for the growing folk audience there, but Doc was dubious. Doc simply could not believe that there was anyone there who wanted to hear it.

Fortunately, Rinzler prevailed. In the spring of 1961, Doc Watson made his urban debut at a Friends of Old-Time Music concert in New York. He was accompanied by Ashley, Clint Howard, and Fred Price. A year later he gave his first solo performance at Gerde's Folk City in New York.

Doc was soon much in demand, traveling the country playing concerts and hootenannies and making some television appearances. He was a smash hit at the 1963 Newport Folk Festival, and in November of that year he played a historic concert with mandolinist Bill Monroe at New York's Town Hall. Bootleg recordings of that concert are still surfacing.

About that time the folk music boom began to bottom out. The Beatles had arrived to breathe fresh air into rock and roll, and most of the newly discovered folk artists were returning to a subsistence level as performers. Doc himself came very close to going back to North Carolina for good, though not for lack of an appreciatative public. He was homesick, and with his vision handicap traveling was very difficult.

In 1964 Doc came home from nearly three months on the road to find that his 15-year-old son, Merle, had taken up the guitar. It wasn't too long before Merle was good enough to play rhythm guitar for Doc. At 16, Merle became his father's backup guitarist, road manager, and chauffeur, and the two began spending up to 300 nights a year on the road.

Because of Merle, Doc was able to continue his career, reaching a steadily widening audience even during acoustic music's leanest years.

In 1968 the father-son duo was asked by the State Department to represent the United States in a cultural exchange program with African nations. The Watsons went from snow-covered North Carolina to 100-degree temperatures in Nairobi, Kenya, playing at villages in the bush country of Malawi, Zambia, Botswana, Lesotho, and Swaziland to enthusiastic native audiences.

In 1972 Doc's music touched a new generation of listeners when he participated in the recording of *Will The Circle Be Unbroken* [United Artists], a landmark project organized by the

Arthel "Doc" Watson, shown here with his J.W. Gallagher guitar, established the flat-picked acoustic guitar as a solo instrument when he appeared in the '60s.

Nitty Gritty Dirt Band. The Dirt Band gathered together and recorded with a living country and bluegrass music Hall of Fame that included Doc, Maybelle Carter, Earl Scruggs, Roy Acuff, and Merle Travis. The result was a three-record album that later went gold. Doc's warm humor, his singing, and his remarkable guitar playing sparkle throughout the album.

The burden of travel eased for Doc and Merle in the '70s. Their commercial appeal was such that they flew to their many concerts in a private twin-engine plane. The team was joined in 1974 by bass guitarist T. Michael Coleman, who still performs with Doc today. [*Ed. Note: Merle Watson died in a tractor accident at the family farm in October 1985.*]

Doc's distinctive playing starts with a Herco nylon flatpick, which he favors because of its embossed grip surfaces, its durability, and the cleaner sound it makes against the strings. The strings themselves are medium-gauge D'Addarios (Merle uses medium-light Gallaghers, from the same company that produces the Watsons' guitars). Doc likes his guitars set with an action slightly higher than normal, feeling that the extra clearance produces more punch and volume. He uses a capo—he calls it a "cheater"—occasionally, most often at the third fret. Doc also fingerpicks on occasion.

Although his right arm appears to move very little while he plays, Doc has characterized his technique as three-quarters arm motion and a quarter wrist motion. He leaves the little finger of his right hand lightly touching the pickguard as a depth gauge. Doc believes that flatpicking technique must be light and delicate to be clean, and suggests practicing scales using even up-and-down picking. On the left-hand technique, he advises guitarists against copying his use of the thumb on the sixth string for barred chords. He says that Merle has developed a better reach on the neck by using conventional barre chording.

\* \* \* \*

*C*OULD YOU TELL US A LITTLE ABOUT THAT FIRST BANJO *your dad built for you?*

When I came home that first spring at school my dad said,

"Son, I might make you a little banjo this summer," and I said, "I ain't never seen one of them." He said, "Well, I used to pick a little and I know where to get ahold of some of them tension hooks, so I believe I can make you one." So he commenced to working on it. He carved the neck out of maple and made little friction tuning pegs like dulcimers have. When he got the hoop done he stretched a groundhog hide over it, but that just didn't work right. It was too stiff and didn't give a very good tone. We solved the problem, though, when Granny's 16-year-old cat passed on. That made one of the best banjo heads you ever seen and it stayed on that thing, I guess, as long as I picked it. Dad got it made and tuned it up and the first piece I ever heard him play was "Rambling Hobo." He showed me a few tunes to get me started. Then one day he picked it up and put it in my hands and said, "Here, son. Take this and learn to play it good. You might need it in this world. It's yours now." He never would pick no more after he got me started.

*It seems like your father left you with a fine legacy by giving you that banjo.*

Making that banjo and encouraging me into music, knowing that it was a trade I could learn, was a mighty fine thing he did for me. The best thing my dad ever did for me in my life, though, was to put me at one end of a crosscut saw. He put me to work and that made me feel useful. A lot of blind people weren't ever put to work. I remember the morning when he leaned back in his chair, took a big swig of coffee, and said, "Son, do you think you can learn to pull a crosscut saw?" and I said, "Yeah." I didn't know what I was getting into but I soon found out, I tell you right now.

*Could you run down a progression of the guitars you've gone through since you've been playing?*

Well, I got a Stella when I was 12. I had heard a friend named Paul Montgomery in school playing guitar and learned a couple of chords. When I came home that summer, my brother had borrowed my cousin's guitar. Daddy heard me messing with it one morning and said, "Son, if you can learn a tune on that by the time I get back from work this evening we'll go find you a guitar of some kind." He didn't know that I already knew a chord or two, and when he came home I could pick the chords to "When The Roses Bloom In Dixie Land." That's when we went and got the Stella. I kept that awhile and I worked out a price of my second guitar myself at the end of a crosscut saw. That was a Silvertone from Sears. I traded around a time or two between that and when Mr. Richard Green, an old man who ran a little music store in Boone, helped me get my first Martin.

*Do you remember what model it was?*

It was a Martin D-28. That must have been about 1940. It was a new guitar and he let me have a year to pay it off. I played on the street nearly every Saturday, when the weather was warm, at a cab stand in Lenore, South Carolina. Sometimes I'd make as much as $50.00, and I paid that guitar off in four or five months. I didn't aim to lose that thing. I kept that guitar right up until the time I joined Jack Williams.

*Is that when you bought the Les Paul?*

Yeah. I tried to use a pickup on the Martin for awhile but I finally got up enough nerve to trade it on the Les Paul.

*Did you get into altered chords with the Jack Williams band?*

Some. Jack played pretty decent piano, mostly honky-tonk, and I'd improvise with the three- and four-note chords. I didn't worry about learning all the barre chords because we had a

rhythm guitar player. The hardest chore I got into with that group was playing the lead fiddle tunes for square dancing. That man would just keep you going for twenty mintues. He'd break your arm off.

*What do you think you gained from that experience with Jack Williams?*

I still use some of the hot licks that I played on the electric, but they come out sounding a little different to the ear when you lay them on the flat-top. I got a lot of technical practice with the flatpick during those years. It helped build my knowledge of using the flatpick enormously.

*Did you always flatpick, right from the start?*

I started off playing with a thumb lead, Maybelle Carter style. Then when I began to listen to Jimmie Rodgers I figured out there was something being done there besides the thumb and finger. So I got me a pick and started working on it. It was Hank Garland who inspired me to learn fiddle tunes on the guitar. I did learn some fingerpicking from a fellow named Olin Miller. I loved Merle Travis. That's who I named my son after.

*Was your work with Jack Williams your first real performing job?*

Well, of course there were the street things; and people who heard me on the street invited me to come to amateur contests and fiddlers' conventions, and I went. I began to win a few, but I found that people didn't want me in their shows no matter how good I was because I was a little trouble to them and I didn't have a flashy stage show. It just wasn't accepted then for you to just sit on the stage and pick, unless you were a super musician, and that I wasn't. I did win some contests, though, and I remember one time when I entered once in the professional category and won it. That really helped my ego.

*Your music shows a wide variety of influences. Were you exposed to different kinds of music early?*

We had the records and they were pretty varied. In 1939 we got a battery-set radio and we could pick up anything from Del Rio, Texas, to Minneapolis, Minnesota. I heard a lot of big band music. I remember getting interested in dixieland jazz. I thought that was some kind of fine. And later I began to like the Dorseys and Phil Harris. You name it and I began to like the sound. When you begin to understand music and your ear is being educated to the theory, then you can really learn to love it. You can't really love something until you can understand it.

*At what point did you start using the custom-built J.W. Gallagher [Wartrace, Tennessee] guitar you have now?*

I don't remember the exact year that happened. After I stopped playing electric and went on the road I borrowed a Martin from a boy named Joe Cox who couldn't play a lick. He gave me that guitar to play as long as I wanted and I used that for quite awhile. Then I played some on a D-28 that Ralph Rinzler had. Merle and I both had Martins for awhile. Then, one Easter, J.W. and his son dropped by our house with three or four of their guitars. The house was full of people who had just come back from Union Grove [the nearby music festival]. I played all of the guitars and just before he left he came over and handed me the guitar that I'd liked the best. He said, "I want to give you this, and there are no strings attached except the ones on the guitar. We'll just let the thing endorse itself if it is any good." I used that guitar for eight years. Three years ago this September he came up to me in Nashville and told me he wanted to do something for me because I had sold more guitars than he could make, just by

**Doc and Merle Watson in an early '70s club appearance.**

playing that guitar. I told him he could build me a new guitar with a neck to my specifications, and I sent him my '53 Les Paul to copy. He copied the neck and shape, the fretboard, and the type of frets, and made a guitar to suit himself. That's what I have now.

*Is that what he calls the Doc Watson model?*

Yes. He heard me playing it and asked if he could produce it and put it in his catalog. Then in January he brought me a twin to it and I've got that at home. I played it on the road for two or three months to break it in so if something happened to one, the other wouldn't have to hit the road straight brand new. When a guitar is green you might be able to hear the good in it, but they're not like they are once you've played them awhile and you break them in. They have to be played to season them properly.

*Do you ever play the banjo anymore?*

Maybe one out of ten shows I'll pick it up and play something. I've let Merle do most of the banjo work.

*Did you ever play any other instruments besides banjo, harmonica, and guitar?*

I tried the fiddle for awhile but I never could get that bowing hand right. I've picked around a bit on the mandolin and I do think I could learn to play that. I never could find a mandolin that had a neck wide enough to suit me and a tone fittin' for beings, though. I did find a beautiful old Gibson A model that I done my damndest to buy, but the lady that owned it didn't want to sell.

*When did you get the notion to try to play fiddle tunes on the guitar?*

I guess I actually started trying to do that pretty early. I'd made up my mind that I couldn't play the fiddle, but I wanted to play with the same kind of bounce and rhythm that the fiddle

did so I started working them out on the guitar. You can't do the same things that are done on the fiddle but you can do the tunes to where they are pretty. I spent a lot of time practicing. I hadn't heard anyone else do that on a guitar before, and I'll tell you it really surprised Bill Monroe when we played together at the Ash Grove in Los Angeles. Ralph [Rinzler] had got the idea for me and Bill to do some of the old Charlie and Bill Monroe things together as an extra short set on the shows. The first tune we did was "Paddy On The Turnpike," and all at once I took a break on the guitar. Bill came over after we got off the stage and said something like, "Mighty fine guitar playing." Then in a few minutes he said, "Do you know 'Tennessee Blues'?" and I said, "Yeah, I think I can pick it." We got back up there the next time and we flat got on it and I played just as fast as he could go with it. When we got off the stage he said, "Man, you got after that tune. I've never heard a guitar played like that before." You can imagine how I felt. I'd been listening to Bill Monroe for maybe twenty years.

*What kind of process do you and Merle go through in working out a tune?*

Well, I don't ever tell Merle how to play a tune. I might suggest something like, "Try this and see if it will work," but you can't mold a guy if he's a true musician. He's got to pick the way he picks. We'll sit down together and get the melody line straight and he will pick around a bit on it. I'll let him think about it for awhile and in the next day or two he'll sit down again and he will pick it. He does his own arrangments. He'll play a tune one way one night and a different way the next. Same with me. There are one or two songs that have definite arrangements. I play "Sweet Georgia Brown" about the same way every time, maybe adding different phrasing here and there occasionally, but basically it's the same arrangement. The country songs that

**134**

I'm so used to I'll play a little different each set, depending on how I feel. "Milk Cow Blues" is one we vary quite a bunch.

*Do you consciously do things with your voice and harmonica to play against the guitar?*

I think the combination comes out according to your feelings. If you are really into a tune, not forcing yourself or nervous, and really into playing for an audience, those sorts of musical things happen as a result of your feelings. It's not a conscious thing. You may practice at something to get it a certain way but find it comes out different when you do it onstage.

*Do you use a pickup on your guitar?*

Yes. Merle and I both have Barcus-Berrys installed in our guitars. We got into that because of shoddy sound systems at a lot of the festivals. If you turned it loud enough for them to hear your guitar you got feedback. Well, if you put a padded-down signal into their board you can play as loud as you want. It might not sound as sweet and clean all the time, because of their system, but it will be the sound of the guitar.

*What kind of amps are you and Merle using?*

We've used Fender Twins for years. I don't believe you can hardly whip them for what we do. We rent them wherever we go.

*What is your general opinion of the festival circuit these days?*

I'd really rather not say what I think about some of those festivals. There's about 70 percent of them that I wouldn't take Rosa Lee or my daughter Nancy to. People go to certain festivals just because they can raise all the hell they want. The security is bad and there's a lot of drinkin'. There's too many who don't go to listen who spoil it for those that do. It's just downright rudeness. Those festivals are sure a far cry from the quiet, very attentive audiences of the '60s folk festivals. That Newport festival was something. I remember when Clarence, Fred, Clint, and I played it in 1963. We'd go out onstage and eight to ten thousand people would go dead quiet and listen to the music. Man, you couldn't believe the ovations for those simple old tunes that Clarence did. You knew the people were there to hear

the roots of their music.

*Do you hear many new pickers who excite you?*

Lord, yes. There are a lot of fine ones coming along. Norman Blake is surely one. That last album I heard by him has some licks on there I don't think I could do. The left-hand parts I believe I could handle, but I don't know about that right hand. I'm going to ask him what kind of operation he had on that wrist to loosen it up like that. Tony Rice and Dan Crary are two more mighty fine pickers. In fact Tony is recording a couple of cuts with us for this live album. There's also a real fine young fingerpicker named Guy Van Duser. He can pick himself a guitar. There are so many guitar players that play for a show and then there are some that play for the love. Man, you can sure tell the difference when you sit down and listen to them. Too many people are just trying to see how many notes they can play on the guitar. Fast and tasteful *can* be combined. Two musicians can play a riff and the choice of notes and the phrasing is what makes it tasteful or not—no matter how fast or slow it is played.

*Do you get much of a chance to jam with new musicians these days?*

Once in awhile I will if I'm rested and their playing interests me. I'm ashamed to say, though, that I don't have the passion for the music that I did at one time. I seldom jam anymore because I play so much on the road that I get it out of my system with audiences.

*How much of your musical repertoire is made up of the old-time tunes?*

I'd say about 30 percent of my music comes from family and relatives and the rest from records, radio, and what-not. One new tune we're doing for this live album is the old Everly Brothers song called "Dream."

*Do you have any ambitious concept albums that you are anxious to do? Do you still have a good backlog of old tunes to draw upon?*

Well, there are quite a few old ones that I could dig out. We've got one more album under this contract and I haven't even thought of half of that. We just kind of take them one at a time.

---

### A SELECTED DOC WATSON DISCOGRAPHY

**Solo albums (includes albums with Merle Watson)** (on Vanguard): *Doc Watson*, 79152; *Doc Watson And Son*, 79170; *Southbound*, 79213; *Home Again*, 79239; *Good Deal*, 79276; *Ballads From Deep Gap*, 6576; *Doc Watson On Stage*, 9/10; *The Essential Doc Watson*, VSD 45/46; (on United Artists): *Memories*, LA 423-H2; *Doc And The Boys*, LA601-G; *Lonesome Road*, LA725-G; *Look Away!*, LA887-H; *Live And Pickin'*, LA943-H; (on Poppy): *Elementary Doctor Watson*, 5703; *Then And Now*, LA022-F; *Two Days In November*, LA210-G; (on Flying Fish, 1304 W. Schubert, Chicago, IL 60614): *Red Rocking Chair*, 252; *Doc & Merle Watson's Guitar Album*, 301; *Pickin' The Blues*, 352; (on Sugar Hill, Box 4040, Duke Station, Durham, NC 27706): *Down South*, 3742; *Riding The Midnight Train*, 3752; (on Liberty): *Doc Watson Favorites*, LN 10201. **With Chet Atkins:** *Reflections*, RCA, AHL1-3701. **With Mitch Greenhill and Mayne Smith,** *Storm Coming*, Bay (1516 Oak Ave., Suite 320, Alameda, CA 94501), 215. **With The Nitty Gritty Dirt Band,** *Will The Circle Be Unbroken*, United Artists, 9801. **With Jean Ritchie:** *Jean & Doc At Folk City*, Folkways, 9026. **With Earl Scruggs:** (both on Columbia) *Earl Scruggs, Family & Friends*, 30584; *Strictly Instrumental*, 2643. **With Roger Sprung:** *Progressive Bluegrass*, Folkways, FA 2370. **With Marty Stuart:** *Busy Bee Cafe*, Sugar Hill, 3726. **With David Holt:** *Reel And Rock*, Flying Fish, FF 372. **With Others:** *Banjo Man*, Sugar Hill, 3715; *The Doc Watson Family*, Folkways, 31021; *Country Music And Bluegrass At Newport*, Vanguard 79146, *Greatest Folksingers Of The Sixties*, Vanguard, 17/18; *Old Time Music At Clarence Ashley's*, Folkways, 2359 & 2355; *Old Time Music At Newport*, Vanguard 79147; *Old Timey Concert*, Vanguard, VSD 107/108; *Tellulive*, Flying Fish, 224; *The Watson Family*, Folkways, 2366.

# HANK WILLIAMS, JR.

**By Dan Forte**

**M**ENTION THE NAME HANK WILLIAMS TO ANY veteran country music fan, and he'll reel off any number of Hank's compositions—"Your Cheatin' Heart," "Jambalaya," "Hey, Good Lookin'," "Cold, Cold Heart," "Honky Tonkin'," "Kaw-Liga," "I'm So Lonesome I Could Cry"—that have become standards since country music's first superstar died New Year's Day, 1953. But mention the name to someone a bit younger, maybe not even necessarily a country fan, and you're likely to hear an equally long list of hit songs—"Family Tradition," "Old Habits," "Whiskey Bent And Hell Bound," "A Country Boy Can Survive," "All My Rowdy Friends (Have Settled Down)"—that came from the pen of Hank Williams, *Jr.*

Although still a young man, Randall Hank Williams, Jr., has released 50 albums (his latest is appropriately titled *Five-0*), including no less than five greatest-hits collections, and he's been the subject of a made-for-TV movie, *Living Proof.* A subtle but sure sign of his notoriety came almost completely unnoticed when reissues of his father's material began bearing the name Hank Williams, *Sr.* The older Williams lived barely long enough to give his son (who was three when his father died) a lasting nickname, Bocephus, and a formidable legacy that has been both a source of pride and a thorn in the side for Hank, Jr. As an eight-year-old, Hank, Jr., gave his first public performance, singing "Lovesick Blues," a song closely associated with his father. Three years later, he received a curtain call at the *Grand Ole Opry* for singing the same song, and at age 14, Bocephus provided the singing voice to the soundtrack of *Your Cheatin' Heart*, the film biography of Hank, Sr., starring George Hamilton.

At 16, Hank showed that he had inherited more than just a name from his father, when his original song "Standing In The Shadows" (a recurring theme of his original tunes) won a BMI (Broadcast Music, Inc.) songwriter's award. He also began displaying an aptitude that even his father was not especially known for, learning to play guitar, piano, banjo, fiddle, and steel guitar—all of which he employs onstage. Even more eclectic in his musical tastes than his father, he gravitated towards blues and rock and roll, which resulted in his landmark 1976 release, *Hank Williams, Jr. & Friends*, recorded with fiddler Charlie

Daniels, Allman Brothers Band pianist Chuck Leavell, and Marshall Tucker Band guitarist Toy Caldwell—just as Willie Nelson and Waylon Jennings were simultaneously popularizing the "outlaw" image and crossing over to rock audiences. The album was critically acclaimed and would have certainly ensured success for Hank, Jr.—for the first time, on his own terms—but his hopes (and nearly his life) were dashed when he fell head first down a rocky face while mountain climbing in Montana.

The accident changed Hank's outlook on life ("I realized that you better do what you *want* to do," he says), and that was immediately reflected in his music. There were more songs dealing with the relationship between him and his father's legend (including the smash hit "Family Tradition"), and after refusing to perform any of Hank, Sr.'s songs for years, he recorded his own arrangements of several (such as "Honky Tonkin'," "Kaw-Liga," "Move It On Over," and a haunting rendition of "Ramblin' Man"). He also hasn't hesitated to throw in some blues, jazz, or good old rock and roll on occasion—including ZZ Top's "La Grange," Fats Waller's "Ain't Misbehavin'," "The Blues Medley," with John Lee Hooker and Ray Charles, and even Warren Zevon's "Lawyers, Guns, And Money." Bocephus may never eclipse Hank Williams' legacy (and he may always be standing in the shadows, to a degree), but in 1982 he set a record that no artist is likely to duplicate, placing nine of his albums on *Billboard*'s country chart simultaneously.

\* \* \* \*

**I**N YOUR EARLIEST MEMORY, WHAT MUSIC DID YOU *first hear?*

Hank Williams, Daddy. I mean his music.

*You'd hear his records in the house?*

Yeah, oh gosh. And also the type of stuff you hear me doing now. I would be listening to records back then, like Jerry Lee Lewis or Jimmie Rodgers.

*Did your mom try to dissuade you from getting interested in rock and roll?*

No, she liked it when I played that other stuff. But I had a

manager that didn't want me to do anything but Daddy in the show. It was me and the Drifting Cowboys, and just do Daddy. "Don't do nothin' else. Don't play that awful rock and roll." I'd go out there and do "Lost Highway" or "Cold, Cold Heart," and the people would go *nuts*—crying and screaming.

*There's a scene in* Living Proof *where you're recording one of Hank's songs while listening to his original record in the headphones. Did you actually cut any records that way?*

I did two whole albums that way. They'd put his voice in singing one line, and then I'd sing, and then both of us together. You've got to remember I was 17 or 18 years old. I was runnin' around with girls in cars and doin' stuff. I'd run in and do that, and *whoosh*, run back out. But as a teenager, I drove them crazy with the banjo. [*Hums a scale.*] I would drive to Earl Scruggs' for lessons, and I was there religiously on time.

*Did any guitar players give you tips?*

Every one of them. I'd say, "How do you do this? How did you make that chord?" I used to hang out with Johnny Rivers, when he was on a lot of those shows with me.

*Were you mostly around country players?*

At first, but a little later on—like in my mid-20s—it was the Allman Brothers and Toy Caldwell and some others. Although there was a lot of country guitar players that could play anything. Hell, Jerry Reed and Glen Campbell can play anything. Yeah, I was blessed because I had the connection to all these guys. And they got a thrill out of showing Hank Williams, Jr., how to do this.

*If you separate your guitar playing from everything else you do, would you consider yourself a country player?*

Oh, shit no.

*You've obviously been into blues for a long time.*

When I was like 14 with my little band, Rockin' Randall And The Rockets back home, we listened to Jimmy Reed and Lightnin' Hopkins. That stuff's fun to play, whether you're 14 or 35.

*You seem to be incorporating the blues into your playing more and more all the time.*

I really am. I've been gettin' it from the fans. I do that solo stuff onstage, and they say, "Why don't you cut some of that, man? Instead of just doing it on the show, we want to hear it on the tape." And, hell, I think that "Blues Medley" with Ray Charles and John Lee Hooker is the high point of that album [*Major Moves*].

*Hooker must have been a big influence on you.*

Oh yeah. Probably Lightnin' more for guitar—for me and a lot of other people—but maybe John Lee more on the vocals. Listened to a lot of him.

*Was it hard to gradually incorporate that type of influence into your own music without rubbing the country audience the wrong way?*

Was it! There was no way to do it before. See, I was going out and doing tours, doing Hank Williams stuff, as a boy, and then I'd come home and get with my band, and it was "Soul Twist" and "Raunchy" and Duane Eddy. So it was two different entities there.

*Were you playing lead guitar in that band?*

Oh, yeah.

*On your early albums, you were never promoted as an instrumentalist at all.*

Well, I wasn't taking it very seriously. I had plenty of money and cars and *whatever* happening, so I'd just run out and play

Daddy. But on the end of all those shows, I always did "Memphis," and I played every instrument on the stage. To be very truthful, I just didn't get too serious about the music business, because I wasn't doing my music anyway. Later on, I incorporated it all, and that's practically *all* you got, period, from the *Friends* album on.

*Where does the type of picking you do on "Attitude Adjustment"* [Major Moves] *and "Dixie On My Mind"* [Rowdy] *come from?*

Doc Watson- or Jimmie Rodgers-style dixieland. Doc Watson is Mr. Clean. It's all a blend of what I like to listen to. It's country and blues and old rock and roll and dixieland.

*The guitarists you mentioned as early influences were mostly acoustic bluesmen.*

Yeah, them and Chuck Berry. Everybody was trying to do "Johnny B. Goode" or something. I think he influenced a hell of a lot of people. When you turn on your AM rock radio, you sure do hear a lot of Chuck Berry licks. I don't hear that many Elvis Presley licks, but I sure hear a lot of Chuck Berry ones. *He* was the king, as far as I was concerned. You just have to look at the repetition, you know—he gets copied the most.

*Is that the type of material Rockin' Randall And The Rockets did?*

Oh, that's *all* we did—"Roll Over Beethoven," or things like "Stay"—that was our big one—"Blueberry Hill," "Twist And Shout." This was high school—14, 15, 16, 17 years old. We were playing at parties.

*But at the same time, you were still . . .*

Going out on the road—Hank Williams, Jr., at Cobo Hall in Detroit, filled up auditoriums, doing "Your Cheating Heart." And then right back to the party with the little girls and [*hums Chuck Berry licks*]. It was two separate things.

*That must have caused quite an identity crisis.*

It did, later on—because all I'm doing now is Rockin' Randall And The Rockets. All it is is a guy doing what he wanted to do. Yeah, being the son of Hank Williams was real fun for a kid, but it was hell for a man. Especially a man who had people telling him, "Say, you can play, man. Do what you want to do." But I felt a commitment, like, "I should do this for Daddy." Let me tell you something: Hank Williams don't need anybody to do anything for him. When I sat down with the powers that be at Warner Bros., I said, "Do you think if I'd gotten killed in that fall that Hank Williams would be any smaller of a legend?" The deejays would say, "Oh God, Hank, Jr., got killed. That's too bad. Well, here's another great Hank Williams song for you." That's the bottom line [*laughs*]. But I bet Daddy's looking down and saying, "Now you're on the right track." See, when he came to Nashville, he was a little different, too. I got films of him doing "Lovesick Blues," and those knees are going all over the place. He learned to play from a black blues singer.

*You've used the term "white man's blues" for the type of music you do.*

Well, country music *is* white man's blues. Not only mine, but all of it.

*Because, in a sense, it serves the same function?*

Yeah, it serves the same function in society. The black man's gonna go buy Bobby Blue Bland or Al Green or whoever he's listening to, and the white man's gonna go buy Jon Anderson or Merle Haggard or Hank Williams. George Jones—if that ain't the white man's blues, nothing is. Whether he's driving to and from

work or having trouble with the wife or whatever. It don't have to have a steel guitar to be a country song. Let's face it—there's been a pile of country smashes in the last ten years that ain't got no steel guitars or fiddles on them. I think the bottom line is it's white man's blues, but there's a lot of them like to hear something else mixed in—a little ZZ Top or Jimmy Reed or whatever.

*Was it when you started working with* [*producer*] *Jimmy Bowen that you began using Reggie Young on guitar for a lot of your sessions?*

Yes, although we didn't use many people who were there in Nashville. Jimmy transported a lot of players there, and they never went back—like Billy Walker. See, Reggie's a country guitar player, but he can play country, rock, blues—*anything.*

*When you work up tunes on the road and then take the arrangements into the studio, who shows Reggie Young what to do?*

Me or Lamar Morris [guitarist with Hank's Bama Band]. I sit down with an acoustic and say, "Here's a song I wrote, and this is how we want to do it." And those guys just fall right in. I show him—I mean, he can play circles around me, but some of this old "gut" stuff we're doing, a lot of guys just haven't played that in a long time. So it's fun for both of us. Billy Walker has got a good swampy blues feel, in stuff like "I Got Rights" [*Family Tradition*] or "Country Boy Can Survive" [*The Pressure Is On*].

*Where do you get your ideas from?*

The TV and the newspaper and keeping my eyes and ears open. I may be in my prime right now—I don't know—in songwriting. I knocked out two the other day just like *that.* Songwriting is real easy for me, thank goodness.

*One element that does seem "country" about the songs is that you write about everyday situations.*

Absolutely. I love a lot of rock guys, and we communicate on the phone or go hunting together, but some of this stuff on MTV, I can't go for that, man. I hate it. With your hair dyed purple and the devil stuff and the words that mean nothing. I want to be remembered as a damn good songwriter, and if they can't relate to your songs, you've had it. I mean, I've got real good record sales, I hope for that reason. If they can relate to it in the pickup truck or in a Mercedes, then you got something. That's the whole key.

*Do you mostly work them up on acoustic guitar?*

Absolutely. All of them.

*A lot of your acoustic tunes incorporate some unorthodox chord shifts and a lot of wide-open, drone chords.*

Right. I like to use full chords with all six strings. I use a lot of open tunings that I don't even know what they are, but there's a whole bunch of those open D's as I run up and down the neck. Mickey Newberry-style things—some of it. A lot of that is like an autoharp. I like all strings going, not muting anything.

*Do you write songs as a result of fooling around with open tunings?*

Yes, sometimes they come like that—"I Got Rights," "The Pressure Is On" [*The Pressure Is On*], "I Don't Have any More Love Songs To Write For You" [*Whiskey Bent And Hell Bound*]. I love that sort of big concertina drone effect, with all those notes going at once.

*When you come up with the original idea or lyric for a song, do you already know what the arrangement will be?*

Just about immediately. "Attitude Adjustment," for instance, I knew what that was going to be between the hot dog stand and the limo in the airport. That's where I'm blessed—hearing what I want to play. I wrote another one, "I'm For Love" [*Five-0*], and it was very Johnny Cash-ish, right from the start.

*A couple of years ago, you were using a Fender Strat onstage.*

Yeah, and I've still got two here. Well, I've given one away to the audience so far. I've given one [Gibson] Les Paul and one Strat to the audience when I got mad at the sound. I just handed it to them. There's a nice set-up Strat somewhere [*laughs*]. Then on TNN or something, I gave a Les Paul away. A new one, thank God, not a '57. I broke down about ten months ago and got my checkbook out and bought a '57 gold-top and a '58 sunburst. I said, "Holy shit, now I know what they're talking about!"

*Are those the ones you use onstage?*

Hell, yes! You know, if you want sustain, that's the way you got to go. I like to take a Strat and change the pickups to make it sustain—then you've got the best of both worlds. But, I'll tell you, these damned old Gibsons spoiled me. If you're going to do this blues type stuff or Billy Gibbons or whatever, you got to have it. If you want it to hold there and talk to you, you've just got to have it. At least I do. You know, they get a lot of money for those things, and I can see why. I bought them from George Gruhn. He's got some dandies. Like old Dickie Betts said, "You've got a '57 gold-top and that tobacco sunburst—you'll be rarin'." See, that gold-top's hotter, it's got more high-end on it. They've just straightened everything up for me. Instead of running around—"take this DiMarzio out and put this Schecter

**Hank Williams, Jr. onstage at the Concord (California) Pavilion in 1984.**

back in"—I just stopped with the old humbuckers. And God almighty! Maybe that's because of what I listened to on old records that I liked and wanted to hear. They don't give them away, and it's not very smart to take them on the road, but I've got a couple of back-ups.

*What type of lap steel do you play?*

I think I'm about the only one using that old thing like [steel guitarist] Don Helms used with Daddy. I don't know what you want to call it—electric Hawaiian or electric Dobro or whatever it is. I've got an old Fender and an old Gibson—both 6-strings. I've had that old white Fender, I don't know how long. It's just like your el cheapo basic one that they had. That's the only two laps, and I keep about two Strats and two Les Pauls out there. I've played bottleneck-style, but I like the lap better. I like to take out the acoustic on the bus, especially if I'm writing songs, play like Robert Johnson stuff. [*Sings*] "You better come on in my kitchen, it's going to be raining outdoors." Oh, that's fun to fool with. Dickie Betts is just the master on that stuff.

*What tuning do you use on lap steel?*

Open *G* or *A* or open *E*.

*You play through Marshalls. Now, that's not very country.*

And a Mesa/Boogie, too. A lot of the time I use a Marshall on one side and a Boogie on the other. But the speakers aren't Marshalls anyway—that's just the cabinet. I put KT-130s in there—JBLs. The heads are Marshalls, but the bottom is all changed. I like to go with one Boogie and one Marshall, especially on the acoustic parts.

*It sounds like you put the acoustic through a chorus sometimes.*

Yes, a Boss Chorus on "Queen Of My Heart" [*Man Of Steel*] or "Old Habits" [*Habits Old And New*] or "Mister Lincoln" [*Major Moves*]. It makes my Guild sound good. But when I want to go back to the blues thing, I knock it off.

*When did you switch to Guild acoustics?*

I always had Martins, and then I played a Guild in a pawnshop in Spartanburg, South Carolina, about three or four years ago. It really turned me on. They make my model now—a Hank, Jr., model. I want an acoustic to just fill the room up when I'm writing a song. It's got that big early Epiphone or Gibson look. It's like a dreadnought, just bigger. And the back is arched. It reminds me of some Epiphone guitars that Ernest Tubb used to have when I did shows with him when I was a kid. I'm sold on Guild. Yeah, they really turned me around. I was born into thinking that if it didn't say Martin or Gibson, you could forget it. But the Guild will knock your socks when you're sitting in the room—you get a good feeling from it, and you write that song.

*Who designed the Hank, Jr., model?*

I told Guild what I wanted. It's a combination of a couple of their deals. It's got a maple back and a spruce top. It's beautiful.

But most beautiful guitars don't sound worth a shit. Man, this one does. I've got three. They make a tobacco-colored Hank, Jr.; I said, "I'm putting this in the time vault."

*What kind of a pickup do you have in the soundhole?*

Dean Markley. I use his strings, his pickup. I've tried all this other stuff, and I keep trying to find something with a volume control on the guitar, and it never works. I want that clear acoustic sound, so I just use the amp. I like that.

*Do you just use the Dean Markley strings on the acoustic, or on the electrics as well?*

I use them on both. On the electrics, though, I use different stuff, too. GHS, here and there, or Markleys on the basses, or maybe Gibsons. But on the acoustics I really like them.

*At this point, are there styles that you wouldn't do because you don't think a country audience would accept them?*

Oh, God no. Anybody who knows me knows better than that. I'm not looking for a country audience. I don't *have* a country audience that much. I've got a lot of guys who wear cowboy hats and have four-wheel drives, and they got a lot of damn Marshall Tucker albums, too. You know this ain't '53 or '54 anymore. Today's fan goes in and says, "I want Hank, Jr.'s album, I want Stevie Ray Vaughan, Huey Lewis, Willie Nelson, and a Ry Cooder." They don't go in and say, "Give me Dolly Parton and the Oak Ridge Boys and Tom T. Hall." They get what they want. I mean, I'm a pretty country son of a gun, but I can go downtown. I got a jet out back with my name on its tail, and it can land in Montana and it can land in Manhattan. I think the key is, we're havin' fun on that stage, and they know it. Yeah, we don't have many boundary lines in our stuff. It's just American music that people can enjoy. We play for majorities, I guess.

*You went through a period when you refused to sing your father's songs. What did it take for you to accept that you could do them again, in your own way?*

A bunch of hit records of my own. You know, styles have to be made; they don't grow out of the ground. You don't drop a seed in, and put on some super fertilizer, and they pop up in two months. And, you know, this empire [*laughs*] didn't come along from going out there and doing another version of "Hey, Good Lookin'." Yeah, for a while, I didn't do any. After a while, it was almost scary. I started doing some of Daddy's songs again—like a medley of "Cold, Cold Heart," "I Can't Help It," and "You Win Again"—and there was just polite applause. Then I'd do "Whiskey Bent And Hell Bound," and they'd go nuts. Merle Kilgore [singer who opens all of Hank, Jr.'s shows] said, "Listen brother, I was with your daddy, and I been with you for 19 years, and let me tell you something. You see that audience out there? Your daddy didn't fill that auditorium—you filled it up." So it was like making a whole circle, 360 degrees. That was quite a shock to me—a *real* attitude adjustment.

---

### A SELECTED HANK WILLIAMS, JR. DISCOGRAPHY

**Solo albums** (on MGM): *Greatest Hits*, SE-4656; *Hank Williams, Jr. & Friends*, M3G 5009; *14 Greatest Hits*, 1-5020. (On Warner/Curb): *One Night Stands*, 5E-538; *The New South*, 5E-539; *Family Tradition*, 6E-194; *Whiskey Bent And Hell Bound*, 6E-237; *Habits Old And New*, 6E-278; *Rowdy*, 6E-330; *The Pressure Is On*, 5E-535; *High Notes*, E1-60100; *Hank Williams, Jr.'s Greatest Hits*, E1-660193; *Strong Stuff*, E1-60223; *Man Of Steel*, 1-23924; *Major Moves*, 1-25088; *Five-0*, 1-25267; *All My Rowdy Friends Have Settled Down*, Warner Bros., 0441.

# JIMMY WYBLE

**As told to Frankie R. Nemko**

CERTAINLY AS LONG AS THERE ARE GUITARISTS LIKE Jimmy Wyble around, America's Southwest can still lay claim to Guitar Country. From Texas and Oklahoma have come jazz virtuosos like Charlie Christian, Barney Kessel, and Herb Ellis, as well as bluesmen such as T-Bone Walker, Freddie King, and Lowell Fulson. Western swing, of course, is still alive and well down there—bringing to mind its elder statesmen, Leon McAuliffe and Eldon Shamblin.

According to Ray Benson, guitarist/leader of western swing's Asleep At The Wheel, "All the greatest guitar players come from Texas and Oklahoma. The guitar grew up there, and the western swing bands *plus* the jazz bands were what was happening. Down there it's a tradition, and it goes a lot deeper than just rock and roll—which is where a lot of the country picked up on guitar.

"Jimmy Wyble is who I would like to play like more than anybody else in the world," Benson continues. "As far as single-note guitar is concerned, he's my favorite."

Soft-spoken, humble Jimmy Wyble—born in Port Arthur, Texas, in 1922—is a lot of people's favorite guitarist. Over the years he has compiled a resume equally impressive in both country and jazz circles. Joining Bob Wills And His Texas Playboys (the absolute kings of western swing) in 1944, Jimmy would often spice up the western dance numbers by adding Charlie Christian or Django Reinhardt lines to his solos.

The Wills band eventually brought Wyble to California where he came in contact with more jazz and studio guitarists. A short stint with Spade Cooley's country group preceded Jimmy's full-fledged induction into the jazz world when he joined vibist Red Norvo's combo in the mid-'50s.

Wyble played with Norvo for eight years, during which time he also accompanied Frank Sinatra and toured with Benny Goodman. In 1964, when his wife took ill, Jimmy decided to stay in Los Angeles and work in the studios. He played on numerous recordings, television shows, and soundtracks like *Ocean's 11* and *The Wild Bunch*.

Jimmy's most recent endeavor has been with his old friend Tony Rizzi in Tony's Five Guitars Plus Four with its unique harmonized-guitar concept. He also tutors several guitar

students today and has published one instructional book, *Classical/Country* [Playback Music]. His two-line contrapuntal approach to soloing makes for one of the most advanced sounds in jazz guitar's recent history.

Wyble's series of guitar etudes (available on tape, record, and sheet music from Playback) have been highly acclaimed by such artists as Laurindo Almeida, who called them "well-written, pedagogic works dedicated to our instrument, which create new horizons, new ideas—precisely what is needed now," and considers Jimmy Wyble "one of the greatest guitar talents, extremely competent." The Brazilian stylist added, "If anything bad can be said about him it is that he's too shy!"

\* \* \* \*

Where I grew up there were a whole lot of guitarists on the block, so to speak—no organized combos, just dozens of fiddle bands. We'd sometimes drive a couple of hundred miles for a dance and make a buck for the night! But we all loved to play so much it was worth it.

Even though I was occupied with country and western music for a living, all the time I was also listening to such people as [jazz violinist] Joe Venuti and [guitarist] Eddie Lang. I remember hearing [clarinetist] Benny Goodman on the radio and the Red Norvo/Mildred Bailey band—never dreaming that one day I'd be playing with them! I'd send away for every guitar book I heard about and would spend laborious hours picking a measure here and there. I learned the Alan Reuss solos, but was never really able to handle that kind of material at that time.

I was utterly amazed when I first heard Django Reinhardt on records. For a short time, being such a novice, I actually tried to copy a few bars here and there, which was quite ridiculous because at that point I had absolutely no proficiency. Then I heard Charlie Christian, and I was totally devastated. Not that I considered Charlie better than Django—it was just something that happened to me emotionally whenever I'd listen to Charlie play. I spent as many hours as possible trying to learn some of his licks.

There was another guitarist in the Bob Wills band at the same time I was named Cameron Hill, who, like me, was an all-out fan of Charlie Christian. Cameron would copy a chorus of, say, Charlie's "Flying Home," and he and I would play it in harmony. Bob used to refer to us as "twin guitars." That was the good thing about Bob, he didn't restrict us to playing in the country style. Whatever we could bring to the job he'd let us do. Some of us who were really into listening to jazz would take some incredible solos right in the middle of all that cowboy stuff! That was a very swinging band; in those days we were often referred to as the country and western version of the Benny Goodman group. Bob really knew nothing about music, but he was such an emotional inspiration to all of us in the band—that alone made us cook.

Those early experiences in the studios with Bob Wills meant so much to me in terms of meeting the likes of George Smith, George Van Eps, Barney Kessel. Also during that time we'd be playing at these huge ballrooms for up to 7,000 people, and right next door at a smaller jazz place would be someone like [trumpeter] Harry James or [saxophonist] Charlie Barnet. That's how I got to meet so many of the jazz greats and become so influenced by them.

When I decided to stay in Los Angeles I was still working with a country and western band, Spade Cooley's. However, Spade ran a much tighter ship than Bob Wills. He was far more rigid and stuck pretty faithfully to the country and western concepts. It's curious to me now how working in such an atmosphere I always somehow managed to be taken into areas

where I'd meet the jazz people. Like [reed player] Jimmy Giuffre—he and Barney Kessel were on the faculty at the American Operatic Lab in L.A., so I went there for a while and studied with them.

My ambition was really never anything other than to play guitar—I didn't even know what a studio guitarist was, much less a whole orchestra of guitars. I just had a burning desire to play, no matter how or where. But in the '50s I was listening to Tal Farlow who at that time was with Red Norvo at the Haig Club in Hollywood. I used to go and listen to them, and that became quite a turning point for me. When Tal left Red for a few months, he was replaced by Jimmy Raney. Once again I'd sit in front of the band all night long, absorbing every note that Jimmy played. This was also around the time Jim Hall was playing with [percussionist] Chico Hamilton, when [flute and reed player] Buddy Collette and [cellist] Fred Katz were in the group. I was learning so much from all those guys. And it was during that period that I frist met Tony Rizzi, who was just so far ahead of the game then.

Those years were very important to me, because after Tal left Red Norvo in 1956, a young guitarist named Bill Dillard joined Red and made two albums with the group. We were close friends and jammed a lot. Then Bill was tragically killed in a fire, and Red asked me to take over Bill's chair. I was absolutely overwhelmed. My reply was, "I'd like to, but I can't play like Tal or Jimmy or Bill." Red told me, "I'm not interested in that; all I'm concerned with is whether you're interested in growing and learning."

I have to confess here and now that that man, Red Norvo, literally saved my life. At that point I had become a thoroughly, emotionally-frustrated, mixed-up person—to the degree of becoming an alcoholic. What a task for anyone to undertake: Here was this young, inexperienced, emotionally-disturbed musician, and Red virtually taught me how to function in his wonderful trio and quintet. So in addition to what I gained musically—which was vast, believe me—just learning to accept myself and making an honest effort was all attributable to Red Norvo.

I stayed with Red for eight years, traveling extensively throughout the U.S. and abroad. In 1964 the band went to Australia where we accompanied Frank Sinatra. During that period with Red I was fortunate to have the opportunity to take part in several tours with Benny Goodman as well, and record with his orchestra.

So you can see my musical life was taking on a very different look and sound. Before I joined Red, and after I had gotten to hear all those guitar greats like Charlie Christian, Barney Kessel, Herb Ellis, and numerous others, I became bent on playing like them. I was just obsessed by the need to copy my idols. Coming under Red's influence—at the age of 35—I found myself being awakened for the first time to the fact that we have to grow as individuals. I learned that even if I'd had the proficiency to emulate those idols, it wouldn't have been the right thing to do.

The last time I officially worked with Red's group was in 1964. And it has been since then, really, that I've become more and more involved in the studios, playing on numerous television shows, record dates, and movie scores. Probably one of the most exciting projects I ever had in the studios was with Laurindo Almeida. He had written a score for three guitars, so Laurindo played classical, I was on electric, and Bobby Bain handled the bass guitar.

I gradually developed my own style and approach to studio work and began experimenting with different kinds of instruments. When I first arrived in Los Angeles way back in 1944, I had just one guitar: the Johnny Smith Artist Award model made by Guild. I had met Johnny in Denver, fell in love with his sound, and decided I had to have that for myself. But as soon as I began freelancing I realized I had to get into the electric instrument, so I got myself a Fender. Incidentally, when I was with one of those cowboy bands, Leo Fender came and gave each of us guitarists one of his very first Telecasters, which he made practically in his garage. I still have it and occasionally play it on a record date or something.

I also knew that I'd need a lot of gadgets in studio work, so I got a Fender amp, a wah-wah pedal, fuzz boxes, and a Small Stone phaser [Electro-Harmonix], an expanded reverb unit. I must admit in all honesty, though, that I'm not that much into rock playing. I used all these accouterments from time to time but I'm really not that adept at the new music. I mostly enjoy playing my acoustic guitars. I have a 6- and 12-string, a Martin flat-top, a Howard Roberts jazz model, and a custom-made Guild Mark 7 classical instrument.

I finally gave up my Fender amp and bought a Benson 300 amp. Now I have an early vintage Polytone 102 amp, which I use almost exclusively for jazz, and a Polytone Mini Brute.

Another instrument, a new innovation that I'm just getting to know, is the Guitorgan. It's made by a company in Texas called MCI, Inc. Basically, it's like a Hammond B-3 organ built inside an electric guitar. It's played the same way as guitar, with no difference in tuning or in the fingerboard; however, there is a preciseness that's *really* required in the left hand. In playing guitar you can anticipate the note, and it doesn't play until you actually pluck that string. However, with the organ attachment, as soon as a string makes contact with the fret it's playing that note. You can't accidentally bump into things. I would say that for a good technical player it would present no problems—in fact, it would force a person to play correctly.

I was involved in Tony Rizzi's Five Guitars right from the very beginning, and it's been a tremendous experience. Playing with Tony after all these years of admiring him so much is like a dream come true—a great privilege. As the readers probably know, Tony has taken those early recorded solos by our mutual idol, Charlie Christian, and harmonized them for five guitars. The challenge involved in playing those charts really keeps me on my toes.

I firmly believe that the whole music scene is changing so much now that someday very soon Tony's contribution to the guitar world will be available in schools for ensemble playing. When I first started out, I didn't have the opportunities to be exposed to such things. In fact, I was never formally trained in music. I did take a few lessons from a man named Raymond Jones, a machinist who was also an avid guitarist. He's a fine craftsman and is still building beautiful guitars. He taught me the rudiments of reading and the first legitimate aspects of playing guitars. He took me through the Nick Lucas and Nick Manoloff books.

Now *I'm* involved in teaching. Since the advent of my first published book, *Classical/Country.* I've been virtually forced into teaching. The material in the book isn't really country or classical, but because of my background, it cuts across all the lines—classical, country, jazz. The basic concept involves a two-line contrapuntal approach, creating pianistic sounds on the guitar. I've been asked to demonstrate and speak about this innovation at such prestigious places as Lee Ritenour's master guitar class at USC and Dick Grove's Workshop in North Hollywood. I'm also passing it on to some of my private students who are interested in this form. My involvement with the contrapuntal writing has become almost an obsession; but I can see great potential. It could quite easily lead to being able to improvise with two lines instead of one.

Today my heroes are many. Of course, Jimi Hendrix was a tremendous innovator and stylist, and we always need to have those kinds of people in any art form. None of us could help but be influenced in some way by his contribution. I really like to listen to all the new people, like Eric Clapton, Robben Ford, Lee Ritenour, Tim May and Mike Rosati [both with Tony Rizzi's group], and Jay Graydon, who did the *Andy Williams Show* with me—you'll be hearing a lot more of him. All the people in the rock scene—so many of them have tremendous musicianship and taste. I also have the greatest admiration for some of the studio guitarists, like John and Tom Morell, Tommy Tedesco, Mike Anthony, and, of course, Howard Roberts, who, by the way, was very helpful in the publication of my books.

I do want to stress, though, that the greatest lesson I have learned over the years is to not become so completely enraptured by certain heroes that your playing is exactly like theirs, because that could turn out to be a stumbling block, a dead end. I'm so glad that my experiences have broadened my horizons. There's just so much variety in music today, the resources are endless.

---

## A SELECTED JIMMY WYBLE DISCOGRAPHY

**Solo albums:** The Jimmy Wyble Quintet, *Diane*, Vantage [Box 126, Reseda, CA 91335], LP-502; *Classical Jazz*, Jazz Chronicles [6226 Santa Monica Blvd., Hollywood, CA 90038], JCS 77-IN2. **With Red Norvo:** *Naturally*, Rave, RLP-101; *Red Plays The Blues*, RCA, LPM 1729; *Windjammer City Style*, Dot, DLP 3126; *Dinah Sings Some Blues With Red* (with Dinah Shore), Capitol, T1354. **With Benny Goodman:** *Into The Seventies*, Time-Life (Capitol), STA 354; *Benny Goodman And His Orchestra*, MGM, E3810; *Benny Goodman Swings Again*, Columbia, CL 1579. **With others:** Eydie Gorme, *On Stage*, ABC-Paramount, ABC 307; Bob Harington Quartet, *Jazz a la Carte*, Crown, CST 388; *Tony Rizzi's Five Guitars Plus Four Play Charlie Christian*, Milagro [dist. by Ray Lawrence, Ltd., Box 1987, Studio City, CA 91614], 1000; *Dirty Old Men* (various artists), Nocturne [same address as Jazz Chronicles], NRS 902; *The Bob Wills Anthology*, Columbia, PG 32416.

# REGGIE YOUNG

By Jas Obrecht

AROUND NASHVILLE, REGGIE YOUNG IS KNOWN AS the first studio musician to call for a tasty guitar part. One of the busiest and most respected players in town, he regularly backs the biggest names in the business: Willie Nelson, Waylon Jennings, and Hank Williams, Jr., to name but a few. Although he's best known for his work in country circles, Reggie's distinguished career traces back 30 years to the first wave of Memphis rockabilly. Later in the '50s, he cut hits with the Bill Black Combo, and accompanied the band in '64 when it went on the road with the Beatles and the Yardbirds. In the 20 years since then, Reggie has devoted himself almost exclusively to the work he loves best—session guitar.

Producer Jimmy Bowen has worked with Reggie on dozens of albums. For him, the soft-spoken guitarist's greatest strength lies in his sensitivity. "Reggie's guitar playing is the ultimate complement to a singer," Bowen explained to researcher Dino Bradley. "He's the most melodic player. If you hire a rhythm section on Monday with people like Reggie Young, by Wednesday these guys will sound like they've been together for 20 years. Reggie walks into the studio with a true focus on what music is being made in *that* room at *that* time. He will sit there for ten seconds and listen, and then he'll play a note or phrase that you just can't live without."

For Reggie Grimes Young, Jr., 48, a life in music seemed almost pre-ordained. His dad, who hosted a radio show in Arkansas when Reggie was young, still plays Hawaiian-style guitar. Reggie was born in Caruthersville, Missouri, and at 14 moved to Memphis, Tennessee. There, while teaching himself to play, he came under the influence of Chet Atkins, Django Reinhardt, and B.B. King. "B.B. was my hero," Reggie recalls. "I used to chase his bus up and down Beale Street, and I'd see him every time he was in town. He made a big impression on me when I started playing."

Reggie's earliest gigs were with western swing bands. The first regional hit he played on, though, was roots rock and roll: Eddie Bond's "Rockin' Daddy," cut in Memphis in '56 for Mercury Records. As part of Bond's four-piece rockabilly group, Young spent the rest of '56 opening shows for Carl Perkins and Roy Orbison. He then worked with singer Johnny Horton in

Shreveport, Louisiana, and in 1959 moved back to Memphis, where he joined the Bill Black Combo. One of the city's top bassists, Black had already achieved fame as a member of Elvis Presley's original lineup. When Elvis was drafted into the Army, Bill formed his own rock-a-boogie band. One of Reggie's early singles with Black, Hi Records' "Smokie (Part 2)," sold over a million copies and became 1960's top R&B hit. Following an appearance on *Dick Clark's Christmas Show*, the guitarist was inducted into the Army in late '59.

After serving his hitch in Ethiopia, Young rejoined the Bill Black Combo in 1961. By then a top concert draw with several gold records to its credit, the band toured frequently and made many TV appearances. In sessions during this period, Reggie cut several instrumentals with trumpeter Willie Mitchell, including the hit "20-75." By 1964, the Bill Black Combo's popularity was so strong in Europe that the Beatles themselves requested that the band open their U.S. tour. "We started things off, playing about 15 minutes of instrumentals—which was *boring*," Reggie laughs. "Then we backed the Righteous Brothers. They'd take a break, and then have the Beatles. It was a lot of fun, but it was really spooky, too, especially when the Beatles came on; they had to have barricades up in front of the stages. The Beatles had big old Vox amps; it was the first time I had ever seen amps that big. It was kind of the beginning of that kind of rock and roll."

Reggie's fondest memories of the month-long experience are the days off in Key West, Florida, during which members of the bands jammed in a small motel cafe. As part of a fair-trade agreement between American and British musicians' unions, the Bill Black Combo followed its Beatles dates with a 30-day package tour of England. Sharing the bus and billings were the Ronettes, Billy J. Kramer, and the Yardbirds with Eric Clapton on guitar.

Once home in Memphis, Young made a career decision: "Around '65, I knew that being a studio player was the way to go. You could make a lot more money doing sessions than you could traveling—at least I could. And it was easier." He settled into producer Chips Moman's American Studios, becoming part of a rhythm section that came to be known as 827 Thomas Street. Its core players included drummer Gene Chrisman, organist

Bobby Emmons, pianist Bobby Wood, and bassists Tommy Cogbill and Mike Leech. "We started the first in-house group," Reggie explains. "We just bound ourselves together, and we wouldn't work outside the studio unless they used the rest of the band."

During the next seven years, 827 Thomas Street played on more than 30 gold records and 500 others that made it into the charts. Reggie's Top-40 credits from this stint include Elvis Presley's "Suspicious Minds" and "In The Ghetto," Wilson Picket's "I Found A True Love" and "I'm A Midnight Mover," Dusty Springfield's "Son-Of-A-Preacher Man," and Neil Diamond's "Sweet Caroline," "Holly Holy," and "Brother Love's Travelling Salvation Show." In 1968, he became perhaps the first session player to use a Coral electric sitar on Top-40 hits, giving the instrument a prominent role in the Box Tops' "Cry Like A Baby" and B.J. Thomas' "Eyes Of A New York Woman."

With the decline of Memphis' recording scene in the early '70s, Reggie and the rest of 827 Thomas Street moved to Atlanta. When that didn't pan out, Reggie moved to Nashville in '73. He arrived in town just as Danny O'Keefe's "Good Time Charlie's Got The Blues" broke into the Top 10. "A lot of people thought I was a steel player on that tune," he notes. "I was using a volume pedal, just squeezing out notes; nobody else in town was using one. A lot of the country singers said, 'Boy, we want to get that guitar player,' so that helped me get work when I moved here."

Within a few months, Reggie was back in the Top 10 with his first hit with Dobie Gray, "Drift Away."

Since then, Young has appeared on hundreds of albums and scores of hits, including Waylon Jennings' "Luckenbach, Texas," Willie Nelson's "Always On My Mind," and every Hank Williams, Jr., release since the late '70s. He recently returned to Memphis to back Roy Orbison, Johnny Cash, Jerry Lee Lewis, and Carl Perkins for an album and film, and he'll appear on the forthcoming release credited to the Highwaymen, which bands Kris Kristofferson, Willie Nelson, Johnny Cash, and Waylon Jennings. Here, Reggie updates the state of Nashville studio guitar and offers essential information for all aspiring studio musicians.

\* \* \* \*

*WHAT ARE THE MOST IMPORTANT ASSETS FOR SOME-one in your line of work?*
Attitude is a key factor, and you have to be versatile. Most of the sessions here are head arrangements; there's very little reading. You just work things up, but throughout the week, you could go from bluegrass to rock and roll. I don't think the old hillbilly country music is selling like it used to. To me, what's happening here is like what was going on in the '60s in Memphis and California. Some of the "country" music I've been on sounds to me like '60s pop music. They're just calling it country.

The music has gotten better; it's a little more involved than just three chords.

*Do you consider yourself a "country guitarist," or is that a label you've picked up because you happen to work in Nashville?*

I wasn't country until I moved to Nashville [*laughs*]. Yeah, if it's cut in Nashville, the first impression people have is that it's country music, even though there's a lot of music here that is not necessarily country. But I think the image will always be that way because of the *Grand Ole Opry*, Opryland, and other attractions, and because all of the TV shows coming out of here relate to country music. In fact, when I first came here, I thought Nashville would be like what I'd seen on *The Porter Wagoner Show*; I figured everybody had crewcuts, sat around on bales of hay, and played guitar.

*Years ago, there was a so-called "A Team" of Nashville studio musicians. Does that still exist?*

No. The scene is more open now; there's all kinds of players. The old A-Team consisted of guys like [guitarists] Grady Martin, Hank Garland, [drummer] Buddy Harmon, and [bassist] Bob Moore. It was six or seven guys, and they did all the work. They were doing three or four sessions a day, and Owen Bradley was producing the bulk of it. The first bunch of guys to infiltrate that old A-Team was the rhythm section that [producer] Rick Hall was using down in Muscle Shoals in the mid-'60s: [bassist] Norbert Putnam, [keyboardist] David Briggs, and [drummer] Jerry Carrigan. They moved up and broke through that wall. And then I moved to Nashville with the Memphis rhythm section by way of Atlanta in '72. We had an R&B background mostly, and pop. We kind of influenced that into the Nashville thing. Luckily for me, I brought work with me. Some of the people I worked for in Memphis had already moved here, so I didn't knock anybody out of work or have to fight to get in the door. In the last few years, a lot of tremendous players from California have come here, like [bassist] Dave Hungate.

*Is the studio scene still highly competitive?*

Not really. There's still only a handful of players doing the bulk of the work, but it's more than just six or seven guys, like it was years ago. The producers don't have in-house sections, but they use the same players over and over. It's not a clique, but I know there's guys trying to get in. Seven years ago, I was all over the place. I used to do a 10:00 A.M. date at one studio, a 2:00 P.M. date somewhere else—I could do three or four sessions a day. I was scooting around all over town, but that's not happening anymore. I'm working more than I used to, but instead of it being spread out among a lot of producers, three or four producers do just about all of the work here.

*Are you a solo specialist?*

Yeah, probably. When people hire me, they kind of let me do what I do best—I don't know what that is [*laughs*]—without just dictating, "Play this, play that." I guess I'm somewhat of a stylist.

*At what stage of the recording process are you called in?*

Basic tracks, and then I go back over-dubbing. Most of my sessions are block-booked a week at a time, so I usually go in on Monday, and I'll be through Friday evening. In the first week, I do most of my basic tracks and some solos. I may also do overdub sessions later on. For example, I was working with [singer] Mac Davis recently. We started Monday, did a couple of songs a day, and wound up at the end of the week with ten or 12 songs. For a ten-song album, you have a couple of throwaways.

That was just for basic tracks. We could probably spend that much time again overdubbing and sweetening. And then you've got your vocals, mixing time, and whatever else.

*Are chord charts or demo tapes prepared before you show up for a session?*

Sometimes. Mac, being a writer, just played some of the songs on guitar while we took chord changes. We use a number system in Nashville—instead of letters for chords, you do it in numbers. A 12-bar blues, for example, would be a 1 4 5 progression. That way, if they want to change the key, you don't have to do any transposing: "1" becomes whatever key you're in. Sometimes you see charts with note values under the numbers. This system really makes it a lot quicker, and most of the songs are not that difficult. You can do number charts out of your head pretty quick.

*Do you splice different takes to create one solo?*

I do, but not very often. It all depends on what it is. If it's kind of free and I can just do something off the top of my head, I really like first and second takes. It's good when it's *new*. You can really get bogged down doing it over and over, while still trying to make it sound spontaneous.

*Jimmy Bowen recently said, "If you hire people like Reggie Young on Monday, by Wednesday these guys will sound like they have been together for 20 years."*

[*Laughs.*] When you're in a basic rhythm section, by the end of the week, you really do get locked into each other. This is especially true with head arrangements: You run it down and work out the parts that don't feel good. It's trial and error. Bowen's always joking about how he has to have everything ready—the sounds on all the instruments—because when we get it together and run it down, the first take usually comes off because the band gets so locked into the artist. And you try to relate to the *artist's* music instead of making the artist go to where the band is. Once you lock into what the artist's music is about, you're home free. That way, even with the same players, you don't sound like the same band all the time.

*Bowen added that you usually have a true focus on what the artists are trying to do.*

That's flattering, but that's what it's all about. It's the artist's career. They are going to live with that album for the rest of their life. Why would I want to throw myself into their life? It's their music. I need to get into what they're doing and to try to adapt to their style, their way of interpreting what they've written or the way they are hearing things.

*When you're hired to work with an important musician for the first time, do you listen to some of his previous work?*

I think you should know somewhat of what he's done. If you're not very familiar with it, you should maybe get an album and listen to it, especially if it's a writer/artist. If he has a concept or a style of music, you try to lock in on that. But I'm always open. If I have an idea, I ask the artist and not the producer. Bowen works that way. As a matter of fact, he's told various rhythm sections I've worked with: "Go to the artist, and then let the artist come to me."

*This seems the opposite of sessions where the producer calls all the shots and the musicians have to play exactly what's written.*

Yeah, but there's a lot of that here, too. I prefer the other way. Why dictate *everything* that's going to be played, especially in a creative situation with head arrangements? When you've got

**Reggie had an immediate impact on the Nashville guitar sound when he arrived in 1973.**

people who could probably come up with something better than you could think, why put a blanket on them and say, "Play this"? A certain direction is okay, but to just have a dictator over a session—yuck.

*Do any of the artists you work with ever know exactly what they want?*

Exactly? I don't think so [*laughs*]. Everybody's open for suggestions. To hear something in your head that's just preconceived and you know how it's going to sound—no, I don't think I know anybody like that.

*What is the best attitude to have when working with musicians of the caliber of Willie Nelson and Waylon Jennings?*

I think where a lot of players get really frustrated is trying to play something *they* want to play. Then somebody says, "No, I don't like that. Would you try something else?"—and they don't know how to handle that; they get offended. I just try to feel people out and figure out what they want and then play it. If it doesn't come out, well, at least I tried what they wanted.

*Is there a common mistake made by studio newcomers?*

Probably being too aggressive, trying to get their foot in the door. I've seen players come in who completely destroy the rhythm section and everybody's creative ability. They just try to

take over; they're real aggressive people. Even if you can provide *great* guitar fills, if you act like you're the only person in the room, you won't work very long. If a producer hires somebody who doesn't get along with the guys, he won't be there the next date. If the producer doesn't figure it out the first session, he will eventually. And you won't get work in this town by going to a producer. A lot of people go at it backwards. Guitar players call me a lot, saying they have a tape or something and want to know if I would recommend them taking it around town to producers. I tell them I don't see how that would help at all.

*What would help?*

Getting to know the players. Usually, most of the work comes from the musicians talking. Like, if I work with somebody who is a good drummer, the next date I might recommend him: "Man, this guy's great. He works good in the section, and he's not trying to take over." If you can get on demos or get with anybody that's playing, talk to them. It's like one great big band here, and different people work out of it. You can call a lot of different players, but usually they've all worked together and know how to get the best out of certain things. You need to be song-conscious, too. Instead of being just a "session musician," you really need to know something about songwriting.

**Reggie's studio career extends back 30 years to the first wave of Memphis rockabilly.**

*Should a potential Nashville session guitarist master reading music?*

The first priority today should be learning how to read. I think my day—like the old barnstorming days of the record business—is coming to a close. Everything is getting real technical and specialized. Music is getting a little more complicated, and it's hard to throw a bunch of guys together to do a difficult piece unless it's written out. But I'm sure there will always be three- or four-chord songs in Nashville. I don't think you could survive in L.A. without being able to read, and

eventually it's going to be that way here. So, number one, learn how to read; I wish I could.

*How do you handle a written cue?*

Luckily, I haven't run across that. Nine times out of ten, they know I can't read, or if not, someone tells them. I get hired a lot of times anyway, and they just leave a place to let me play whatever I want through the chord changes. But as far as playing notes goes, I'd have to sit down and really figure it out or get somebody to play it so I could memorize it.

*What's the favorite guitar among Nashville session players?*

Probably a Fender Stratocaster. There are a lot of guys using them, and I hear them on records a lot. The Les Paul and Telecaster, too—it all depends on what you are doing. There aren't many Gibson ES-335s anymore, although that was all there was back around '72. When I first moved here, every guitarist in Nashville sounded and played like Grady Martin, and that's what he had, with an Echoplex.

*Are you ever told what type of guitar to use on a session?*

No, it's up to my own discretion. I usually play a '57 Stratocaster with EMG pickups. It has a whammy bar tailpiece, but I don't use it. I took a couple of springs out of it; it isn't blocked, but the tailpiece touches the wood. That guitar doesn't have any special electronics or anything. I was using a Les Paul, too, but right now I'm also playing a Kramer Pacer with EMG pickups—a humbucker on the back and two single-coils. That guitar has a Floyd Rose bar and stays in tune real good. The only feature I don't like about it is that if you bend one note and hold the other, the note that's not being bent goes flat. But I like the sound of that guitar, especially with those pickups. It's got 3-way switches, and a midrange boost in one of the tone controls—that's good for overdriving the pickups. The Kramer's not as thick as a Les Paul and not as thin as the Strat. It's a real nice guitar. And I use a '65 Tele sometimes; it has EMG pickups, too. I like EMGs, especially with digital recording. They get rid of all the noise, and still make it sound like the guitar.

*What's your choice in acoustics?*

I've got a Hohner. I'm not a big Martin fan, I guess because so many people have Martins, especially in Nashville. When I first moved here, I did a jingle where everybody on the date had to play a Hohner instrument. They brought in this prototype—a real pretty little guitar—and I really like it. It sounds great, and I use that or a Daion steel-string. But I don't play acoustic that much.

*What's the rest of your setup?*

I've got two Fender Concert amps. I use the TC Electronic Stereo Chorus/Flanger box, a Korg digital delay, and a Rane G-14 stereo EQ. My effects rack also has an Ibanez UE-405 multi-effects unit, but I'm not using it. The last stage of my rack is a Rocktron Hush II noise reduction unit. I'm really fond of that thing because you can run your phase shifters and all your old noisy gadgets through it, and it filters out certain frequencies. It's just great. Since everything is digital, I eventually want to come out of my rack and go directly into the board. I could just have some kind of monitoring system out on the floor and not even use amps.

*Do you ever have trouble coming up with creative parts?*

Yeah, I have good days and bad days [*laughs*]. Sound has a lot to do with it. When everything sounds good—I plug it up, and it all works—I get real creative. If the phones sound bad or I have a bad mix in the studio, it's kind of a downer. I don't get as aggressive. When things sound good, I just get a big charge of adrenaline. I really want to play.

*Since the '50s, what changes have had the most impact on studio guitarists and bassists?*

The bass going direct—instead of through an amp—was a big, big thing; that happened in the middle '60s. Going to headphones was another one. Our horn section in Memphis was always in the back of the studio, and there was a little delay—they were always behind the beat. Using phones pulled everybody together, and that was a big improvement. Equipment is still getting crazy; I don't know where that's going to stop. When I started out, we cut in mono. Going to two or three tracks was incredible. With 8-track, I said, "Well, it's got to stop here." Then we started filling up all eight tracks and looking for others. Then it was 16, 24, and, locking two 24s together, 48 tracks. And you can still find things to do. It was a big thing when we got our first 8-track. I got a little paranoid at first because you could hear everything I did. But the great thing was that it made parts repairable: I could fix a part without losing an otherwise good take.

*Do you ever miss playing onstage?*

No, because I really enjoy studio work. I've been doing it a long time. I'd rather do that than play live all the time. I've become a homebody; I like to be around my family. I can get as much enjoyment being on a fun record date as I can playing live. I don't need the applause. About seven years ago, we got a little hot country group together—[drummer] Larrie Londin, [pedal steeler] Buddy Emmons, [bassist] Joe Osborn, and me. We went to England with a singer named Tompall Glazer. It was sort of fun for a while, and then I was ready to come back home. I play and write a lot at home.

*Have you ever considered doing a solo album?*

Yeah. I've been approached by a few people who want to do it for their label, but I just haven't had the time. I don't know what would drive me to want to do that. I would want it to be good. I don't think an instrumental album would sell very much, and I'm not that big of an ego person. But last summer, Larrie Londin, Dave Hungate, a synth player named Shane Keister, and I played some live things. We want to come up with an album, but we just all can't get together, because we all work so much. We did about six tracks, and we just have to put solos on and try to get a label deal. We sort of sound like the band on *Late Night With David Letterman*. I don't know if anything's gonna come of that. I've written four or five instrumentals recently that I like for my own enjoyment, and who knows—maybe one of these days I'll get it together and put them down.

*How far in advance is your schedule booked?*

Right now, I'm booked up through the next three months. It's been really busy for me, and I'm thankful for that, because there's a lot of guys that aren't working. It's hard to regulate: If I'm not working, usually somebody else is working all they can handle. But it's been pretty even for me the past few years.

*Can you cite a favorite period in your career?*

Probably the Memphis years, especially at American from '65 to '72. That was a big learning experience for me. Sometimes people listen to those records and say, "Man, it sounds like you guys were really having a good time," but it was a lot of *hard* work. We'd go in the studio and stay weeks at a time. I'm proud of that, because I had the privilege of being part of records that are going to be played for years and years. I'm enjoying myself now, too. I've been working with a lot of young guys, and I still feel fairly current because I like the music that's happening. I haven't found the shutoff point yet to where I say, "Gosh, I can't stand that." I like to listen to outstanding musicians, and I love good solos—I don't care what instruments they are on or what kind of music it is.

---

## A SELECTED REGGIE YOUNG DISCOGRAPHY

**With Jimmy Buffett:** *Living And Dying In 3/4 Time*, ABC, D 50132; *Last Mango In Paris*, MCA, 5600. **With J.J. Cale:** *Okie*, Shelter, 2107; *Troubadour*, Shelter, 52002; *Shades*, MCA, 5158; *Grasshopper*, Mercury, SRM 1-4038. **With Jessi Colter** (on Capitol): *I'm Jessi Colter*, ST-11363; *Jessi*, ST-11477. **With Neil Diamond** (on MCA): *Gold*, 37209; *12 Greatest Hits*, 37272. **With Crystal Gayle:** *True Love*, Elektra, 60200-1. **With Dobie Gray:** *Drift Away*, Decca, 7 5397. **With Waylon Jennings** (on RCA): *Waylon Jennings*, AYL1-5126; *Honky Tonk Heroes*, APL1-0240; *Ol' Waylon*, APL1-2317; *I've Always Been Crazy*, APL1-2959. **With Tracy Nelson:** *Tracy Nelson*, Atlantic, SDD-7310; *Sweet Soul Music*, MCA, 494.

**With Willie Nelson** (on Columbia): *Always On My Mind*, FC 379951; *City Of New Orleans*, FC 39145. **With Mickey Newbury:** *I Came To Hear The Music*, Elektra, 7E-1007; *Rusty Tracks*, ABC, ABL-5215. **With Elvis Presley** (on RCA): *From Elvis In Memphis*, AFL1-4155; *Greatest Hits, Vol. 1*, AHL1-2347; *Golden Records, Vol. 5*, AHL1-4941; *Worldwide 50 Gold Award Hits*, LPM-6401. **With Eddie Rabbitt** (on Elektra): *Rocky Mountain Music*, 7E-1065. **With Kenny Rogers** (on United Artists): *The Gambler*, 934; *Kenny*, 979. **With Joe Tex:** *Spill The Beans*, Dial, 6004. **With B.J. Thomas:** *B.J. Thomas*, Everest, 4101; *Pick Of B.J. Thomas*, 51 West (dist. by Columbia), QR-16053; *Reunion*, ABC, 858. **With Bobby Womack** (on United Artists): *Understanding*, 5577; *Safety Zone*, LA-544. **With Hank Williams, Jr.:** *Family Tradition*, Elektra, 6E-194; *Habits Old And New*, Elektra 6E-278; *Rowdy*, Elektra, 6E-330; *Five-O*, Warner/Curb, 25267-1; *Greatest Hits—Vol. 2*, Warner/Curb, 25328-1. **With others:** Bill Black Combo, *Cookin'*, 51 West, 16243; Box Tops, *Box Tops' Greatest Hits*, Rhino (1201 Olympic Blvd., Santa Monica, CA 90404), 161; Billy Burnette, *Between Friends*, Polydor, 6242; Johnny Cash, *Rainbow*, Columbia, FC 39951; Joe Cocker, *Civilized Man*, Capitol, ST-12335; Crusaders, *Standing Tall*, MCA, 5254; Jackie DeShannon, *Jackie*, Atlantic, 7231; Don Everly, *Brother Juke Box*, DJM, 20501; B.B. King, *Love Me Tender*, MCA, 886; Kris Kristofferson, *Breakaway*, Monument, 33278; Herbie Mann, *Memphis Two-Step*, Embryo, SD 531; Wilson Pickett, *Greatest Hits*, Atlantic, 2-501; Johnny Rivers, *Road*, Atlantic, 7301; Cat Stevens, *Izitso*, A&M, 4702; George Strait, *Does Fort Worth Ever Cross Your Mind*, MCA, 5518; Conway Twitty, *Crosswinds*, MCA, 3086.

# ABOUT THE AUTHORS

**Dix Bruce** is the former Editor of *Mandolin World News* and the author of a mandolin instruction book.

**Annemarie Colby** is a freelance writer based in San Francisco.

**Bob Doerschuk** is an Associate Editor of *Keyboard Magazine* and has been on its staff since 1977.

**Steve Fishell** plays pedal steel, lap steel, and Dobro in Emmylou Harris' Hot Band and has written numerous articles for *Guitar Player Magazine.*

**Dan Forte** is an Editor At Large for *Guitar Player Magazine.*

**Doug Green** is a past President of the Country Music Foundation. He is best known as the leader and guitarist of the western band, Riders In The Sky.

**David Grisman,** leader of the David Grisman Quintet, has been a major force popularizing the mandolin in jazz and New Acoustic Music.

**Jim Hatlo** is Senior Associate Editor of *Frets Magazine.*

**Dennis Hensley** is a freelance writer.

**Mark Humphrey** is a freelance music writer and radio show producer. He is a regular contributor to *Frets*, *The LA Reader*, and other publications.

**Frank Joseph** is a freelance writer.

**Rich Kienzle** is the author of *Great Guitarists: The Most Influential Players In Blues, Country Music, Jazz, And Rock* (Facts On File), co-author of *The Country Music Book* (Scribners), and a regular columnist for *Country Music Magazine.*

**Bob Krueger** is a well known freelance writer and photographer.

**Richard Lieberson** is a freelance writer.

**Don Menn** has been associated with *Guitar Player Magazine* since 1973, rising from Editorial Assistant to Editor in 1978. He is now the Director of Finance of GPI Publications.

**Frankie R. Nemko** is a freelance writer in Hollywood.

**Jas Obrecht** is a Senior Assistant Editor for *Guitar Player Magazine* and a columnist for *Frets.*

**Robert K. Oermann** is one of the most prominent freelance writers in Nashville today.

**Jon Sievert** has been *Guitar Player Magazine*'s Staff Photographer since 1976. He is now a Contributing Editor for both *Guitar Player* and *Frets* magazines.

**Roger Siminoff** is the author of several books and Director of Operations of GPI. He was the founding Editor of *Frets Magazine.*

**Tom Wheeler,** the current Editor of *Guitar Player Magazine*, has been with GPI since 1977. He is the author of *The Guitar Book* and *American Guitar: An Illustrated History* (both published by Harper & Row).

**Chapters reprinted from:**

Chet Atkins: *Guitar Player*, October 1979; Jethro Burns: *Frets*, October 1979; James Burton: *Guitar Player*, June 1984; Carter Family: *Guitar Player*, March 1979; Roy Clark: *Guitar Player*, November 1978; Floyd Cramer: *Keyboard*, March 1977; Charlie Daniels: *Frets*, October 1983; Don Everly: *Guitar Player*, June 1977; Lester Flatt: *Frets*, August 1979; Hank Garland: *Guitar Player*, January 1981; Emmylou Harris: *Guitar Player*, November 1978; Waylon Jennings: *Guitar Player*, January 1984; Doug Kershaw: *Frets*, October 1981; Albert Lee: *Guitar Player*, May 1981; Barbara Mandrell: *Frets*, March 1984; Joe Maphis: *Guitar Player*, August 1981; Sam McGee: *Guitar Player*, June 1976; Bill Monroe: *Frets*, May 1979; Ricky Nelson: *Guitar Player*, September 1981; Willie Nelson: *Frets*, December 1984; The Grand Ole Opry: *Frets*, December 1982; Tex Ritter: *Frets*, July 1979; Hargus "Pig" Robbins: *Keyboard*, July 1977; Roots Of Rockabilly: *Guitar Player*, December 1983; Earl Scruggs: *Frets*, March 1985; Hank Snow: *Guitar Player*, May 1976; Sons Of The Pioneers: *Frets*, April 1979; Merle Travis: *Frets*, October 1980; Doc Watson: *Frets*, March 1979; Jimmy Wyble: *Guitar Player*, June 1977; Hank Williams, Jr.: *Guitar Player*, May 1985; Reggie Young: *Guitar Player*, January 1986.